Suicide Angels
and the
Silent Terrorists

A Story about Bullying

By author and poet

ANNETTE EVALYN SWAIN

iUniverse, Inc.
Bloomington

Suicide Angels and the Silent Terrorists
A Story about Bullying

iUniverse books may be ordered through booksellers or by contacting:

iUniverse
1663 Liberty Drive
Bloomington, IN 47403
www.iuniverse.com
1-800-Authors (1-800-288-4677)

ISBN: 978-1-4697-3239-8 (sc)
ISBN: 978-1-4697-3240-4 (hc)
ISBN: 978-1-4697-3241-1 (ebk)

Library of Congress Control Number: 2012900358

Printed in the United States of America

iUniverse rev. date: 02/24/2012

CONTENTS

Chapter One

Where Memories Began

Remembering the way her mother sung her to sleep as a one year old, Annie lay in her glossy, white cot, just inside the nursery door. Baby Annie cooed, as she so warmly smiled up at her mother, who lovingly and adoringly smiled down on her. Annie's big sleepy eyes began to feel heavier and heavier.

With every pat of her mothers ever so tender and caring hand, baby's eyes now fully closed. Annie could still hear the song of her mother's soft, sweet lullaby. The serenity as she drifted ever so cosily into dream land. In her memory she could still hear her mothers voice singing, "Twinkle, twinkle little star, a little star is what you are."

Her infant days, were helping her mother make her older siblings beds. There was Lewis, Lauren, Lucy and Lindy. Annie at this stage was four years young. As a young child, Annie found it quite amusing that all her older brother and sisters names started with the letter L. She also had a younger sister Maralyn, a much younger brother Kenny and by the look of mummies tummy, another one on the way.

Annie also remembered over hearing an adult conversation as she was growing up. Something about her mummy saying, "daddy didn't believe in waste." She didn't know what this meant (at the time)

When Annie was a little four year old, she helped her mother make all of her siblings beds. It was hard work for a little four year old but Annie was willing to learn from her mother.

"That's how you fold the corners, just the way the nurses do, it's called a mitre corner," her mother would say. "It helps keep the corners of the bed nice and tidy and tight," Annie knew from this moment on, even at such a young, tender age, that she would one day, become a nurse. Mother always looked at her with a smiling, cheerful face, even first thing in the morning.

Education came easily to Annie, happiest to be learning, she remembered following her older brother Lewis and sisters, Lauren, Lucy and Lindy to school, well before she was old enough. Her mother would panic, when Annie was no where to be seen, sneaking out the door with the older children.

"Oh you naughty, little scallywag," her mother would say. "Don't be in such a hurry to grow up sweetheart, your time will come soon enough," she smiled.

Annie always remembered feeling so very close to nature, a sense of universal protection, of course she felt her parents protection but also from something much greater. Even though her father instilled in her great faith and religious beliefs, it was a greater power, an assurance she recalls, even before Sunday school days. There was a knowledge to be gained and much to be learnt.

Often the church would visit the family home and share fellowship. Annie met many different and interesting people of all ages, cultures and several different religions as she was growing up. One couple in particular stuck very clearly in her memory, they were friends from America, Mike and Penny. Mike and her father owned a fishing boat together. According to her father, the boat capsized, during a storm, in the marina, where it was moored, Annie was about seven years of age at this stage. She always wondered, why they never saw much of Mike and Penny after that?

By the time Annie was eight, she took delight in planting her own little shrubs and flowers. Her father would lead her around the garden by the hand, picking berries from all around the garden. So many beautiful berries, blue berries, raspberries, golden berries, strawberries, mulberries, just to name a few.

Her father worked long hours, building in the country. He'd be gone, off travelling before dawn and wouldn't make it back home until after dusk. He absorbed himself in his garden, as one of his much loved hobbies. He always said it was the closest place to God when he was in his garden.

Annie had many fond memories of her father, kissing her on the cheek. Each morning before he left for work, he would kiss all of his eight children goodbye. She remembered the smell of his clean soapy skin and tooth paste breath.

On Saturdays father would pile all the bikes into a trailer. He joined all the family up in a bike racing club, all eight of them. Annie loved the cycle club, it was called Skid Kids. The cycling was great for health benefits and the fact Annie was competing with boys made Annie feel confident and strong. She also loved the name of her team, Fire Birds.

The kitchen at Annie's home was always abuzz with activity. Her mother worked tirelessly and relentlessly, preparing meals for such a large family. One of her favourite sense memoires, was the smell of her mothers Sunday Roasts and hot Apple Pie wafting through and out of the house. She loved helping to prepare meals and believed her mother was magic, the way she could get so many special dishes out of a few vegetables and pieces of meat. Everything her mother made tasted divine and her pasta bolognes', Oh, was to die for. All made with such tender loving care. Annie gained so much skill and knowledge. Some of her best memories, were with her mother, in the kitchen preparing meals together.

On Sundays of course, there was church and Sunday School. The mad rush to have everyone up and ready, dressed in their Sunday best. After Sunday School and Church service, weather permitting, father would take the whole family to the country, to finish off some of his building jobs.

Annie remembered being absolutely terrified of this huge cow, she sat on the roof of the parked car, the old Austin Healy, to try and get away from it, only because her brother Lewis told her it was a vicious, charging bull. She never lived that one down, boys will be boys.

If her father had a free week end, they would pack a picnic basket. The family would drive down south along the beautiful coast. Lots of fresh air and long walks along deserted beaches, creating calm and many memories in time.

Learning from her mother and father was very important to Annie. She tried so hard to impress both of her parents as she was growing up, after all it was tough competing with so many brothers and sisters. She was always being challenged. It made her more co-operative and yet some how resilient. Even her baby brother Terry, was always trying to compete with her, wrestling with her, always great fun, they would role around, wrestling on the floor, laughing so much until they cried.

Chapter Two

How Time Flies

Sure enough, as usual, Annie's mother was right. Before she knew it, Annie was seventeen and finishing the end of her eleventh year at High School. She'd already applied for her first part time job. She'd applied as a Nurse Assistant, in a little nursing Home down the road, Weringa. She had her learners permit to drive and hoped to soon be successful in passing her license test. She didn't mind walking to work though, it was only a couple of kilometres from home, and it was only during the school holidays.

The walk to work was a pleasant one, there were many pretty gardens and rivers with bridges, the weather, was usually fine, very fine.

Annie arrived at Weringa, for her very first morning shift. She was directed by the busy, senior, registered nurse,who ran the nursing home, to a little cottage at the very far corner of the block where the nursing home stood. As she entered through the back door, of the cottage, there was a distinct smell of strong urine, like the smell of ammonia, it took her breath away, she coughed briefly and caught her breath.

The young girl that had worked the night shift, was busy running bed pans and potties, back and forth to the bathroom. She looked like she had just woken up herself. Her eyes were bloodshot and her thin, gold rimmed spectacles, hung crooked on her freckly, pug, button nose.

Her short, mousey, brown hair, sat ruffled on her head, something that resembled a birds nest. She only stood about five feet tall and for a change, Annie found herself looking down at her, only standing at five foot five herself.

"Good morning, you must be Annie? Hi I'm Missy, I always save this job for last," she smiled, "It's the pits."

"Smells like it," Annie smiled back.

"Nearly finished," Missy yelled out, as she took another dive into the bathroom, appearing to hold her breath, emptying another smelly potty. "Then I will give you a run down on these wonderful, little old ladies."

"No problems, don't rush on my behalf, after all, I wouldn't want you to spill any of that," Annie cringed slightly.

An echoed voice came from the bathroom, "And I wouldn't want to clean it up either, it's bad enough having to empty these things, let alone playing with it but it's all part of the job, I'm afraid."

Annie heard sounds of gushing water, Missy yelled out, "won't be long now, just giving my hands a good scrub."

Missy came from the bathroom looking very flustered, Oh that last one was a stinker, I had to hold my breath, Mrs. Mac, massive bowel action, better remember to write that one up in the bowel book while I'm think'n about it."

Missy continued to give Annie the run down for the day.

"Now," Missy smiled, "once you've assisted all ten of these lovely ladies up out of bed, set them up for breakfast, made their cups of teas and coffee, then you have to start peeling all the veggies for Sunday roast."

"For these ladies?" Annie inquired.

"No, for the whole nursing home," Missy confirmed.

6

Missy grabbed a large cloth that was thrown over a small, folding, card table, exposing three rather large pumpkins, at least two dozen potatoes, ten onions and more carrots than a Annie wished to count, never too fond of carrots herself.

"It's only 0730 hrs now, you'll have these completed by 1000 hrs, that will give you plenty of time to help everyone finish showering and dressing ready for lunch; are you okay Annie?",

Annie stood there quiet for a moment. She hadn't envisaged her morning, being filled with a couple of hours of peeling pumpkins and crying caused by chopping, stinging onions.

"Oh, yes, yes I'm quite alright, I'm sure I'll get through all of this with out to much ado!" She replied, trying to sound as keen as possible about the task presented before her.

"You look a bit daunted," Missy smiled again, "don't worry, it's not as hard as it looks. I must admit, peeling and chopping pumpkins, is no ones favourite job but it's not as hard as it looks, here let me show you how easy it is."

Missy picked up, what had to be, one of the most gigantic, hippobotanic pumpkins, Annie had ever seen.

"Follow me." Missy exited the back, glass, sliding doors to the nursing home cottage.

Annie followed, expecting Missy to go over to the main kitchen in the nursing home, to show her some whiz bang machine that helps to chop and peel pumpkin! But no, that wasn't to be the case.

Missy stood there, outside the cottage, on the foot path, she lifted that massive pumpkin, way over her head and threw it down with as much force as she could muster. Annie stood there, with her mouth gaping open, some would call it gob smacked. Looking down curiously at that poor pumpkin, shattered in pieces, all over the ground. Annie didn't know whether to laugh or cry, she'd never seen her mother do anything quite like that with a pumpkin, all over the dirty ground!

"There you go," Missy laughed, "all you have to do now is peel it."

Annie laughed, more from shock, than amusement.

"Thanks for your help," Annie smiled as politely as she could.

As Annie made her way around the cottage that morning, she introduced herself to all ten elderly ladies. They were all very sweet and unique, in their own individual way. For the following week, Annie was able to experience, first hand, a taste of what it would be like to become a real nurse.

Some of Annie's other experiences were quite nerve racking, for instance; One night, while she was scheduled on to do a night shift. Mrs. Welker, a well spoken elderly lady, with her long grey hair in plaits, climbed out of bed and bumped her head. She struck her head hard on the sharp corner of the bedside cabinet, giving herself a nasty gash.

Annie called for the Sister on duty in the nursing home immediately, then grabbed a handful of combine and a pair of gloves from the already prepared dressing trolley, she began to apply pressure to the gaping wound.

As the Sister, otherwise known as the Registered Nurse, arrived to assess Mrs. Welker's, she apologised, as she called the locum. He wouldn't be arriving for at least two hours and there wasn't a doctor on site. "But your doing the right thing Annie, just keep applying that pressure," Sister smiled, reassuring both Annie and poor old Mrs. Welker.

"Here, take your hand off for a moment and let's see if that bleeding has slowed down a bit?" Sister continued.

Annie removed the pressure as the wound gaped open once again, the blood profusely spurting out. Annie quickly re-applied the pressure back on the wound.

Holding Mrs. Welker's head as comfortably as possible, Annie began to feel a little dizzy and clammy.

"Are you alright?" Sister asked. "you're looking a little pale, perhaps you'd better sit down for a moment."

Annie had never seen so much blood before, she thought that the combination of applying all that pressure and all that blood, may have contributed to her wooziness. Sister grabbed two crepe bandages and some more 20 by 20 combine from the dressing trolley and began applying a pressure bandage.

"Now I've applied this pressure bandage, you can relax a little. I hope you've enjoyed your lesson on how to apply a cranial, pressure bandage," Sister said assertively, admiring her own handy work.

The doctor arrived and quickly and efficiently sutured the wound, twelve sutures in all. Thank goodness, by that time, the bleeding had subsided. Doctor left orders to observe Mrs. Welkey with hourly neurological observations, checking for signs of confusion and loss of motor response, as well a further bleeding of course. Temperature, pulse, blood pressure and respiration, along with pupil reaction, were also monitored hourly for the rest of Annie's night shift.

As if that didn't keep Annie busy enough, all the commotion had unsettled another one of the residents. Little Miss O'leary, a petite old Scottish women, with very thick, curly, fluffy, dark hair, not an ounce of fat on her frail little body and as wrinkly as you please. Annie had never experienced someone talking to them selves in such detail, she was almost convinced that little Miss O'leary was actually having a conversation with someone real, as she wandered down the halls of the cottage, looking up at the walls, in the dark. As a matter of fact, the one way conversation was quite convincing, if not a little scary for a young nurse assistant. Little did young Annie know, it was only a taste of what was yet to come.

It turned out this resident was a very heavy drinker in the past, because of the damage to her brain, she suffered from hallucinations. Annie was concerned, this lady usually confused but pleasant, was becoming extremely unsettled, talking louder and louder, her conversation with her imaginary friend was quickly becoming an argument! Annie was worried she would wake more of the other residents.

Not wanting to bother the sister on duty but Annie had no choice. She once again rang across to the main Nursing Home. Sister was accustomed to dealing with this little old lady. She more than gladly came across to administer an injection of haloperidol, which helped to settle her and assist in her cooperating.

Sister popped in quickly to also check on Mrs. Welker and her observations, satisfied that she was now stable, she returned to the main Nursing Home.

Annie found getting to know each of the residents enjoyable. Annie loved their individuality. Each of them came from different back grounds, different nationalities. She absorbed their uniqueness, sensed their spirit, she saw beyond their warn out, withered, wrinkly exteriors.

What she saw, were beautiful, young beings in warn out shells and that is something that time can not change, the interior spirit. They all treated Annie like their very own granddaughter and in return, she treated them all with the utmost love and care, compassion, kindness, dignity and respect.

They laughed together, sang together and had some of the most interesting conversations. Annie was sometimes shocked that little old ladies knew such crude language. It didn't take her long to realise, yes, they were certainly human too and on the odd occasion, would let off wind, as well as steam.

After working many week ends and night shifts, Annie finally met Matron on a day shift during the week. She was so typical of the Matrons of this time. Not very tall, broad shoulders and as solid as a brick out house, grey, short hair with glasses.

Fortunately for Annie, Matron Tremopeth, wasn't as stern as she looked. Of course she was strict enough when required. Her serious spectacle—laden face, was authority enough, to have even the bravest of big men, shaking in their boots. She did though have a heart of gold and mothered all of her staff, as well as loving all her residents.

Annie was overwhelmed with excitement, when she'd heard Matron Tremopeth, complimented her work. She had heard many good reports over the past weeks. So much so, she offered Annie a full time job in the Nursing Home's Cottage. Apart from peeling large pumpkins and the thought of smelly onions wafting through Annie's mind, she was happy to accept the position, in view of gaining more experience. To continue on with further nursing studies.

Chapter Three

Never A Dull Moment

Annie was extremely excited about venturing on to do her training a s fully qualified nurse. It was in one of the states biggest hospitals. She had great success with her training, so eager to learn. She wanted to have as much understanding and knowledge as possible, so she could do the utmost to care for her patients, physically, emotionally and spiritually, mind, body and soul. She enrolled in a health and fitness course also, this enabled her to learn more about the human body and revised more anatomy and physiology. It was also great, because it also kept her fit, for some of the heavier tasks in nursing.

She was famished after a very busy morning in the Emergency Rooms. She'd only grabbed an apple for breakfast, from home. At lunch time she decided to grab some lunch from the hospital cafe'.

As she was standing in line, waiting to be served, she had noticed out of the corner of her eye, the handsome, dark haired police officer. He had previously been guarding a prisoner in the ER, where she had been allocated that day.

As Annie turned to face him, he smiled over at her. She noticed, at that moment, his warm, beautiful smile and welcoming eyes, they were smiling too. Annie smiled gently, if not a little shyly in return.

After collecting her standard double cut, chicken and salad roll, with an orange juice, she was about to exit the café, to sit out in the sun with her other nursing colleagues. Suddenly she noticed, that tall, dark, handsome police officer, coming towards her. She was very nervous but excited all at once.

"Excuse me," he said, in a very deep manly voice, "you can join me, if you like!" He smiled as he gestured over to the table where he had previously been sitting, "I don't bite, honest."

"Oh, okay then," Annie replied. She felt a little uncomfortable in male company. Although she had three great brothers, this was different. She noticed the older she became, the more attention males appeared to pay her, not that she encouraged it, it just seemed to happen. As she went to sit down, she held out her hand, "Hi, I'm Annie," she smiled again, this time with a little more confidence.

"Hi, I'm Mitch; Very pleased to meet you Annie, have you been working here long? You seem to to be very efficient at what you do. That was the first thing I noticed about you in the Emergency department, apart from your stunning good looks of course," he smiled again.

Annie could feel herself blushing, hoping it wasn't showing through her make up. "Oh, thanks for the compliment but a little polly filler helps," she laughed.

"Polly filler?" Mitch mused.

"Yes, make up!"

"Ha Ha,Ha," Mitch laughed again. "So, you're good looking and funny as well."

Mitch had such a sexy deep laugh, she found herself being instantly attracted to him.

"Well," he continued, "You really look like a girl who looks after herself. You look pretty fit, are you into gym training?"

"Well," she smirked, "I am a gym trainer, actually, a fitness instructor."

"And a nurse as well," Mitch replied with interest; "Gee, I was hoping to ask you out for dinner, if you could possibly squeeze me into your busy schedule?"

"I might manage to fit you in?" she smiled, as she once again, found herself looking into those sexy, smiling eyes.

"You'd be on shift work too, wouldn't you?" he asked.

"Yes, that's right, morning, evening and night shift," she replied.

"Are you free this Friday evening?" He smiled a humble smile.

Annie could not believe, this gorgeous, young, handsome police officer, was actually enquiring into asking her out on a date. She answered him, trying not to appear like a desperate young, school girl.

"Yes I am free, although I have a class to teach at the gym at 1800 hrs, that goes for one hour. I can't get out of it either because it's part of my training hours to becoming a fully qualified instructor."

"That's no trouble, we can have a late dinner, or supper if you'd prefer. I know a cosy little place," Mitch explained, "North of the city, it has lighter type meals and the best ice cream sundaes. You don't have to rush either, because it's open until 0200hrs."

Mitch sat up even taller, as he clasped his hands together, leaning closer to Annie over the table.

"So," he said, "how about it then? Are you going to let me take you to dinner?"

"Well, I am a sucker for a good sundae, especially chocolate." Annie had hardly touched her roll or her juice.

Annie Glanced down to her nurses watch, sitting on her left bosom. "Oh my goodness, I have to get back to work, where did that time go?"

Annie stood up and started leaving the cafe'.

"So is that a yes?" Mitch called out to her, so everyone else in the cafe' could hear.

"Yes," Annie gave him the biggest smile as she turned and ran out through the double glass doors. He smiled back at her with relief. Her smile remained with her for the rest of the day, no matter how hard she tried, she couldn't wipe that smile from her face.

At the end of the day she went to grab her bag from the staff locker room. As she was heading out of the double glassed emergency, sliding doors, she heard a deep manly voice calling her name.

"Annie, Annie, wait up, "Mitch called out.

Annie turned to see him coming towards her.

"Hi again." She beamed.

"Here you go." Mitch handed Annie a piece of paper with his name and number on it. "Call me and I'll make arrangements with you, for our dinner date, if that's O.K. With you?"

"I don't usually ring boys," Annie sighed. "I guess this once, I'll have to make an exception."

She gave Mitch a cheeky smile and giggled, amused at his attention.

"Great, I'll look forward to hearing from you then." Mitch once again smiled, that sexy eyed smile.

"I'll ring you this evening, I promise." Annie sweetly smiled back.

As nervous as she was, about ringing Mitch for the first time that evening, Annie picked up the phone receiver and dialled his number. Eight, double four, nine, she took a deep breath and hung up half way through dialling. What's the big deal, she thought to herself, "he's probably just as nervous as I am." Once again she picked up the receiver, this time completing the number. She could hear the phone ringing at the other end, then an answer.

"Hello, Hello, Mitch speaking."

"Hi Mitch, it's me Annie, the nurse from the hospital."

"You don't have to remind me Annie, I certainly wouldn't forget you in a hurry. So, how does that little cafe', North of the city sound to you? It's very casual, cozy, laid back sort of a place."

"Sounds great to me," she replied promptly, without delay. "Maybe it would save some time, if I showered and got ready at the gym after my class. Would you like me to meet you at the cafe'?"

"I can pick you up from the gym if you like?"

"Sounds like a plan then! How about you pick me up from there at 1930 hrs, that will give me plenty of time to get ready. Is that O.K. With you?"

"Your the boss, ... Annie can you hold on a minute? I've got a call coming in on my mobile."

"No worries, I'll hold."

It wasn't long before Mitch was back on the phone to Annie.

"Look Annie, I'm so sorry to cut our conversation a bit short, but I'm down for recall and work requires me as soon as I can get there. So I'll see you Friday evening then!!" Mitch's voice rose at the end of the sentence.

Annie quickly gave Mitch her phone number and address of the gym.

"See you at 1930 hrs on Friday then," she said, before saying goodbye and hanging up.

Annie cradled the receiver to her bosom. "Oh he sounds divine," she thought, as she sat peacefully, with her heart slightly racing, still unable to wipe that smile from her face.

Friday night couldn't come quick enough for her.

The conversation flowed extremely well, when the night arrived. There was definitely a lot of emotional chemistry between them. Even after the cafe' closed, Annie and Mitch walked the city streets, window shopping and chatting into early hours of the morning.

When it came time to say goodnight, neither one was keen to bring the night to an end. They stood closely by the passenger side door of Mitch's car, an old red Holden Gemini. He informed Annie, he was soon to purchase a new black Holden Ute, with a double cab.

"Holdens never die," he laughed, "they just go faster."

"It doesn't matter what car you drive," she assured Mitch. "Why it wouldn't bother me, if you didn't drive at all."

"You're so sweet Annie," he whispered as he gently pulled her closer to him. "Can I see you again?"

Annie will never forget that red Holden Gemini, or the galvanised, high iron fence beside where the car was parked. Most of all, she will never forgot that long, lingering, passionate kiss that continued on and on and on.

From that evening forward, she felt like she was walking amongst the heavens, on cloud nine, her whole life just seemed to fall into line.

The very next day, after their first date, there was a knock at the door. Annie's mother answered it.

"Nennie," Her mother called, "there's a delivery for you."

Annie approached her mother at the entry way of their family home, holding a beautiful arrangement of long stem red roses, amongst white forget me nots.

"HMMMM Delivery for Annie." Her mother smiled. "Well, I wonder who they could be from. Couldn't possibly be that policeman friend of yours, you can't stop talking about, could it?"

Annie opened her mouth in awe at the beautiful dozen red roses, "WOW."

"Hurry up Nennie, what does the card say?"

Annie read the card in her head, before reading it to her mother, "Awwww that is sooo sweet."

"It says, Dearest Annie, Thank you for a great night out and the best date I've ever spent with a girl. Love Mitch. XXX

"Oh that's so nice." Annie took a second and third sniff of the beautiful sent of the roses.

"What did you get up to on your date?" Her Mother asked.

"We had a lovely meal at this sweet little cafe' in North Adelaide, then we walked and talked for hours. He kissed me good night and dropped me at my car at the gym, where I left it."

"That's all?" Her mother questioned her again.

"Yes mum, that is all, he was a total gentleman, opened my doors and everything. Treated me like a perfect lady, it was a great night."

"Don't go rushing into anything Neenie dear," her mother said, as she kissed her warmly on the cheek.

"Don't worry mum, I won't." Annie reassured her.

"I'm very happy for you dear, here let me put those beautiful roses in some water for you, I will add a little sugar to make them last longer." Her mother smiled.

'Thanks mum, I love you," She gave her mum a big hug.

"Oh I love you too Neenie, sweetheart, I'm glad you've found someone nice."

Annie and Mitch spent many more evenings together. They were so much in love. They began spending more and more time together. They played golf together, lawn bowls together, jogged together and even worked out at the gym together. They became best friend as well as romantic partners. Mitch would invite Annie to all his social and police work functions and Annie would invite Mitch to all her social functions and nursing shows.

She was quite nervous at her first police function. There were so many big, brawny blokes, so many new faces and so many names to remember. At the first police function she attended, the police officer sitting to the left of her, looked quite authoritarian, not to mention the size of a yeti. Thank goodness the female police officer to the right of her was Jenny, Mitch's patrol partner, who she'd met several times before. Mitch was sitting directly across, facing Annie. They sat across from each other as often as they were able, so they could look into each others eyes and play footsies under the table.

Mitch, being a bit of a lad, let out an almighty belch, after sculling down his chilled glass of West End light beer to quench his thirst.

"Oh you pig," Annie laughed, jokingly.

Mitch and Annie laughed together, knowing it was a private joke they had between them.

The police officer to the left, the big brawny yeti, frowned down at Annie in disgust.

"Do you mind," he peered down some more. "Excuse me, do you mind, I resemble that remark."

Resemble, resemble, Annie thought to herself for a second.

Barry the big brawny bloke still looking down at a Annie, now engaged in a smile, bellowed out with laughter, as did the rest of the crowded table along with.

"Oh resemble, I get it." Annie joined in the laughter and stopped shaking in her boots, she really thought she had offended him but he was having a joke with her.

Annie was quite relaxed in their company from that moment on, it was a real ice breaker.

Chapter Four

Graduation Day

During her nursing training, Annie had a wonderful time. There was so much socialising and camaraderie. She was enjoying every moment with her beloved Mitch. Everything seemed to be going extremely well, absolutely incredible.

It was time for Annie's graduation day. All The nurses went to the Adelaide International Hotel for dinner. Mitch was so proud to be at her side, to see her graduate, as well as escorting her to the dinner.

Mitch hired a tuxedo for the occasion. Annie had looked around for months, to find the perfect dinner dress but couldn't find anything that appealed to her. She ended up recycling one of her old favourites. It was a beautiful black, body hugging number, with a slit up one leg, a pretty white, satin collar, sexy but sophisticated, quite low cut in the front. A large, gold and pearl button finished the outfit at the waist, where the large white satin, open collar ended. A pair of black, suede court shoes finished it off nicely, topped off with a pair of tear drop, pearl ear rings and neck-let to match. With Mitch also in black and white, they looked like the perfectly matched couple.

By the time they got through the tedious formalities of the graduation ceremony, Annie was so thirsty. As soon as she sat down beside Mitch at the dinner table, she begun guzzling down her celebration, sparkling,

Australian wine, she'd almost drank the whole flute glass, as though it were water. Mitch grabbed her gently by the wrist and pulled the glass away from her lips.

"Hey," he grinned, "don't skull that too fast, you might choke on something!"

He held the flute glass up to Annie's nose, until she was staring cross eyed, down to the bottom of it.

"Oh my goodness," Annie gasped, "Oh my God."

As she held Mitch's hand around the flute glass, she trembled, as tears began to well in her eyes. In the bottom of the glass, sat a perfectly cut, sparkling, white gold, diamond and sapphire ring.

"Wow, what a day this has been, oh it's just beautiful," Annie gasped sobbingly as she placed her other hand over her mouth, slightly trembling.

"It's eighteen carat, white gold," Mitch continued, "with sapphires and an eighteen point, rose cut diamond, a family heirloom in fact. You'd have to go a long way to find another like it," Mitch smiled, his eyes sparkling as he watch the expression on Annie's face intensely.

Annie felt some what embarrassed, as she thought back to when her future mother-in-law had first shown her this beautiful, antique ring, not aware of the fact, she would end up with it on her finger. At the time Annie had said,

"Oh it's beautiful but I prefer my diamonds mounted."

Mitch's mum Marie had actually gone to all of the trouble to have it mounted, just the way Annie wanted it.

Mitch pulled her hand away from her mouth again, this time tipping the flute glass up, so he could clasp the shiny ring in his fingers. Holding it in front of her, everyone around the room went silent, awaiting in expectation.

"Annie," Mitch spoke softly, in his deep, sexy voice, as he usually did when he was serious about something. "We've been really great friends for quite a while now, we get along extremely well. I would like you to be more than just a girl friend. Annie I would be really honoured, if you would accept this ring and sincere proposal, for you to become my life partner and my wife."

Mitch sat there with the ring in one hand and Annie's hand in the other, eagerly awaiting a reply.

Annie paused for a moment, taking it all in, almost choking on her tears of joy.

"Yes, my answer is definitely yes," she sniffled, "yes." She pushed her finger swiftly into the ring.

By now, the whole ball room full of graduation dinner guests, had the gist of what was going on. They all started tapping their glasses with their cutlery. The whole room filled with chime sound and they all began chanting, Kiss, Kiss, Kiss,Kiss, in rhythm with the chiming. Suddenly, they all cheered loudly, as Mitch and Annie's lips fell together, passionately. By the time the dinner celebrations were over that evening, just about every guest had come over and congratulated the couple on their engagement.

Mitch and Annie had decided to set their wedding date two years from the date of the proposal, which was absolutely perfect timing, as it fell on a Saturday, in the month of June, June the eighteenth in fact.

Annie was so excited, she couldn't wait to start planning everything. The following morning, after her graduation, Annie got straight on the telephone and called her life long friend Leane.

"Hey Leane, it's Annie."

"My goodness Annie, how are you? I haven't heard from you in ages, I've missed you!"

"Oh I've missed you too and I think of you often." Annie had known Leane since she was only nine years old.

"It's so funny, you know Annie, I was just thinking of you and then the phone rang, it's so weird the way that always happens," Leanne laughed.

"Leane do you remember the promise we made each other, when we were just kids?"

"Yeah, the one about promising to be bridesmaids in each others weddings?" Leane squealed excitedly down the phone." Annie laughed as she pulled the receiver away from her ear, at the sound of Leane's deafening squeal. "Oh you're kidding did Mitch propose already? Oh Annie I'm so happy for you, that's wonderful, congratulations."

"Well, will you be one of my bridesmaids?"

"Oh absolutely, I wouldn't miss it for the world my friend. How many bridesmaids are you going to have?"

"Well I'd better do the honourable thing and ask my four sisters, with my oldest married sister being the Maid of Honour. Maids of Honour are meant to be married, aren't they?" Annie questioned.

"Yes, that's right, my goodness, this wedding is going to be huge Annie," Leane giggled. "I mean even just with your immediate family, it's one big party."

The moment Annie hung up the phone, she thought she'd also better ring and inform her parents of the exciting news.

"Hi mum."

"Hi Nenny, what's up Love?" Her mother asked.

"Mum, Mitch proposed to me last night, at my graduation dinner."

"Yes we know Nenny, Sweetheart."

"How do you know?"

"Mitch snuck around and spoke to your father and I one day last week. You were at your hairdressing appointment. He asked your father for your hand in Marriage."

"Oh you're joking," Annie laughed out loud. "See, I told you he was a gentleman."

"Yes I must admit," her mother laughed along with her, "even your father and I were surprised."

Annie sat for a moment, after saying goodbye to her mother. She felt so inspired by her good friend Leane, Mitch and the warm relationships with her parents, so much so, she decided to write a poem. She hadn't written a poem for quite a while, a long time actually, what with study and Mitch and all.

She got out her favourite pen and one of her many scribble pads, as the words began to flow through her mind, heart and spirit.

© Friendship

Isn't it miraculous, the way some people enter your life,
Or how if you turned that corner, you could have ended up in strife.
Things happen for a reason, that's the way it's meant to be,
And if things didn't happen the way they did,
then I wouldn't be Friends with
Thee.
Sometimes when we've been troubled, and we wonder
on earth what For?
We realise further down the track, This opens another door!
This door is one of progress, a step in the right direction,
A room filled with inspiration, admiration and affection.
It doesn't make you an instant millionaire, or give you instant
Wealth.
It has no monetary value, all you need is
Yourself.
A friend is someone special, whom you hold close to your heart,
And you will always remain close, even when physically far apart.
The strength of ones spirit, is what keeps a friendship alive,
And with the strength of ones friendship, for perfection yea shall
Strive
So on this special day, and the day that yea were born,
The spirit of your friendship, hath brightened up every dawn.
It has created a new dimension, one that I never would have known
And It is all because of your friendship and the way that yea have
Shown.

Chapter Five

(Two Years Later) June Wedding

Annie couldn't believe two years had gone so quickly. It was the eighteenth of June, her wedding day. Traditionally Mitch and Annie had decided not to see each other for twenty four hours prior to the ceremony, at the Brohem Place Uniting Church.

All Annie's sisters, Laura, Lucy, Lindy and Marolyn, along with her good friend Leane, were at the hairdressing salon with Annie, when she received a big bunch of assorted roses, carnations and forget me nots from the florist. At The same time her mobile rung. Carmen, Annie's hairdresser, answered it for her. She smiled over at Annie, who had already started sipping on some white, sparkling, Australian wine with her bridal party.

It was her future mother in-law Marie on the phone. She had flown in from Gosford, New South Whales, along with other family and friends, to celebrate Annie and Mitch's special day.

"Hi it's mum, just ringing to make sure you received the flowers!"

"Yes mum, they've just arrived actually, a moment ago, they're gorgeous, thank you so much, you didn't have to do that mum."

"I didn't," Marie replied.

"Oh you didn't?" Annie paused briefly.

"No, read the card love, I rang for Mitch because he knew how strict you were about not speaking to, or seeing each other until you get to the church."

Carmen carried the big bunch of flowers over to Annie and handed her the card.

"Not that I was ears dropping or anything," Carmen smiled as she winked.

Annie laughed as she opened the pretty, floral card, it read,

To my Dear darling future wife, looking forward to our life together, can't wait to kiss my bride, I love you. Your future husband, forever yours, Mitch. Xoxoxo.

"Oh I can't cry," Annie grimaced, "I'll ruin my polly filler." Annie flapped her hands in front of her face, trying to prevent her tears from smudging her make up. All the girls in the salon laughed together.

Carmen handed her a tissue, Annie dabbed the corners of her eyes and thanked Carmen.

"Oh mum, tell him thank you and tell him, I love him. Thank you for calling mum. See you soon. Love you too, bye mum, bye."

She smacked her lips together and kissed her future mother in-law, Marie, through the phone and then hung up.

After the beauticians and hairdressers had finished pampering Annie, her mum and her bridesmaids, they were chauffeured by limousine, to the Intercontinental Hotel in the centre of the city. There they would make final preparation for the wedding ceremony.

All the bridesmaid's dresses, the page boy, Annie's nephew Dill's outfit and flower girl's, Annie's niece Samantha and God child Rebecca's outfits, along with flower arrangements, were all delivered to the penthouse suite earlier that day.

"Oh my God, the flowers are exquisite," Annie said out loud as she entered the penthouse, the scent of red roses and white carnations filled Annie's nostrils.

The room was filled with bouquets large and small. The girls just stood there for a moment, admiring the beauty and aroma of rich, freshly cut flower arrangements.

It didn't take long for the bridal party to get into their matching teal green, silk Bridesmaids outfits. The dresses had box sleeves, with sweet heart neckline, fitting, three quarter length, with a slit up one side. Matching silk court shoes and a little cocktail hat to top it all off. They all looked so elegant, with their hair done up in French rolls.

Annie thought it would be a good time to give her girls a little gift each. She had bought a little something to thank them all for being her bridesmaid and helping her with her special day.

"Here you go girls, let's pour a glass of bubbly and propose a toast to a job well done in preparing for my big day."

Annie filled all seven glasses, including one for her mum and handed them out. As they took their first sips of icy cold bubbly, Annie gave them all a little gift box.

"Oh how sweet," Laura thanked Annie as she kissed her gently on the cheek, being careful not to ruin her make up.

"They're adorable," Lindy also kissed Annie. The other girls all thanked her with a light cuddle and kiss. Leane held the pretty pearl drop earring's up to herself in front of the full length mirror.

Marolyn joined her as she helped Leane do up the divine, fine necklace of pretty pearls, matching the earrings.

All the girls came rushing toward the full length mirror to admire their little gifts.

"I've got a grand idea," Lucy smirked at the others in the mirror, as she stood with one hand on her hip and the other securely holding her bubbly glass. "Let's all wear our pretty gifts down the aisle, that way we will be perfectly coordinated."

"Good thinking ninety nine, I was hoping you'd say that. Of course, if you don't like them, you don't have to wear them." Annie smile serenely.

"Don't be silly Annie, they're gorgeous," Leane commented and commenced taking off her own regular jewellery as not to clash with her little gifts.

The young ones arrived at the hotel suite forty five minutes before they were due to leave for the church. Everyone assisted in helping the wee ones to get ready. They looked so adorable, almost like little, animated Disney characters. Little Dill, with his white blond, curly hair and big blue eyes. He wore a tuxedo and tails, with bow tie and teal green cummerbund and cravat, the top hat looked wicked. He perfectly matched the grooms-men.

Samantha and Rebecca, the flower girls, wore pretty white, frilly, satin dresses, with wide silky green ribbons, to match the bridesmaids teal green, which in turn matched the grooms-men's cummerbund and cravats. If there was one thing that Annie was really fussy about, it was colour coordination.

The last thing to be done, before the limousines arrived, was for everyone to help Annie to get into her wedding dress and help her place on her tiara and veil.

All the bridesmaids helped Annie step into her traditional wedding gown. Silk and lace, with strings of pearls, draping down her bare back, off the shoulder, sheer lace covered the arms and flowed down to the fingers. The girls placed her mother's pearl broach on a velvet choker and placed it around Annie's slender, bare neck. They slid a blue, satin garter belt upon her left leg, which was also borrowed from her sister. Then finally, a pretty pair of pearl drop earrings, that Annie's parents bought for her as a personal gift on her special day. So finally she was wearing, something old, something new, something borrowed and something blue.

Annie slipped her silk, stocking feet, into white, satin shoes. The last piece of her family's tradition, was to have all the girls assist the bride, too place on her tiara and veil and then, to hand her, the enormous bouquet of flowers.

For the first time in her life, Annie felt like a real life, fairytale princess.

There was a knock at the door. It was the photographer, wanting to get some video footage and a few stills before the ceremony was to take place. He sat Annie by the big glass window, it overlooked the Festival Theatre and the River Torrens, a very pretty view.

From the window you could also see North Adelaide and the Broham Place Uniting Church, where the ceremony was to take place. A perfect view for Annie's first wedding photo. The river was reasonably full after the first sign of the winter rains. Green grass and foliage, followed the water's edge.

It was quite an overcast, rainy day but that didn't worry Annie in the slightest. One of the other family traditions, or beliefs, was that if it rained on your wedding day, it lead to a long, prosperous marriage!

The limousines arrived at the hotel, at the same time as Annie's father.

"Go on mum," the photographer said smiling, "give your daughter a nice big kiss on the cheek then, beautiful, now your turn dad, hop in there on the other side of your gorgeous daughter, you must be so proud to have so many beautiful daughters." The photographer smiled again. "Now you girls come and kneel down in front of the bride, place the wee ones on your laps, mum and dad, you stay either side of the bride. That's great, fantastic, perfect. Now I want everyone to say, Mount Barker Matured Cheese."

By the time everyone had finished saying Mount Barker Matured Cheese, all were smiling and laughing naturally, so it was a great shot. It was a bit of a private joke, as the photographer was from mount Barker and Annie always bought Mount Barker Matured Cheese.

"Time to go Miss," the limousine chauffeur knocked on the now open doorway to the hotel penthouse suite. "As it is, you're already going to be traditionally twenty minutes late."

"Not Miss for long," Annie beamed. She took a few deep breaths. "Well I guess we best get going then!"

Everyone piled into the lobby lift, they noticed Annie looking a bit pale, smiling nervously.

"Are you O.K. Annie?" her oldest sister Laura asked.

"I'm a little nervous, extremely happy and excited all at once," Annie giggled. "All of you have been great. Thank you for all being part of this day, a very special day, group hug."

They all quickly huddled together in the large, lobby lift, before it reached the ground floor. Annie managed to contain her tears to once again, avoid ruining her so called polly filler. She had tried so hard to keep herself looking as close to perfect as possible for her husband-to-be.

The two limousines pulled up, one behind the other, alongside the high staircase leading up into the church's huge double doors. Annie was to enter through the left aisle, with her dad and exit down the right aisle with her new husband. There were twenty two steps, to get to the door and with children in tow, it took longer than expected, they had already began to get restless.

The children, page boy and flower girls, seemed to be a little confused about what to do but once they approached the big doors to the church, they heard the organ playing the wedding march and they just followed it up the aisle. Without a problem they just breezed slowly up the aisle and followed the music to the front of the church, just like following the pied pipers flute, it was amazing.

All Annie's family and friends, thought she was mad having little children participate in their wedding. Annie had decided that children were a big part of what marriage was all about and couldn't understand why more people didn't involve these special little human beings in their special day. She had also invited children along to with the parents to the reception, although some parents still preferred to get sitters and come on their own.

Annie walked the walk, arm in arm with her dad up to greet her husband-to-be. She was pleased to see he was looking as nervous as she. She kissed her dad on the cheek as he handed her over to Mitch, he shook his hand. She squeezed Mitch's hand and gave him a reassuring smile.

The ceremony was short, enlightening and told a story of marital wisdom. Everyone cheered as they kissed and then cheered even louder when Pastor Stephen introduced them as Mr. and Mrs. Paggett. They were so busy holding each other tight and smooching, as the crowd of one hundred and twenty guests continued clapping and cheering.

Annie walked proudly on her husband's arm. Once all the paper work and signing of the marriage certificate were out of the way, they had time to say hello to everyone as they left the church, on their way for more photos. They then made their way to their wedding reception.

As Annie and Mitch had both enjoyed South Australian wines, they decided on the vintage hall, at the Old Stoneyfell Winery. They had previously been to a fund raising masquerade ball there and really enjoyed the wines, as well as its lay back but slightly formal atmosphere, with a barn feel. It was exactly what they wanted. Not to starched and not to formal either. She wanted everyone to relax and have a great time, celebrating this very emotional, spiritual day.

There was a reasonable sized stage for their three piece band, The Defenders, an appropriate name for a policeman's wedding and boy did they have the crowd up rocking and a rolling all night long. Everyone kept coming up and telling Annie and Mitch, that it was the best wedding they'd ever been to. Everyone was enjoying this very special occasion. Annie couldn't have been happier, than she was at this moment. Little did she know the best was yet to come.

Mitch had been so blown away by the sight of Annie, his bride and he said so in his speech. Sometimes during the evening of their wedding reception, they were being separated as they socialised with their guests. Mitch would throw Annie little sexy glances across the room, just to let her know she was on his mind. Mitch couldn't wait to see what Annie's reaction would be, for he had something special planned for her, awaiting her back at their Honeymoon, Pent House suite at the Intercontinental Hotel. He couldn't wait to get her back there this night and have her all to himself.

John Farnham started to play out loud.

"It's time for the wedding waltz everyone," the DJ announced, "clear the dance floor for the bride and groom."

Annie couldn't believe her ears, as Mitch swooped across the room and took her hand. Mitch had been left to pick out the song for their wedding waltz and Annie had no idea until this moment, what he had chosen. As they entered the dance floor, Mitch held her close.

"Mitch, this is John Farnham isn't it."

"Listen to the words as you dance with me babe."

Annie's eyes began to tear up as she listened to her favourite artist sing out the wedding waltz tune. Mitch had chosen the perfect wedding song. She had never heard this particular John Farnham tune before. It was so sentimental and rang so true, she couldn't have possibly picked out a better song herself. She continued to listen to the lyrics, word for word and with each word, she could not hold back the tears of joy.

The song played on," I lost this heart of mine, the moment you arrived. You're the reason why, my love will never die."

They danced on and on, until the whole dance floor was over full with their wedding guests.

Chapter Six

Exploring One Another

Annie's long, shiny, raven black hair, had been pulled up softly into a curly bun, high on her head. Delicate ringlets fell around her high cheek bones and strong jaw line, flowing onto her shoulders. Her neck and shoulders bare, apart from the velvet choker and pearl broach her mother had given her as something old. She had already removed her veil in the limousine, on the way to the hotel. The honeymoon suite awaiting her.

Mitch lifted Annie out of the limousine, then carried her through the foyer, into the beautiful, dark, marble atrium, towards the lobby lifts. It was a very busy Saturday night and many of the guests were gathered around the hotel piano bar.

Many whispers and comments could be heard about the bride and groom. Annie was very flattered but also embarrassed, by all of the attention from total strangers.

"Oh she looks like a real live princess," one female patron gasped.

"Isn't she stunning!" another commented.

Another couple rushed towards Annie and Mitch.

"You look so beautiful together," the young woman smiled.

"Congrats," the young man added.

"Thank you," Annie and Mitch replied at the same time.

Before anyone had a chance to say another word, Mitch quickly swept Annie into the lobby lift and pushed the top floor to their penthouse suite. Mitch looked into Annie's eyes, hungrily. Holding her tightly now, he kissed her wantonly and so passionately on her eager lips.

A porter, who Mitch had hired, greeted them at their penthouse door.

Mitch quickly whisked Annie over the threshold, she squealed with laughter, excitedly and playfully, she giggled and giggled.

"That will be all thank you porter," Mitch winked.

The porter winked back, then efficiently disappeared down the corridor.

Mitch kicked the door shut and carried Annie to the middle of the room.

"Annie," he whispered in his deep, sexy voice.

"Yes darling."

"Have I told you how beautiful you are to me?"

Annie's eyes smiled, sparkling. "As many times as I've told you how beautiful you are to me baby."

"Well," Mitch grinned cheekily, "I'm telling you again and tonight I'm going to show you, just how precious you are to me and will always be."

Annie's smile beamed from ear to ear, "God I love you so much."

Tears welled up in her eyes.

"Baby there aren't enough words to express how much I love you, so tonight my beautiful wife, I am going to show you." He kissed her sensuously on her red, painted, glossy lips, as he held her in his strong, secure arms.

Annie wrapped her slender arms snugly around his strong, manly neck.

At the bar chilled two glasses of golden, sparkling, Barossa Valley wine. He placed Annie down on the prince sized bed. The bed was adorned with white linen and lace. Her olive complexion, glowing more so now against her white wedding gown, white surrounding her.

Mitch kissed her again deliciously on the lips, before stepping over to the bar to get their celebration drinks. He brought both the glasses to the bedside.

Entwining their arms around each other, they sipped from the cold, sweet but sour, golden liquid. It was very refreshing, considering they'd hardly had time to drink the celebration wine at their wedding reception because they had been so occupied with socialising and catching up with their guests.

"Well, Mrs. Paggett," Mitch chuckled, amused at Annie now having his name. "Finally, I have you all to myself."

Mitch took her wine flute from her hand and placed both their glasses on the bedside table. The table held a huge white bowl of ruby, red strawberries sat with an identical white bowl of freshly, whipped cream.

Mitch then picked up one of the juicy looking strawberries and began dipping it in the whipped cream.

"MM they look delicious," Annie groaned. As she went to take a bite Mitch moved closer to her.

"Not as delicious as you my darling wife." He placed half the strawberry in her mouth, placing his own lips directly over the other half.

Their lips were moist with the juices of the fruit. Divinely and gently they kissed, as the sweet tangy-ness of fresh strawberries tantalised their taste buds.

Mitch pulled her to him and stood her up beside the bed. He clasped her firmly around her slender waist with his strong, comforting arms. He then slid his clasped hands down under Annie's bottom. Picking her up, he spun her around once. As he slid her down, placing her feet back on the ground, she could already feel his excitement firmly against her.

Annie could feel her spirit elevate as her heart began to beat even more rapidly.

Mitch's hands travelled around to the back of her waist. He slowly began to unzip her white satin and lace wedding gown, sliding it off of her shoulders, to reveal her naked breasts. Her gown now hung from her hips, enhancing the slimness of he waist line. Placing his hands gently around the nape of her neck, he looked deeply into her eyes. Slowly and delicately he kissed her soft, moist lips.

Brushing his hands down over her shoulders, he now followed the curves of her hips. He pushed the bulk of the white satin and lace all the way to the floor. As he slid down he kissed her delicately to her navel. On the way up he kissed each of her breasts with feather like touch. Feelings of warmth and tingling filled Annie's being.

Pheromones working overtime, passion and spirit filled their senses. Gently he kissed the place of her heart, then listened to it beating rapidly inside of her. He softly brushed his left hand over her breast and pulled her closer with his right, clasping her firmly against him, kissing her insatiably.

Pulling himself away from her lips, he whispered so hot but so sweetly in her ear.

"I love your heart, step this way my gorgeous wife."

Annie stepped out of her wedding gown, now a pile of white satin and lace in the middle of the penthouse floor. Wearing her white satin court shoes, her white stockings and suspenders covered most of her tanned legs. A sheer pair of high cut, satin, French Knickers was all she wore.

Mitch gently slid his fingers inside her, slowly moving to feel her moist warmness. He moved further in between her thighs. As he kept touching gentle, precious, soft touches, Annie began to moan with pleasure. Mitch kept moving his fingers softly around and around, every now and then he would place another finger further and further inside of her. All the while they kissed warm, moist, hot kisses.

Annie went to feel for Mitch's now hard, hot, throbbing manliness. She only touched it for a split second, before he grabbed her hand away.

"Oh no you don't baby," Mitch growled at her in his deep, sexy voice. "I want this to be a night that you will remember for the rest of our lives."

He took her by both hands and drew her nearer to the welcoming bed. He slowly slid off her white, satin and lace, French knickers, flicked the clips on her suspenders and lay her on the bed, removing her stockings, suspenders and white satin shoes. They kissed each other long and intensely. Annie now lay fully naked but warm. She slowly helped Mitch undress out of his tuxedo and tails. She grabbed him firmly around his waist and pulled his hot naked body next to her now tingling, buzzing skin. She placed her head on his firm, toned, masculine chest, she could feel his heart beating so very loudly with in him.

"I will always love and take care of your heart, my beautiful husband," she whispered softly.

She kissed his chest with gentle lips, then moved up on his warm skin, kissing him passionately on his mouth. She kissed his neck, with slow, subtle touch, as she moved slowly down once again.

"Where do you think your going young lady? I haven't finished with you yet." Mitch smiled mischievously down at her, as he rolled Annie over onto her tummy. "Now you just lay there and behave yourself and enjoy it."

Starting at her lips, he then kissed the nape of the neck, he kissed her from head to toe. He then picked up the bowl of ruby red strawberries. One by one, he began dipping them in a generous amount of thick, whipped, cream, placing them carefully over Annie's bare back.

With every placed strawberry, Annie tingled with excitement and from the sensation of the cool whipped cream. Three strawberries across her naked shoulders, and three down the middle of her naked back.

One by one Mitch devoured each and every one of those strawberries. Licking away every last ounce of evidence of cream, licking and licking and licking, every lick excited Annie more and more. She moaned in ecstasy.

When Mitch had finished devouring the strawberries on Annie's back, he slowly turned her over.

He kissed her, she kissed him back. She tried to get a taste of him. He placed her arms way above her head as he succulently placed his mouth over her breasts.

Mitch sat straddled over Annie's pulsing body. Feeling his erection against her, she looked into Mitch's sexy eyes and groaned.

"Oh baby, this isn't fair, it's torture not being able to touch you. After all, you are my hubby now, I'm allowed to touch you!"

Annie gave Mitch that sad but cute puppy face.

"You must promise not to touch me Annie, you have a whole life time to touch me, this is a night for you to remember. Don't worry, you'll get to touch me soon enough and believe me, I'm going to enjoy it too."

He placed another strawberry dipped in cream between her lips, once again they kissed with the juices from the fruit, tantalising touch, taste sensations. Mitch then one by one again dipped the ruby red strawberries in the thickly whipped cream, placing only four this time.

He place one on each nipple.

One in her navel.

And one on her mount of women.

This time he added a little more whipped cream to each strawberry.

Starting at her lips, he kissed her long and moist, long and warm, long and tender. As he bent over, still straddling her now quiveringly, excited, hot body, she could feel his hot, hard, firmness, rubbing against her abdomen. It excited every nerve ending that existed in her being. She wanted him so much. She had waited so long for this special moment.

Mitch devoured the rich strawberries from her breasts. Licking away the cream and sucking her succulent breasts as though they were themselves, juicy fruit.

He quickly and ravenously devoured the third strawberry from her navel. He licked his tongue firmly from her navel to her mount of women, his licking and sucking becoming stronger and harder.

As he licked away the last traces of cream with his firm tongue, he gently placed a gentle finger inside of her warm moistness. With firm hungry lips, he kissed his way down to her warm, moist place.

Annie could feel her womanly juices flowing and her womanly fruit throbbing with anticipation. She could feel herself blossoming, blooming, ripe for the picking.

Mitch placed another gentle finger inside, he licked her labia softly as he twirled his finger around and around, exploring every inch of her.

"Oh my darling bride, you are so wet," he said as he continued to gently stimulate her with his fingers, licking from the juices of her womanly fountain.

"Oh Mitch, Oh Mitch."

"Ok then, my gorgeous wife, you can touch me now. Do as you will. What would you like to do baby? I'm all yours."

Annie could not hold back any longer, she wanted him inside of her so desperately, she urgently held Mitch's hot, throbbing, erect penis with both hands, feeding it deep inside of her. They kissed ferociously.

She had never felt closer, than than she did with Mitch at this moment. Two lovers intertwined, heart, soul, body and mind.

OOOOOOOOOOOH Mitch!

Chapter Seven

The Honey-Moon Phase

Annie and Mitch had decided to have two months off for their honey-moon, with plenty of time to explore the beautiful Australian land they were both born in. Though Mitch was born in Tamworth, New South Whales, the Country Music Capital and Annie was born in Adelaide, South Australia, The City of Churches, there was still so much of Australia to explore.

They had both agreed to begin their honeymooning in a warmer climate, in North Queensland, the weather being tropical. It was paradise on earth. They stayed in a modest resort called the Radison Royal Palms, in Port Douglas. It was a little cheaper than the Mirage Resort, room there, were $2,000 a night, which is probably money for jam for the rich and famous.

One thing was for sure, Annie and Mitch had promised each other a game of golf at the Mirage golf course, for a small fee of $200 for 18 holes. A casual game, a once in a life time opportunity.

The first day on their honeymoon was spent four wheel driving. The tour guide took them through some of the most stunningly, beautiful, spectacular, huge, tropical rainforest, in all its natural wonder. Annie was amazed at all the overwhelming serenity she could feel.

Hot water springs surrounded by glossy greenery and fernery. The hot water springs, known to have great healing powers. Many of the elderly would come from far and wide to bathe there, in hope of having their ills cured. Some people called it heaven on earth. They swore by it.

The rainforests had trees as high as the eye could see. Natural gushing water falls and mineral falls. Annie and Mitch's professional tour guide, explained that there were many species of plant life, that were becoming endangered. There were many places that the tourists weren't allowed to walk and plants that weren't to be touched by human hands.

They went bird watching and listened to all the different birds and animal sounds of the forest. It was so calming to the soul. The guide led them through an area of forest where there was one extremely large, colourful bird; it was one of the few prehistoric birds left on earth. It was covered in almost shimmering black, blue feathers, with a very large bony horn coming from the top of its head. Annie and Mitch were asked to keep very still, as these large birds were known to be able to claw a human to death. They had thick triple claws and extremely strong kicking action that could tear a human in half.

Annie had heard of these cassowaries, but never in her life, had she dreamt that she'd be standing in a rainforest right next to one.

All of the other tourists and tour guide, finished off a long days touring, by relaxing in the hot water spring. It was like soaking in a very, very warm bubbling spa bath.

Annie lay in in the water in Mitch's arms, her head resting on his chest. Looking up from the forest floor, she could hardly see the sky. The warm bubbles tingled on Annie's relaxed skin. She lay there, in the middle of the vast forest, just being, being part of the greatness.

Glancing up at Mitch, Annie's face glowed peachy and healthy, shiny with steam. Mitch looked down into her eyes, kissing her gently on her forehead.

"This is so totally awesome," he said as he turned his head from left to right and then gazed up at the tall, tall trees.

"Isn't it paradise," Annie replied, as she twisted, turning her head and kissed Mitch on his moist, salty lips.

Silently sitting there, still, in the middle of the forest. Beautiful smells, beautiful sights, beautiful sensations, beautiful sounds. They were lost in the moment.

Well they say that all good things must come to an end. Before long, it was getting dark. The tour guide coaxed everyone back on the four wheel drive coach. It had been a long but extremely, pleasant, enjoyable, relaxing day.

Arriving back at their resort, Annie and Mitch showered and headed straight to the resort restaurant. They were famished. The dining area was open air, with water features and fernery all around. Once again a setting of tranquillity.

They chose from a menu of the freshest seafood and the finest wines. The region well known for freshly caught barramundi, amongst many other tantalising tropical, seafood delicacies. Also being on Australian soil, Annie and Mitch were spoilt for choice when it came to choosing a great tasting, fine, Australian, white wine, to compliment their seafood dishes.

What a very romantic dinner it had been, hand feeding each other their individually chosen dishes and chatting about what an exhilarating day it had been. Annie and Mitch decided to try a few tropical fruit cocktails at the bar before heading back to their room. Both feeling a little tidily, they giggled walking arm in arm."

"What are we going to do back at the room," Mitch smiled as he whispered in Annie's ear.

"My you are good, you must have read my mind, are you think'n what I'm think'n?"

Mitch grabbed her playfully on the bottom.

She squealed, giggling.

As soon as they entered the room, Mitch embraced Annie. Their lips locked as they moved together in harmony, their tongues continued tantalising with the taste of one another. They traced each others lips, over and over, in sweet synchronisation.

Mitch ran his warm, strong hands down over Annie's toned thighs, as they continued to embrace each other tighter and tighter. She could feel his body becoming harder and harder, his muscles firm against hers, holding closer and closer. They had captured every single sensation this day and this was the grand finally. With their warm, moist kissing, they explored each other deeper and deeper, physically, emotionally and spiritually.

Moving as one, they stood there once again, motionless, in the moment. They hadn't even started and their souls began to sore. This is the way Annie always hoped love making would be with her life partner. Not just using her physical body but her heart, mind and spirit all as one with his.

Annie held Mitch's strong broad shoulders. Mitch pulled her up onto him, he held her and spun her around, spinning, spinning and then fell with her giddily onto the bed. Frenziedly but passionately, they continued to make love, franticly pulling at each other's clothes like there was no tomorrow.

Slowly and sensitively he penetrated her, slowly and excitedly she received him. Pleasurable moans, outstretched arm, hands now clasped with their bodies pressing firmly to each other.

Legs and feet intertwining, Annie wrapped her legs tightly around Mitch's waist, bringing him deeper and deeper inside of her.

Mitch moaned and groaned deeply, gasping pleasurably, as he moved in a rocking motion, slithering up and down on Annie's hot, hard, toned yet femininely, soft, smooth body. Moistness of their skin in the tropical, balmy air removed all friction.

"Oh Mitch, don't stop, don't stop, Oh Mitch, Oh Mitch."

Annie's moans becoming louder and louder, holding inside screaming ecstasy, he penetrated her gently, deeper and deeper, rocking her world with every motion, rocking her soul, his hard erectness, moving in rhythm to her thrusting pelvis.

Their spirits united, as only two true lovers can. Their spirits had reached the heights no other spirit could reach. Like some magical explosion, the hot throbbing began, pulsating movement, in and out.

"Oh Annie, Babe, AH, AH Baby," Mitch called loudly, as he gasped for more breath. "Oh God, Oh God, keep going, don't stop,"

Annie drew breath desperately.

Mitch's hands clasped Annie's toned, rounded buttock cheeks, pushing him harder and harder and deeper and deeper inside of her.

Suddenly their moans harmonised, as they held each other, twitching in each others arm. Slowly they released their grip. They gently cuddled into one another, as they lay there exhausted but spiritually energised.

"Thank you, my darling wife," Mitch whispered softly, as he bent over and kissed her on the corner of her mouth, then on her temple and forehead.

Annie always loved it when Mitch kissed her on the forehead like that. Her mother always told her, that it was a sign of respect.

"I should be thanking you," Annie smiled sweetly. "That was amazing." She then kissed him on the nose and in return on the forehead.

Annie lay in Mitch's comforting arms and before long, he was fast asleep. She was laying there thinking to herself, drifting into her subconscious mind. Drifting back to one of her last ward placements as a nurse. Even she thought herself a little strange, thinking of work, especially after such a wonderful, erotic lovemaking session with her gorgeous, new husband.

Crossing her mind were the amount of deaths there had been on her last ward. She remembered that there had been three staff suicides. What she couldn't understand was, why no one liked discussing these matters.

Why were people so afraid of discussing death? Here we all are, the human race, the most communicable beings on the earth, if not in the universe! For goodness sakes, we still can't talk to each other, we still don't really know how to clearly communicate.

Why do people procrastinate about nothing, gossip about another, cause heart ache and sorrow?

Annie always believed that hypocrisy bred procrastinators too. So, in other words, people who stand around gossiping, causing misery, to another almost always innocent, harmless soul, is wasting precious working time, so, therefore, becoming a hypocritical procrastinator.

Why is it, human beings, have trouble talking about the things that really matter the most, the real deal? Death and dying, or the high percentage of young, adult suicides in the world today, especially amongst young males?

If I ignore it, would it go away?

If I don't think about it, would it never happen to me, or someone I really love?

Annie continued to lie there and wonder. She knew people could do better, but maybe themselves, didn't think they were worth it?

Before long, Annie had also drifted off into a deep sleep.

Suddenly, she woke with a gasp, she sat up abruptly in the bed.

"Mitch wake up, wake up," She screamed. She shook him vigorously. "Please darling, please wake up." Tears began to well in Annie's eyes and a hard, aching lump started throbbing in her throat, she found it difficult to swallow. Her heart was pounding out of control. "Please Mitch, wake up, wake up." As she shook him harder, Annie began to sob.

Mitch sat up in a state of shock.

"What is it Annie, what's going on?"

"Is someone trying to break in?

He looked over at the door and then back to her, not knowing what to think.

"Oh Mitch," Annie gave out a big sigh of relief. "Thank God your O.K. I had this awful dream, well, it was more of a nightmare really. I was helping to lay out the dead and then I woke up and I, I, Oh it's so awful, I can't even repeat it. You see, I looked over at you and I couldn't see you breathing. I thought . . . ."

Mitch held his finger up to her trembling lips.

"As you can see, Pumpkin, I am alive and well," Mitch smiled reassuringly at her.

"I'm so sorry to wake you Baby, It's just that you looked so glazed and I swore I couldn't see you breathing. So sorry."

"I'm afraid you're not going to get rid of me that easily, believe me," Mitch grinned cheekily. "I've got plenty of life left in me yet."

Mitch pulled the sheets over both their heads and grabbed Annie to bring her closer. Placing both her hands down into his hot groin, he cupped her hands in his and held them over his hot, hard manliness. "Feel what I mean?" His warm breath tingled in her ear.

"MMM, that's much better," Annie giggled, "I can feel your life in my hands."

Chapter Eight

Back To Reality

The honeymoon was drawing fast to a close and there was still so much to explore. Annie and Mitch had decided to finish their honeymooning in Adelaide, South Australia. They had decide to base their lives there, being a great place to raise a family. The cost of living wasn't as high as the other states or Territory.

The bed and breakfasts on offer were plentiful, it was so nice to have all the vineyards at an easy distance. All within a reasonably driving distance too. Country, beaches and waterways and a stones throw away from the CBD. Tasting and collecting wine was one of the highlights of their honeymoon.

They spent a few days hiking in the Flinders Ranges, absolutely spectacular surroundings. It was quite the opposite of being in the tropical Port Douglas of North Queensland, although nothing could top the wonder of the Great Barrier Reef, where Annie and Mitch spent quite a lot of time scuba diving.

Aaah, but the camping under the stars, with no one in sight, not even a tour guide, was really a place you could lose yourself in nature, or as Mitch and Annie found it, losing themselves in each other. It was a known fact that the stars appeared clearer and brighter here, than anywhere else in Australia, along the mountain ranges, it was absolutely breathtaking. They were lucky enough to be there during the night of the large, yellow, fully illuminated moon. It lit up the night, making everything so much more romantic.

Time was running out. Catching up with family, before getting back to the daily grind, was a priority on Mitch and Annie's list.

Mitch's Mum was first on their visiting list. She had recently come over from Gosford, New South Whales. Gosford was a pretty place, a little town, not far from the beautiful Central Coast. Annie really loved Marie and Marie treated her as if she were her own daughter.

Annie had much hope for Marie, who had recently been diagnosed with breast cancer. She'd already undergone quite a lot of treatment, including a radical mastectomy, lyphectomy, radiotherapy and chemotherapy. Now on Tamoxyfen tablets, she still wasn't very well.

Mitch was ecstatic when Marie told him, she had finished her treatment but Annie new when they stopped treatment, it meant there was nothing else doctors could do for her. Mitch was in denial and would only accept that his mother was in remission.

Annie didn't have the heart to tell him otherwise. She thought by telling Mitch the truth, it would be like wishing death upon his mother.

Annie was very spiritually connected to Marie, they shared a special bond. Having many a deep and meaningful, private conversations about her situation and condition, it gave Marie a comfort that her four sons just could not provide.

Annie and Mitch decided it would be a nice idea, to take Marie on a little holiday before they returned to work. Marie had been in and out of hospital of late, she wasn't drinking enough fluids after her treatment and this was making her extremely ill.

Taking her to Kangaroo Island, just off the South Australia coast, was just what she needed. It's a very natural and tranquil place to visit. They had also told Marie the good news, that they were trying to start a family, in hope of giving her a grandchild to look forward to.

It was a wonderfully busy week, squeezing in attractions from all over Kangaroo Island. Thank goodness Marie was feeling a little brighter to be able to enjoy it and the company of her youngest son and his new bride.

Annie was very impressed with Marie, as she wanted to get involved with everything, like she was on her last wing. They went hiking in the dark, with the tour guides, through the Kelly Hill Caves, looking at all the formed stalactites and stalagmites. All the torch's and hard hats were all provided by the tour company.

Seal Bay was amazing, with seals of all shapes and sizes, lolling all over the seashore. The tour guide had warned all the tourists not to make any sudden moves, otherwise the adult seals may attack.

They went out in the middle of the night, to spot the ferry penguins, doing their march. An army of penguins marching all in a row. They were so adorable and so cute but not in the dictionary meaning of the word. Each penguin, made sure they didn't leave one another behind, all taking good care of each other. Human beings could really learn a lot from these beautiful creatures.

Kingscote, the main town on the Island, was full of tourists from all over the world. A lot of them came to have their photo taken with the cuddly Koala, especially the Japanese.

One day in particular, was set aside for a fishing expedition down American River. They couldn't have chosen a more perfect day for their fishing cruise. When they returned to the Island Resort, later that afternoon, all the fresh fish they'd caught, was specially prepared by the head chef, free of charge, for all the fishing expedition clientele to enjoy. It was a nice way to finish the day and very tasty indeed, a wonderful but exhausting day.

Annie and Mitch certainly left Marie with some happy memories. It wouldn't be long now, they had to return to the real world, to continue with their careers.

Annie decided to apply for a nursing position in one of the local, general hospitals, so she could gain more experience in clinical areas. She was now almost twenty two years of age, more confident now, than when she was a young nurse assistant three years ago.

She felt she was ready for a challenge. If only she realised, what she was getting herself into. It all began, when she went for a job interview at the Lake View Hospital, or LVH as some people called it.

Pulling up in the LVH car park, Annie admired the fancy, expensive cars parked there. SAAB, with white a Corvette, she recognised as being Doctor Albertoss's car and other brand new, seventy thousand dollar four wheel drives.

She always thought her white convertible, Holden Astra, was good enough for her, after all, it was Australian. She'd washed, polished and detailed it for the occasion. She had also washed polished and detailed herself for the interview, adding a little polly filler, wanting everything to be just right.

Under the shade of a big, old gum tree, was just the right shady place for her to park. It was a warm, spring day, with clear, blue sky. The sun glistened through the fresh, new green gum leaves. There was a soft, undisturbed, northerly breeze. It made Annie tingle with good health.

Dressed smartly, in a fitting, light cream, linen jacket and midi skirt, cut just above the knee, it complimented her well kept figure. Her hair pulled back neatly, into a French roll. Shoes cream with a slight heel, colour coordinated, of course, to match the rest of her outfit, just as her mum had taught her.

She swiftly hopped out of her vehicle, not thinking about those pre-interview nerves, she strut towards the entrance. On the way, she did a postural check, making shore she was standing straight and as tall as possible. It's something she had done as a small child. It was the way she approached everything in life. She could hear her mother singing to her. "Walk tall, walk straight, and look the world right in the eye. That's what my mother told me, when I was about knee high!" Annie smiled to herself. Even though her own mother, still physically alive, she could feel her walking beside her this day in spirit.

She approached the big, double, glass, sliding doors, the main entrance to the hospital. The glass doors slid open slowly. As Annie entered, she could see that the main building was about fifty years old and in ill repair, the interior design, left a whole lot to be desired. "Yuck," Annie muttered quietly to herself. Grey walls, grey floors. Don't think that's colour I'd want to be looking at, if I wanted to get well in a hurry, she thought.

The LVH was a very busy institution. People sat along the corridors, waiting to be admitted, or waiting emergency treatment. Young, sick children crying, their parents with worried, concerned looks on their faces.

Relatives of dying patients, huddled together, in support of one another, eagerly hoping for some good news from the doctor, news that would never come, the doctor only telling them what they didn't really want to hear.

"Sorry, but there is nothing else we can do."

Annie continued walking down the long, cold, grey corridor. The sign ahead directing her to the administration office. She took several deep breaths, standing tall, relaxing herself for what she hoped would be a cool, calm interview. She slowly but assertively pushed the administration office open. A young attractive secretary sat behind the desk.

Annie smiled.

"Good morning," she said, "My name is Annie Paggett and I am here for an interview, in regards to the nursing position advertised in last Saturdays paper."

"Certainly," the secretary replied, returning her smile. My name is Kate, just take a seat and Miss Saij, will be with you shortly."

"Thank you."

"You're welcome."

Suddenly, a stern looking woman appeared in the door way, inside the administration office.

"Hello, I'm Miss Saij, you must be Annie Paggett!"

"Yes that's right."

"Just step into my office and take a seat, I just have to pull up your file and references." She concentrated on flicking through the filing cabinet, before swiftly keying information into the computer in front of her.

Annie sat breathing easily, much more relaxed than she'd expected.

"Serenity costs you nothing my dear."

What a wise lady her nanna was, all that old fashioned common sense and wisdom. She could hear her nanna, as if she were sitting on the seat right beside her. Annie recalled many of her nannas sayings, the older Annie became, the more sense they made.

Miss Saij began by asking, "What makes you think you are the right person for this position Annie?"

"Well," Annie replied, "for a long time now, I've wanted to be a nurse, hence the reason I continued on from my nurse assistant position to do my full nursing training. From a very young age, I've always enjoyed looking after people, even when they're not sick. The sheer job satisfaction, that comes with helping someone in their time of need, comfort and support that can not be replaced by any computer or machine. Thanked for no other reason, than just being there. The touch of a caring hand, reassurance in your eyes and peaceful, compassionate smile on your face. It's a big ask to help protect another human beings emotions, emotion that comes from more than just flesh and blood . . . I believe compassion runs deeper than that. I believe, it's a very spiritual experience, it touches your soul and changes your life forever.

"For I believe we are all of one soul and what we pass on to others, how we treat each other, will affect us as a whole"

Annie continued.

"During my time in the work force, I've had other opportunities to take other pathways, but I feel, I was always led back to nursing. I really enjoy it. At the moment I am training to be a fitness trainer, it keeps me healthy and fit for my job, plus it also teaches me more about anatomy and physiology and biochemistry. I find all of the human body so very interesting. I also believe it will help me become a better nurse. At this stage, I'm teaching seven sessions a week. It's part of my training, to gain hours towards my certificate. Will this affect my chances of getting this nursing position?" Annie asked.

"No, no, of course not," Miss Saij assured her, "Anything you do in your own time is your own business. Besides, you could go horse riding tomorrow and fall and break your collar bone any day of the week. We have roster request, so if you want to, you could request where you want days off, afternoons, day or night shift, to fit in with your teaching."

"That sounds excellent, thank you. I thought it might jeopardise my chance of getting the position?"

"Of course not," Miss Saij grinned forcibly. "If you were to get the position, when would you be able to start?"

"When ever I am required."

Miss Saij smiled, this time a little softer. "How does twenty seventh of October sound to you?"

"That's great," Annie replied not to sound to over excited. "Do you mean I've got the job?"

"Yes, If you don't mind me saying so, your references, are amongst the best nursing and personal references, I've ever seen."

"Really," Annie couldn't help but smile. "Thank you, thank you so much, I hope I will be of credit to you."

"Here, take this," Miss Saij handed her an identification security card. "Go down to the basement to collect your uniforms. You can collect your personal ID and roster, on your orientation day. Be here at 0900hrs on the twenty-seventh of October. You will be starting with one other new comer. Congratulations and welcome aboard."

Ms Saij got up from her desk and leant over to shake Annie's hand.

"See you in a few weeks," Annie smiled as she once again tried to contain her excitement. "Have a nice afternoon. Thank you for your time today Miss Saij."

"Your welcome Annie, see you in a few weeks time."

"Bye Katie, nice meeting you." Annie smiled at the receptionist as she prepared to exit the office.

"Nice meeting you too Annie, I gather by the look on your face, everything went well!"

"Much better than I expected, I didn't think I'd find out today, that I got the position, but I did. See you on the twenty-seventh of October."

"See you then." Katie called as Annie left the office.

Finding the lifts, Annie took herself to the basement to collect her uniforms.

The Basement was freezing. She could see that compared to the basement, the rest of the hospital was a five-star hotel. Annie walked along the cold, grey, cement walls, until she came to a caged enclosure.

A sign hung on the caged door. SEWING ROOM, PLEASE RING THE BELL. Annie pushed the buzzer.

"Hullo, hullo," said a chubby little Italian lady approaching her.

"Hullo, howa are you today? My nama is a Malina, Hospitala sewinga lady."

Even though Malina's Italian accent was quite heavy, Annie could still understand her quite clearly. Annie had grown up with many Italian friends. Fond memories of one of her Italian primary school friends, Maria, swept passed Annie's mind . . . Annie would swap her vegimite sandwich, for Maria's chunky, Italian bread with tuna, just about every day at school lunch time.

Annie was fitted with her white, nurses uniforms, some of the hems were a bit shabby. She didn't trouble Malina about this, as she was able to blind stitch her own hems, her mother had taught her well.

Malina folded the uniforms with care and placed them in a clear, plastic bag.

"Thera you go Bella, "she smiled at Annie, as she handed her the bag. "Gooda lucka hey, witha you new jobba, aha." Malina's dark eyes sparkled.

Annie was eager to get home to tell Mitch the exciting news.

This was a good day and it just kept getting better. Annie found herself day dreaming, thinking about how Mitch would react, when she told him she'd got the job.

She new he would want to take her out to celebrate. One of the favourite restaurants, was the Broham Place, at the top of the Adelaide Hotel. It overlooked the beautiful church they were married in, The Broham Place Uniting. You could see the whole city from the dining room window. The river Torrens glistened at night, with the lights of the city.

Annie continued to daydream, as she drove home in a very relaxed manner, enjoying the warm spring breeze, sweeping across her face. Occasionally she glanced down at the speedometer, to make sure she wasn't going over the speed limit. She so hoped and prayed, that Mitch didn't get overtime, as she could not wait to tell him the good news, she was absolutely busting, like a kid in a candy shop.

As she pulled into the driveway of their modest, two story, suburban home, she saw Mitch's black, Holden Utility. She smiled, remembering the night they kissed beside his old, red Holden Gemini and how he told her he was getting a new car. She remembered his excitement when he purchased it, he was such a lad, a real man's man.

Jumping out of her car, Annie couldn't make it to her front door quick enough. Not quite placing her key in the door lock, the door swung open. There stood Mitch as tall and as gorgeous as ever.

"Hi there darling," she gasped, "home already?"

"Yes," Mitch replied, "we actually got off early for a change. It was a quiet day, so there wasn't a lot of paper work to do, thank goodness."

Annie placed her arms around Mitch's strong, masculine neck. Mitch held Annie's little waist in his two hands, then clasped them behind her, pulling her closer. Looking up at Mitch, with a mischievous smile, Annie said,

"I've got some great news."

"That's right, you went for that job interview at Lake View Hospital today didn't you?" He looked down at Annie and kissed her sensuously and squarely on the lips.

"So, how did it go? By the look on your face it went well?"

"Of course not silly, I've got this look on my face because I'm pleased to see you."

Annie's smile beamed from ear to ear. "And of course I got the job."

Mitch raised his eyebrow, in that sort of cute, sexy way he did, whenever he was surprised.

"You mean they've already told you?"

"Yes, they accepted me today, straight after my interview. I start in a few weeks time on the twenty seventh of October. Look here's my uniforms."

"MMMM White ones. Now you should feel like a real nurse." He smiled. "By the way, you look gorgeous in your white suit. He frowned at Annie, as he gave her another cheeky smile. "Got the job already hey, boy they must have been desperate for staff," Mitch chuckled.

"Thanks a million darling." Annie rounded her mouth in an O shape, at Mitch's sarcastic remark.

Mitch pulled away and started running up the polished wooden entryway. He glanced back at her, teasing her with his sexy eyes, teasing her to chase. She dropped her bag, slammed the front door behind her and hurriedly kicked off her shoes. Running down the hall, she began to slip and slide all over the place in her stocking feet, she was belly laughing so much, she almost lost her balance and fell over.

Mitch jumped out from behind the living room doorway, letting out an almighty growl. Annie squealed. They grabbed hold of one another, laughing uncontrollably, wrestling each other to the floor. They landed on the big, fake furry, white rug, in the centre of the room. Annie was laying flat on her back now, laughing and panting, smiling with her mouth wide open. Her rib cage expanded with every breath, she laughed and laughed and tears welled in her eyes.

Mitch clasped Annie's hands to the floor, he looked down at her with solemn sexiness. He sat firmly over her hips. They were lost in each others eyes.

"I love you Annie." He bent over and gave her an open mouthed kiss, long, luscious and lingering.

"Annie whispered sensuously in Mitch's ear."

"Love you forever Babe."

"I'm such a lucky man."

Mitch groaned in his deep voice, "I love you more."

He slowly lay gently on her, their lips once again meeting sensitively, only this time, it seemed to linger, much, much longer. Mitch's legs clasped tight on either side of Annie's tender body. Lips pressing more firmly now. Annie unclasped Mitch's hands from hers. Sliding her hands freely and firmly over his broad, strong shoulders, down past the curves of his back, firmly grabbing his cute firm gluteus maximus. (Buttocks)

Mitch took his hands and ran them softly through Annie's hair, removing the clasp that held her French roll. Her hair tumbled long, dark and shiny onto the fluffy white rug.

Their kisses became more excited now. Mitch began gently kissing, sucking along Annie's slender neck. He new that this was where Annie was the most sensitive. If there was any such thing as a G spot, this was definitely one of her most sensitive, for Annie anyway. It aroused her during love making and sent tingles all over her being. Annie gasped, as Mitch continued to kiss her neck. He began to undo her white polished cotton blouse, as her white suit jacket fell open. He slid his warm hand inside her white satin and lace bra and caressed her breast ever so gently.

Annie smoothed her hands back over his body, placing her hands on his jaw line, she kissed his mouth and his lips, licking them playfully, inside and out, not missing a trace, with her soft moist, warm tongue.

Mitch slowly continued to unbutton her blouse, it gaped open to her belly button, he rubbed his strong hands over her firm flat tummy. Grabbing hold of her waist, he lay sweet kisses lower and lower. When he realised he could not go any further because of the restriction of her well fitting skirt, he slowly slid a hand down her hips and up under her skirt. Releasing one of her suspenders, he reached her bare legs. He rubbed his manly fingers up and down the inside of her thighs, running them smoothly, up and down inside of her now, throbbing, hot groins, exploring her now.

He pushed her skirt up to her waist, he once again came up and kissed her passionately on her lips, kissing down along her neck, gently caressed both her breasts, unclasping the front of her pretty lace bra, nibbling, licking and sucking her now very erect nipples.

Annie placed both her hands inside Mitch's police uniform shirt and ran her hands over his pectorals. His nipples were hard, she unbuttoned his shirt and pushed it back over his masculine shoulders. She kissed and licked his chest and flicked her tongue over his nipples. She kissed his whole body down to his naval.

Holding his stomach in, Annie found space to fit her hands down the front of his police trousers, she could feel the heat, even before her hands got passed his loosened belt buckle. Frantically she undid it all the way. Suddenly she could feel it, it was so warm and so, so hard, it felt wonderful in her hands. She rubbed and rubbed it, up and down, so firmly up and down.

Mitch was licking and cupping her breasts in his manly hands as she held onto his penis now with both hands. Annie moved further down to feel more of his pulsating manliness. Quietly they groaned, pleasurably together. Mitch continued to gently manipulate Annie with his fingers. Annie pushed Mitch's satin boxers and police trousers down to his thick, toned thighs and tight quadriceps. She held his large, hard, hot, throbbing manhood even more firmly in her hands.

Annie played her fingers over his large erect organ, like a piano. Feeling over his every bump, his every groove, exploring and enjoying every morsel of her tantalising investigation. Gently she sucked and licked his soft parts below his hardness.

Her excited husband now had his strong hands on the inside of Annie's G-string knickers, slowly and gently twirling his fingers around and around her soft, moist labia and then her erect clitoris. He twirled faster and faster, until Annie could stand it no more.

"Oh Mitch, Oh baby, I'm going to explode if you keep that up. AHHHHHHHHHH Ah Ah Ah OH God Ah Ahhhhhhhhh."

Mitch held Annie Tight, she kissed him lusciously on the lips and then slid down his torso. She reached his thighs and delicately kissed both his hips. She slipped his trousers all the way off and removed his boxers. Running her hands up and down the inside of his thighs. Every time she would move her hands upwards, she tantalised his manhood and then she would move down again. She began stroking his hard now hot penis, the hot, long, hard, throbbing shaft, she gently flicked her tongue over its tip. She softly sucked and licked over his knob, moving her hands alternatively over his body, licking and stroking with one hand and then the other.

Annie licked and sucked his firm, smooth, soft knob more and more and then licked down the length of his shaft.

"Ahhhhhhhhh," Mitch flinched for a moment," Aahhh Annie baby, "he squinted sexily down at her, if you keep that up baby, there's no telling what I might do?"

Mitch pulled Annie up onto him. She spread her legs, straddled his thighs and fed that beautiful, throbbing, hot, long, hard, manhood, into her warm, very lubricated mount of woman.

Like a physical, moving, human orchestra, they began to play in tune. Their bodies moving in poetic rhythm. Pumping together as one. Hips thriving and heaving, their hearts beating out of control. Lips warmly pressing, pressing hard, as warm as the sun. Then finally a synchronised explosion between two spirit's of the soul.

Annie lay limp upon Mitch. He held her in his arms, in awe of their passion for one another.

Mitch rarely smoked cigarettes but enjoyed the odd one after their extravagant lovemaking sessions. He lay there puffing away with a pleasant smirk on his face, occasionally blowing smoke rings in the air. Laying contently beside him, Annie began to poke her finger through his smoke rings and watched them disperse into the warm atmosphere.

"Come on now," Mitch grinned, "That will be enough poking for one day. O.K. Gorgeous.

Lets get up and shower together. How about we go to dinner, to celebrate your new career?"

Mitch took Annie in his arm once more, giving her a huge hug, smooching her on her cheek.

"I'm such a lucky man."

"And I'm very blessed to have you my darling. Where would you like to go for dinner?" Annie asked.

"Where else is there? The Broham Place Restaurant, or is there somewhere else you'd rather go my darling wife?"

"No, NO, Broham is great, fine, I'll make a booking, then I'll meet you in the shower, O.K. Gorgeous?" Annie rubbed her nose with Mitch's nose, like the Eskimos.

She quickly gathered up her clothes from the fluffy, white rug, dumped them in the the laundry and proceeded to the bedroom to fetch her pink satin wrap.

She loved the feel of satin against her naked body. She remembered the day Mitch gave the pink, satin wrap to her.

"Try it on," he insisted.

She recalled how he told her, she looked like a movie star, she was so flattered, she blushed. He said some of the sweetest things.

She dialled the restaurant on their bedroom, cordless phone.

"Hello, Yes it's Annie Paggett here. I'd like to make a booking for two, preferably a window seat please. Yes for this evening, seven thirty please, that's excellent, thank you, bye bye."

Annie swiftly hung the phone up and rushed to the bathroom to shower with her beloved.

There was plenty of time to get ready, as it was only four o'clock in the afternoon, or as Mitch and Annie would say by the twenty four hour clock, 1600hrs. Mitch preferred to use it as he was required to use those times at work and so was Annie with her nursing. It just seemed easier for the two of them.

As she approached the shower, she began to slip her satin wrap from her naked body. It dropped to the shiny white, French tiled floor. She snuck up to the shower alcove, slid a naked leg in and rubbed it up and down on Mitch's strong, lean legs. He opened the door wide to invite her inside.

He kissed her with his very wet, soft lips. Mitch looked into her eyes, as he held her closely and rocked her to and fro under the warm water. The invigorating, hot water spray felt wonderful as Mitch held her in his embrace.

"What times dinner beautiful?" he asked.

"1930 Sargent Paggett," Annie smiled cheekily up at her husband.

"MMMMM Then we have plenty of time," he mused as he glanced at the mirrored ceiling, continuing to hold her lovingly.

"May I have the soap please darling?"

Mitch passed the soap but not before lathering it well in his own hands.

He began to massage her shoulders and up onto her neck.

"MMMMM, that feels wonderful honey, don't stop, "Annie moaned, "MMMM"

Annie lathered the soap and in return began massaging Mitch's shoulders. She massaged his firm bulging pectorals.

Mitch slowly and feelingly slid his hands down to Annie's firm perk bosom, slipping sensuously with the slither of the soap. Slippery all over now, their naked bodies touching, sliding, naked and close. Slithery hands, frantically moving all over each other. Holding one another's bottoms tightly, pushing pelvis on pelvis.

Mitch rinsed his hands a little, before grabbing Annie's thighs, as he slowly slid her up to sit on his hips. She held onto his broad shoulders and kissed him with her open, wet mouth. Annie wrapped her arms and legs more tightly around him, increasing her leverage. Pushing herself up on him, she sat dangling over his erection. It was rubbing against her, teasing her, inviting her. He long wet hair, clinging to her breasts. Mitch pushed the hair aside and began lifting her even higher, pressing her breasts towards his waiting mouth. He pressed them juicily into his mouth as he sucked on them and flung his tongue around on her erect, extremely excited nipples.

While Mitch held her tight, in his secure muscley arms, Annie reached down between her spread legs and placed his penis closer to her vagina, letting it sit just so. She continued to move her hips and rub her pelvis up and down on his big erection.

The temptation was so great, neither of them could wait any longer. Annie reached down again, this time placing Mitch inside her very wet, womanly entrance, feeding it deep inside her. Warm and inviting, there was no stopping them now. It was as though at that moment, nothing could tear them apart. Moving up and down in rhythm, Mitch placed

Annie up against the wall. Still slithering over one another. The harder Annie thrust, the deeper Mitch entered and entered and entered her, deeper and deeper and deeper.

Annie suctioned her lips to his neck, as she tried to smother her moans of divine ecstasy. Mitch moving deeper and deeper inside of her, as she clung to him, sucking onto each others lips, smothering moist kisses, delicious and juicy, they devoured each other.

Mitch lifted her higher and more physically and spiritually, as he pressed her harder against the wall, pressing his delicious penis, harder and deeper inside of her now saturated, swelling, tightening vagina. She gasped for breath.

Groaning louder and louder, now they lifted together. Moving in sequence with each other. Songs of pleasure, with desperate, opened-mouth kisses. Throbbing, tightening and pulsating strongly through every part of their bodies.

"Oh my God, Oh my God, Ah Ah Ah Ah," Annie cried out.

"Come baby, come, Oh Oh I'm gonna come baby, come with me." Mitch's deep, sexy, voice was enough to tip Annie to the point of no return.

"Oh Mitch."

"Oh God Annie."

Ahhhhhhhhhh

Ahhhhhhhhhhhhh.

Groaning louder and louder, until, they synchronised their orgasms together.

Then silence, as Mitch fell against the opposite wall. Annie slid down from his wet, pumped, athletic body. She found the floor, her head still spinning from all their love making and creating all those feel good moments. Their bodies saturated with lovemaking hormones and their spirits soaring to the sky.

Annie leaned against him and they lay against the wet, steamy bathroom wall, loosely holding one another. Annie let out an almighty sigh.

"Oh my God, that was the most thorough wash I've ever had." She smiled and let out a little giggle. She lay her head restfully upon Mitch's tanned, toned chest and placed her hand over his heart.

""Mmmmmmmm, yes indeed," Mitch replied. "Very, very nice," he groaned.

Leaning over, he smooched her on her wet cheek and wrapped his arms all the way around her, giving her a big squeeze. "I guess we'd better get a move on darling, if we're going to dinner!" He rest his head on top of Annie's. Annie grabbed Mitch's wrist watch, to check the time. "1800hrs goodness, time does fly when you're having fun." She smiled and winked at Mitch, quickly kissed him smack on the lips, before getting out of the shower.

Annie stood before the mirrored robes in the bedroom, holding up her two favourite evening gowns, still hanging on the pretty pink, satin, padded hangers that one of her patients had made for her, as a wedding gift.

While Annie was putting on her polly filler(make up)and doing her hair, Mitch had already fully dressed, apart from his dinner jacket and tie. Standing next to Annie as she stood there in her pink lacy G-string and halter bra, with her black stilettos, Mitch admired his wife's reflection in the mirror before admiring his own.

"Annie," he said, "you'd better hurry up and get covered up, or else we won't be going anywhere."

"Oh I can't decide what to wear," she frowned. "Should I wear this black and white halter dress, that one I wore to my graduation dinner, or this royal blue one, I've hardly warn?"

"Look babe," he looked at Annie adoringly, "you'd look great in anything, or nothing, you'd even look good in a potato sack."

Smiling back at his reflection, Annie laughed, "It's funny you should say that darling. My dad said that to me when I asked if I could have a new dress for my high school formal. I think he only said that because he wanted me to feel good about myself, as our budget was pretty tight with so many children. Lucky for me, mum's a good seamstress and dress maker; she bought the latest fashionable material and whipped me me up a great little off the shoulder number, you remember the ones with the frills right around. I was the best dressed there."

"I'm sure you would have been the best looking girl in the room, without a doubt." Mitch pointed to the black halter neck. "Wear that one, then we'll be colour coordinated," he raised his eye brows. Now hurry up and dress before I keep you here all to myself."

"Oh you promise," Annie smiled cheekily.

Chapter Nine

The Pathway Of Uncertainty

What a beautiful spring day it was. The weeks had gone by so quickly. Annie could not believe that the orientation day had arrived already. She pulled on her freshly ironed nurses uniform. Mitch had already left for work, as he had been rostered on a special policing task and had to start very early.

Annie checked the time on her nurses watch, as she carefully pinned it on the left side of her breast.

"Great," she chatted to herself. "Time for some breakfast and coffee." She had a bit of a laugh to herself, she was so like her nanna, always reminding and talking to herself, as well as her higher power. She figured it kept her nan sane for ninety six years, so it wouldn't do her any harm.

She quickly pulled her hair up into a ponytail and twirled it around the top of her head to create her bun. It was always the same, ever since the day she started nursing, always wanting to look as professional as possible. She couldn't believe how many nurses wore their hair down theses days. Sticking in the fourth bobby pin, she smiled at herself in the mirror, "That'll do."

As the day was so brilliant, Annie decided to have her coffee in the back garden. She sat there happily sipping away. The birds were singing, she could see a Rainbow Lorikeet playing amongst the gum trees, gliding from one tree to another, it was so peaceful to watch. Annie always loved the approaching warmer weather, it brought out the best in nature. So many colourful birds and beautiful blooms. On this glorious day, Annie felt so centred. She was more than ready to start her new nursing position.

After setting the house alarm and locking up, Annie approached her car, which Mitch had already parked in the driveway. As she got closer, she noticed something on her windscreen wiper.

"Oops, didn't see that one," she unwrapped what she thought was a parking fine. To her surprise, it was a sweet little not from Mitch, written on a police calling card, it read,

"Officer 45872/2 Loves You, good luck on your first day, look forward to seeing you when we get home, hugs and kisses, Mitch Xoxo."

Just when Annie thought the day couldn't get any better, it did.

The drive to work only took about twenty minutes, that was mainly because of the seven sets of lights, not to mention the goods train, the draw bridge, then the passenger train and then another set of lights. It was quite a busy little run in inner suburbia.

Here she was once again, in the big car park of the LVH; Lake View Hospital. She parked in the staff area, under a big shady tree, she was lucky enough to find one just before 0900hrs as many other staff would have already started at 0700hrs.

Feeling quite comfortable in her nursing clobber, Annie once again made her way to the nursing administration to commence her orientation. She remembered their would be another new nurse being orientated this day.

When Annie arrived at the office, it was empty. Just as she sat down, the office door swung open. Annie watched eagerly to see who would enter.

She couldn't believe her eyes, it was one of her good friends Lindsy, they had been friends since they were nine.

"Lindsy, my goodness, what are you doing here?'

"That's funny Annie," Lindsy smiled from ear to ear, "I was just going to ask you the same question!"

"Well," said Annie, "I applied for a nursing position in the paper."

"So did I."

"And I got the job," Annie said excitedly.

"Guess what/ So did I."

"Wow," Annie could not believe that her best friend had also applied for a nursing position in the same hospital and was starting on the very same orientation day. Their friendship had always been marked by a series of coincidences. Sometimes Annie would just be thinking of Lindsy and the phone would ring, or Annie would pop in to visit Lindsy, when she was in the middle of a situational crisis and needed a shoulder to cry on. Lindsy always said that Annie had perfect timing a sixth sense almost. Today was no different. Annie always believed in destiny and there would be a perfectly good explanation further down the track.

"Where will you be working," Annie asked her.

"I've asked to work in the Emergency Department, besides, I've heard there are quite desperate for staff there, so I guess I'm lucky in that respect." Lindsy sighed.

"Are you nervous?" Annie asked.

"Not yet."

"Nor me either." Annie said.

"If we are working in separate departments, there would be no reason for them to know we are friends, would there?"

"I guess not," said Lindsy, looking at Annie quite peculiarly.

"You know," Annie smiled reassuringly at her friend, "Just in case some time in the future we could end up working together. If they know we are friends, they might be reluctant to put us in the same department.

"Oh, that's comforting to know," Lindsy giggled. "For a moment there, I thought you were disowning me."

"Don't be silly," Annie replied, as both of them sat laughing together.

"So, mums the word," Said Annie, as they sat there shaking hands and giggling like a couple of school girls. Understandable as they were both only just twenty.

Annie really appreciated her good friend being there with her, it was like starting year four all over again.

The good Lord works in mysterious ways, Annie thought to herself as they sat quietly.

The office door swung open again, this time abruptly.

"Good morning girls," It was Ms Saij.

"Good morning Ms Saij," The girls replied in unison.

"Come into my office girls," Ms Saij waved to them, directing them through her office doorway.

"Just a little bit of paper work to complete, then we will give you a quick tour of the facility, before directing you to the areas you have been allocated."

Annie and Lindsy filed through the doorway one after the other.

"Now Annie, you will be working in the Gynaecology Unit and Lindsy, you will be in the Emergency Department as you have requested. Bare in mind girls, that you will be supernumerary, so if people are busy, which they are more often than not, don't feel obligated to take on their work load. Just let everyone know you are on orientation and as part of occupational health and safety, you must read up on all policy manuals. Now, before you go, sign yourself in so you are counted in staff numbers, in case of an emergency and then I will give you a guided tour of this wondreful facility." Ms Saij smiled at the pair. She seemed to be quite an authority figure but in a gentle sort of way.

"Right then girls, grab your bags and we'll be on our way.

As the three of them walked the long secluded corridors, Annie could see the dark dingy décor, which started at the entrance, continued through the clinics, along every corridor and many empty wards. Finally they came to a ward that was actually occupied by patients.

"As you can see girls," Said Ms Saij, "Some areas of the hospital are rather quiet, while others are extremely hectic. We have had several cut backs due to the sizing down of this enormous hospital. Unfortunately even some of our busiest wards have had to close, due to lack of funding. It's been quite tough for everyone, quite sad really." Ms Saij continued.

"This ward is also one of our busiest, at the moment, we are running five different clinics, so it is on a pretty tight schedule, not to mention a tight budget. Of course the staff here are wonderful and they do a fantastic job considering. They are continually monitoring funding for each patient. Staff also take it upon themselves to do fund raising for new equipment, desperately needed by the ward. One can never tell how long before another ward closure will occur."

"What happens to all the staff, when the wards close Ms Saij?" Annie asked with concern.

"Unfortunately the staff get split up and moved to other areas. Most of the time we can allocate them to a place of their request. We do our best to satisfy everyone."

Just as the three of them were about to move on, a strange, scruffy looking, grey haired man, dressed all in white, approached them. He was about fifty five, perhaps closer to sixty, sporting a hair do from the flower power era(Not much taller than Annie.)

"How ya going ladies," He mumbled.

"Oh, Annie, Lindsy," Said Ms Saij, "this is Benson, he is the head of this ward."

"You girlies coming to work for me." Benson asked.

"No," they said hastily in one voice.

"That's a real shame." He stood and looked them up and down as they left the corridor.

Annie couldn't help but feel a little creepy. She didn't know why, she couldn't quite put her finger on it.

While the tour continued, a young male nurse came up and introduced himself.

"Good morning ladies, I'm Dean."

"Good morning Dean," Ms Saij smiled at him. "These girls are commencing full time employment with us today, Annie will be working with you on 2B."

"Welcome aboard Annie. I guess I will see you soon."

He had a slight lisp which suited his boyish features.

"Enjoy the rest of your tour ladies, see you again." Then he was off in a mad dash down the corridor.

Skimming over the departments, Ms Saij pointed out where Blood Transfusion was, Haematology, close to the Operating Theatres,

Day Surgery, Maternity Wing, Critical Care Unit, or CCU, High Dependency, Gynaecology, Staff Facilities, Physiotherapy, Pharmacy, Nurses and Doctors Quarters, Oncology, Radiology, Neurology, Psychiatry, Palliative Care, Gastroenterology, Respiratory, Plastics, Rehabilitation, Research, Pathology, Sterilisation Department, Thorasics and finally the Emergency Department, where Lindsy would be working. There was also the LV Cafe' or Lake View Cafe', running along side the E.D.

Annie and Lindsy looked at one another.

"It's a big place, isn't it Annie?" Said Lindsy, wide eyed.

"Yes, I think it might take me a while to work out where I'm going."

"Don't worry to much girls," Miss Saij laughed, "I've been here for over twenty years and I still get lost." She laughed.

She introduced Lindsy to a short, pug nosed nurse, who walked with a waddle, she had thick, black, bobbed hair and very thick rimmed glasses, with the glass itself looking about an inch thick. It appeared by the way she was squinting though, that she still didn't see things as clearly as she should.

Annie and Lindsy said their goodbyes and wished each other well. They'd planned to catch up in the near future, to see how they both were getting on in their new positions.

Ward 2B was humming with activity, when Annie arrived.

A small obese lady, who looked like she might be some ones grandma, in a white uniform approached her.

"Good morning, you must be our new nurse." She said, talking through her nose.

"Yes, good morning, I am Annie, Annie Paggett, your new nurse."

"Yes good, morning and all that," the stout nurse repeated herself as she replied. "My name is Charlie and I am the head nurse here, welcome to my ward. Right then, follow me and I'll show you where to lock up your bag. Then I'll get you to firstly, read though all the policy manuals. That will probably take you most of the morning." ·

Then Charlie noticed Dean, the male nurse, coming towards them in the ward corridor. Charlie mumbled something about the time,under her breath.

"Ah Dean, just in time," she called out to him even before he was in a conversational distance. "Would you mind showing our new nurse," she paused for a moment, placing a hand to her chin. "What was your name again?"

"This is Annie," Dean reminded her, now standing a little closer. "'We met earlier." He smiled at Annie.

"Yes that's right," Charlie cackled to herself. "Could you show Annie around the office? I forgot I am meant to be in a meeting right now." Then she was gone.

"Don't worry about her," Dean assured Annie, "She's always disappearing for meetings. You won't see much of old Charlie girl at all really, she leaves me to run the ward."

Dean took Annie to the office to show her the policy manuals. He encouraged her to try and get through them before lunch. Annie looked at the shelf of thickly-bound folders, about ten of them filled a huge shelf. She told Dean that she would do her best to complete them, then he left her to get on with the task.

Annie picked up the first manual, thickly labelled Occupational Health and Safety. It weighed a tone, well, probably not a tone but at least five kilograms. She placed it on the old wooden office desk, sat down and began to read. She read, RATS, yuck, they have rats here in the hospital, that's awful, she thought as she frowned to herself. Then she turned the page. RISK ASSESSMENT TEAM, Oooooh R.A.T.S, well there you go, one should never assume, or judge a book by its cover. She smile at her silly thought.

R.A.T.S
Consisting of Management and Employees.

Definition—Hazard—Anything having potential to cause Harm, Injury, Illness or Damage.

Risk—
A Management or likely hood that a hazard will actually cause injury. As in going by previous statistics.

Illness—or Damage compared to degree of injury, illness or Damage likely to occur.

Hierarchy Of Controls-Process for selecting the most effective method of risk control for an Identified Hazard. Annie read on and on, not realising at the time, how relevant this information would be in her nursing future. She was thankful for her speed reading abilities, otherwise, she would have been there until the following morning. She read policies on Fire and Emergency, Evacuation, Medical, Surgical Procedures, Policies on Patient Confidentiality, Policies on Professional Conduct, Hospital Equipment, Staff Safety Regulations, Hazards, Lifting, Meal Break, Work Cover Policies. On and on she read.

Annie hadn't realised when Dean popped his head into the office, she was buried up to her chin reading the last manual. A couple of hour had passed. "How are you going with the reading?" He asked.

"I'm just on my last one now."

He smiled, "You've done well. Not all nurses get through them in the specified time, it's a lot to absorb in one go. When you've finished that one, come and grab me from the ward and I'll take you to the staff cafeteria for lunch."

"Great, no worries," Annie smiled politely, "This won't take me long."

Lunch was a quiet time in the staff dining area. Annie sat patiently and listened to Dean. He voiced concerns about the running of the LVH and how he couldn't wait for his long service leave, so he could resign. Annie thought that it was sad that such a nice, well mannered young man had such low morale and self esteem, although he appeared very knowledgeable and admitted really enjoying nursing.

After lunch, Dean showed Annie all the different fire extinguishers, specifying which ones were for paper or material fires and which were for electrical and fuel fires. He then gave her the run down on evacuation procedures, should a fire occur.

"You will be directed to attend the next up and coming fire and lifting lectures and then annual updates once a year."

Annie was next directed to the treatment room, where Dean left her to get familiar with all the equipment, including the emergency resuscitation trolley.

"You go study all this," Dean insisted, "I've just got to go and do a ward round. I'll come back and check on you in a while, O.K."

"No problems, thank you,"

There was a big stainless steel trolley, stocked with intravenous fluids, needles, syringes, I.V. Lines, bungs, I.V. cannula, adrenaline am-pules, pethidine, morphine for injection. Oxygen masks, one easy flow, vent mask, another full oxygen mask, yanker sucker, Y sucker catheters of several different gauges, gadels airways big and small. There were respiratory bags, to assist the patient to breath during an arrest, where resuscitation was required.

Beside the emergency trolley stood a firm wooden board, about a metre long, hanging from a hook on the wall. It was often used to place under the patient to make sure the surface that the patient was lying on was firm enough to perform CPR. There was also a pat slide, two metres long, used to slide transfer the patient from bed to barouche or stretcher, if they were incapable of moving themselves.

Annie wanted to be sure to study all the equipment, as a wasted second in a resuscitation emergency, could mean loss of life.

She had remembered one of her patients she had looked after during her training, who had collapsed, she had rang three bells and got someone to ring the arrest team. After checking, no response from the patient, no breathing, no pulse, she commenced CPR immediately. One of the ward heads came in and started frantically yelling at her.

"Call the Arrest team, call the arrest team," she screamed in a panic.

The emergency arrest team cam up behind her.

"What's all the screaming for? That's not gonna get your patient back," the emergency nurse assured the ward head nurse.

Annie kept up cardiac compressions until the team took over.

The ward head disappeared and wasn't seen again until the patient had been fully resuscitated. If it wasn't for Annie being on the bell, you never can tell, those seconds may have been vital in the recovery of a precious life. Annie had never been one to waste time.

She was not one to panic, as she recalled another of her nanna's old sayings, panic breed havoc, or haste breed waste, then there was a stitch in time saves nine. Good old nanna. The more life experience Annie absorbed, the more she came to appreciate these short but helpful metaphors.

Remembering year four in primary school, Annie lectured a boy in her class for pulling a chair out from under someone. She warned him of the damage he could do to someone's spine, if they fell on their bottom the wrong way, you could even paralyse them for life, she said. Even though at that time Annie didn't find this amusing, a smile appeared on her face now knowing, that she cared about others safety and well being.

It truly showed in everything she did. She honestly believed, from a very early age, that nursing and caring for others, was to be her life's work.

Annie's eyes once more scanned the stainless steel lined room and the medical and emergency equipment.

Dean appeared at the doorway.

"How are you going with all this gear, Annie?"

"Finished in here, I think, not that I'll remember it all!"

"I'll get you to have a look at the paper work and just have a squizz through some patient's case notes, so you get an idea of how we document our daily nursing units of care. You can familiarise yourself with the charts, as they do differ slightly between hospitals. Also if you notice anyone on a ward computer, ask them if they wouldn't mind you observing what they are doing. Just to get a bit of an idea."

He held open the door for her. "Thank you," she smiled.

"Always a gentleman," he replied with a lisp.

"And thank you Dean, for all your help and direction today, I really appreciate it, I only hope I can can return the favour sometime."

"Don't worry, it gets pretty busy at times, I'm sure you'll have ample opportunity to do so," Dean smirked cheekily, highlighting his dimples.

Dean had a big sigh. "Now we'd better get on with things or neither of us will be getting out of here on time. Just remember in case of emergency, dial 666, I think they're in the mist of changing it to 222 Code Blue. The rest you will learn about at the up and coming fire lectures."

The last hour flew by. Dean re-appeared with the roster, with all of her future shifts, at least for the next six weeks. He then told her to pack up and go home for the day.

Annie was nervously excited about getting her new nursing position and was eager to do a good job. She wrote her roster in her diary, before saying goodbye to all her new work colleagues, thanking them for their assistance.

Chapter Ten

(Six months later)
Bracing A New Reality

Once Annie had settled into her new ward, she decided to continue with her fitness instructor studies. She wanted to finalise a number of electives at the Regency College, so she could continue to go out in the community, to teach people to get healthy and improve their lifestyle.

Annie was much more confident than she'd ever been before. She had learned so much over the past few years, since starting as a nurse assistant. All the staff had been very friendly and helpful, they all worked as a team. She had decided that she would ask her senior for the paperwork for her first nursing appraisal. She was eager to get some feedback from her peers, so she could focus on her areas of improvement.

Once her appraisal was finished by the staff, she gave it to her senior ward head, the clinical nurse manager, Charlie. Annie had been very overwhelmed by the compliments and praise, given to her by other senior nurses on the Gynaecology Unit.

Everything had been running smoothly and Annie was enjoying her work. Unfortunately, there had been some sad moments, some sadder than others. Some patients even lost their babies, before they were even born, some of them had to go through labour just to bare a still born baby.

Others had trouble getting pregnant in the first place and opted for IVF, In vitro fertilisation. But even with I.V.F, there still were no guarantees. The things some women put their bodies through, desperately wanting to have children, even risking their own lives.

Other women came in for elective surgery, including women having anterior and posterior repairs, or what doctors would kindly describe as a coat hanger, sounds charming, doesn't it! Basically it was a procedure to help hitch up a woman's pelvic floor area.

Then there was this ninety three year old lady. Poor old Mrs Swaser, she was so sweet. She had her home invaded, she'd been raped and mutilated by a much younger man. It was a sickening case that made Annie's stomach churn. She had so much respect for the elderly and couldn't understand the mentality of anyone that hurt children or older people, defenceless people. She believed them to be nothing but cowards.

Annie had been allocated to take care of the poor old Mrs Swaser. She had to have her vagina repaired, the rapist had made a terrible mess. Annie tried to show her as much compassion, respect and dignity as possible.

Annie had happened to be very good friends with Bonnie, the female police officer from the sexual assault unit, she'd met her years ago through her husband Mitch, they would often socialise together at police functions. Annie was glad to see someone she trusted to look after Mrs. Swaser, to take a statement from this lady about her terrible experience.

Both Annie and Bonnie tried to make poor Mrs. Swaser as comfortable as could be, under the circumstances. Annie stayed with her, until the patient's daughter arrived.

Annie was also allocated to look after Mrs. Swaser the day after her vaginal repair. Mrs. Swaser said she was feeling much better and wanted to give herself a good shower. Annie explained to the patient, that for her own safety, she had to assist her in the shower, or at least stand by, as the affects of the anaesthetic takes over twenty four hours to wear off. Also due to her going through such a major trauma, there may be a possibility of a bleed.

Standing on the other side of the shower curtain, as to give Mrs. Swaser some privacy, while she had her shower. Suddenly the shower chair slipped, gashing Annie's leg, ouch, right on her shin bone. Annie almost swore but bit her tongue, as to try not to distress her patient.

Mrs Swaser pulled the shower curtain back. "Sorry are you alright? Oh my God, look what I've done to your leg, I'm so sorry dear." She said with sincerity. Annie was in too much pain to to reply and bit on her lip. She stood up against the wall holding her shin toward her chest, trying to apply pressure, to try and stop her leg from bleeding. She started to feel faint and began slowly sliding down the wall and onto the floor. Annie managed to reach for the patients emergency bell, barely having the strength to push it. Her body started to go into shock, she could feel herself getting colder and colder, her eye site fuzzier and fuzzier.

The first nurse to arrive in the bathroom was Katerina, she barged in, noticing blood streaming down the drain, the shower still fully flowing with it.

"My God Mrs. Swaser, are you alright?" Katerina asked anxiously, thinking the bleeding was coming from the patient.

"I'm fine, It's nursey that's bleeding. It's my fault, I went to move the chair out of the way, to wash my feet and it got stuck and flipped outside the shower curtain, the wheels ceased up. I feel terrible."

'It's not your fault," Annie murmured, not feeling to well at this stage, she passed out.

Katerina by now had most of the other staff members gathered around her. While Annie regained conciousness, her leg was numb now.

A few of the nurses got her up and sat her in a wheel chair, then took her to the emergency service, while another nurse stayed with Mrs. Swaser, to complete her morning hygiene.

One of the Interns, under the guidance of another senior doctor, suggested sutures as the gash was quite deep. She needed seven sutures in all.

"Don't be silly," Annie said, "I don't need sutures, just whack on a few steri strips, I'll be right."

The intern looked at Annie inquiringly, as he explained that he was injecting her with some local anaesthetic. "see, I can't feel a thing," she joked.

The injury had actually ruptured a vein, so it was going to take more than a few sutures to repair her leg. The vein that ruptured was not returning the blood as it should and was blocked causing Annie quite a lot of pain. After seeing her own doctor, she was referred to a vascular specialist. It became official, the vein was going to have to be removed.

Annie decided that she would take her annual leave that was owing, rather than take sick leave or claim work cover, besides, she wasn't encouraged to fill out any work cover forms, or anything for that matter. Charlie her boss just let it go, although she'd been aware Annie had injured herself at work. She had appeared to want to ignore the whole situation. Annie believed this went totally against hospital policies she had read but did not want to comment in fear of jeopardising the job that she loved.

By the time she was scheduled for her surgery, Annie was in extreme pain. The blood that was not pumping through her vein, was pooling in her leg, it was agony. She spent many restless nights trying to keep her leg elevated, to try and ease the pain. When she finally arrived at the hospital for her procedure, it was delayed, due to a priority haemorrhage, emergency patient.

Finally laying on the theatre table, she'd arrived for her leg operation. The anaesthetist asked her to start counting back from 100, as he slowly pushed the stingy drug in to her arm. 100, 99, 98, 96, 95, 9 . . . ." There she goes, out like a light." Then her leg was fixed. It was amazing coming out of the anaesthetic, as she could not feel the pain in her left leg any more, it felt like she didn't even have a leg. She felt down her leg, bandages, more and more bandages, good, thank god, all still intact.

Post the operation, doctor Shorame, her vascular specialist, came to check up on her. He explained to her, that she would have to wear anti-embolic stockings for at least four weeks, as they had to strip the whole vein from her left leg. These stockings were to help her with her venous circulation and prevent blood clots occurring. He also ordered her to keep her left leg elevated whenever she was resting or sitting. He suggested she get back into her fitness routine as soon as possible, as this would also help maintain good circulation and speed up the healing process.

While Annie was home recovering from her operation, she decided to utilise her time constructively. She had a big fitness exam coming up at college, for her fitness instructors course. So she got stuck into her anatomy and physiology books, focusing on the energy systems. She hadn't ever failed an exam and passed with comfortable grades. When it came to the human body, Annie was intrigued. There was always something amazing and and Annie always believed that there was something very divine about the human being. She loved to read up everything she could get her hands on, mind body and soul. First and for most, the Bible, little do people know or realise, how many health tips through out the centuries the Bible has.

When returning from her leave, Annie hobbled onto the ward, still wearing her anti-embolic stockings, her leg still a little tender, after all she had been stabbed, wound wise, several times. But all in all, she had recovered extremely well from the stripping of her ruptured, blocked vein. At least the deep throbbing pain had subsided.

It was a very quiet afternoon, the day Annie retuned from leave. Rose the receptionist was sitting at the nurses station. Annie limped past.

"Good afternoon Rose." Annie smiled cheerfully.

"Hi Annie," Rose replied still on her computer.

Annie continued to walk through the ward, trying to make her limp a little less obvious. She locked her bag up in the staff locker room. She smiled in at all the patients as she made her way back down the ward, giving them a little wave and good afternoon as she went.

Annie always felt that a smile helped to make a patients day, helped their recovery and let them know she was approachable, should they need anything. There was nothing worse than a cranky nurse. As a matter of fact Annie could vouch for that. She had copped one of those cranky nurses as she was coming out of her anaesthetic, during her recent leg operation. She remembered the nurse quite well because she had these extraordinary, artificial, bright green, aqua marine contact lenses, a bit scary when you're just waking up in a haze. Apart from that, she wouldn't even let Mitch pop his head in to say good night after he finished an afternoon shift.

Annie had been left feeling quite miserable, as most patients do when they've had a general anaesthetic. At the least, this nurse could have put a smile on her face. Annie hoped she wouldn't have to deal with this nurse again, as she was operated on, at this same hospital she worked in.

As she returned to the nurse's station to receive hand over from the other morning staff, Cartia a nurse that Annie had worked with for about the past six months, was working on the ward computer at the nurse desk.

"How are you today Cartia? Working hard today?" Annie asked.

"I'm O.K., it's quietened down now, but earlier we were run off our feet, lots of surgery, post op and discharge patients. You'll be busy later on tonight, you have a few cases returning from theatre yet."

"That's alright," Annie smiled, "I much prefer it to be busy, it makes the evening go so much quicker."

"By the way, Annie," Cartia informed Annie. "Do you know you're going to 6E?"

"Do you mean relieving?" Annie inquired.

"No, permanently, apparently?" Cartia frowned. "Not a hundred percent sure of all the details. This ward is going Monday to Friday, budget cut backs, you're on a seven day roster, so they had a meeting while you were away and said you'd be going back to general."

"Well thanks for letting me know Cartia."

Annie smiled solemnly, feeling a little sad, as she'd settled into the ward quite well.

"Welcome back Annie and how's your leg?" Annie made this comment out loud to herself. "Oh well, what ever will be, will be, que sera sera and all that.

"What is 6E again?" Annie asked Cartia.

"Orthopaedics I think?"

"Thanks Cartia."

"That should be quite good actually. At least I'll gain more surgical skills and experience. I guess I should start studying up on some of the othopod jargon. I'm pretty keen to learn about hip and knee replacements, as we have a few of those types of rehab clients at the gym where I work. It will probably blend in better with my fitness instructing knowledge too."

Annie cracked a genuine smile. She was lucky she had parents that taught her to look on the bright side and do your best with what you get dealt. See your cup as half full, not half empty, make the most of what you get given. The power of positive thinking.

The evening was just as Cartia predicted, extremely busy. Annie had lost count of the amount of times she had walk/hobbled back and forth down the carpeted corridor. She could almost see where she had worn out the carpet. Thank goodness there hadn't been any emergencies. At this stage the shift had been busy but not chaotic.

Annie made another ward round and finalised her patients' back rubs and medications. She bid her patients good night and God bless. This was no less than standard routine when settling her patients for the evening.

She wasn't normally in a hurry to sit down but her leg was once again beginning to throb and cause her slight discomfort. The anti-embolic stockings were beginning to feel quite tight and uncomfortable.

Annie did one more quick limp around the ward to make sure everyone was settled. It was this time of the night Annie was able to sit down and catch up on some case note documentation. It was like heaven sitting down for the first time that evening. She hadn't even had time for her meal break, nothing uncommon these days. There was no one for meal relief. She made herself as comfortable as possible in her chair, then elevated her left leg under the desk inconspicuously. She tried to hide it, remaining a professional as possible.

Annie was determined to take good care of herself and follow doctor Shorame's advice, especially considering the doctor was a specialist here at this very hospital, LVH.

"Hup," Annie gasped, jumping in her seat. The senior nurse co-ordinator had quietly snuck up on her while she was so deep in thought. She didn't even hear her come through the double doors.

"That's a bit unprofessional isn't it nurse?" Sister downy frowned down at Annie over her tinted rimmed spectacles.

"Oh I'm sorry Sister Downy but I've had strict orders from my doctor, specialist, to keep my leg elevated whenever I'm sitting. It's my first day back at work, since my operation, sorry, I hope you don't mind?"

"Very well then nurse, if you must, carry on then. Is there anything to hand over to me?"

"No sister, all of the patients have returned from theatre and they're all stable. All observations are within limits and stable sister. Everything appears to be in order at present sister."

"Everything but your leg," she laughed sarcastically as she moved away leaving the ward.

For some reason, Annie did not find the funny side to Sister Downy's amusement, as a matter of fact, Annie wasn't amused at all. She believed that Sister Downy was a hard faced so and so and couldn't help but feel sad for her.

She let it go that evening and tried to put Sister Downy's personality down to a warped sense of humour?

It wasn't until Annie was called into Charlie's office the next day, to finalise her ward report, it was then that Annie realised, all was not well. She had no idea of the extent or affect her leg elevation had on her senior staff members.

"Come in take a seat Annie, shut the door behind you," Charlie smiled almost wickedly.

"I've been told you've been stepping out of line with senior staff young lady," Charlie smiled again, this time bitterly.

"I'm sorry, Charlie, I'm not quite sure what you mean."

"Well young lady, I heard you've interfered with a police investigation." Charlie stood over Annie as if Annie her self was being interrogated. Charlie leaned towards her over her desk.

Annie felt astonished and absolutely dismayed. Where on earth was this woman getting her information from. Her facts could not be more wrong. Annie tried to remain stern and voiced concerns in her now nervous state, her voice showing the same. "May I asked who told you that?" Annie replied to her boss's ludicrous comments.

"Let's just say that a little birdy told me." Charlie smirked.

Charlie watched Annie's face intently, waiting for a reaction, a response.

"Well," Annie explained, "I would like the opportunity to clear this up, to tell my side of the course of the events that may have led to your conclusion"

"Go ahead then, I'm listening." Charlie sat down slowly in her office chair and crossed her arms defensively upon her fat bosom.

Annie took a big breath, several big breaths in and out, trying to compose herself.

"Before I had to go on holidays to get my leg fixed, repaired, because of my work injury, I was allocated to look after a ninety four year old lady who'd been raped. She had her home invaded and the sexual attacker had left her pretty damaged. She'd suffered quite substantial physical and psychological trauma. Apart from me being extremely sympathetic, I did my utmost best to make her feel as comfortable as possible. During my time allocated to her, a police woman named Bonnie, who is also a friend of my husbands and I, who would also be-able to vouch for me. She knows that I was not even present during that patients statement, or investigation as you called it.

I don't understand sister? Why didn't some one approach me on the day, if they thought I was interfering in something they thought I shouldn't be? I have done nothing but remain the utmost professional with this matter in question. I was not even in the room, when Bonnie took the patients statement."

It had appeared that Charlie did not even listen to a word Annie had said.

"Annie you do realise, because you've interfered with the police statement, you will have to appear in court when the rape case is brought to trial."

"No I won't," Annie insisted. "As I have already stated, I have not interfered with anything. I was told by the police officer Bonnie, from the sexual assault unit, that if I were to remain present during the statement, that I would have to appear as a witness to that statement, when the case was brought to trial. What I stated to Bonny that day, is that, I would rather not be involved, so once the victims daughter got there, I left the room, then Bonny commenced taking the statement. I did not interfere at all. The daughter came out half way through to ask if they could get a cup of tea. At that stage the tea lady was on her rounds, so I sent her in. I did not enter the room again until the statement was complete and Bonny had left the building."

Annie felt the need to explain herself thoroughly and continued. "I stayed at the patient's bedside for re-assurance. The daughter had phoned ahead and requested I stay with her mother until she arrived. She did not like the thought of her mum sitting in the room on her own with the police officer. As soon as the the daughter arrived, I left the room." Annie finalised.

"Well I'm not sure," Charlie frowned again. "We will have to wait and see. Oh by the way, I've got another bone to pick with you. I've been told, you lase around with your legs up on chairs!"

Annie was feeling rather ill by this stage, her head was now clouded and tears had started to well in her eyes. She was trying her hardest to remain professional and not get upset, just like she was trying her hardest to look after her patient's, as well as herself. She couldn't work out why everyone was giving her a hard time, it seemed pointless. This meeting had nothing to do with her ward appraisal. Of which she'd had great feedback from all the other staff members, this felt like a witch hunt.

Charlie could obviously see that Annie was getting extremely upset and eagerly threw a box of tissues to her across the desk, it seemed also premeditated.

"Go on, why don't you go home and have a nice stiff drink," Charlie laughed arrogantly as if it was all good fun, like she enjoyed upsetting people.

"I don't drink during the week," Annie sniffled, she felt choked up inside. "Besides" she added, "I've got a big exam tonight, so I couldn't have a drink even if I wanted to."

Annie went home from the ward that last day on 2B, feeling rather lost. She had worked so well on the ward and had done her best to remain professional and as caring as possible. She didn't understand what was going on. She'd had nothing but positive feed back, the whole time she been on ward 2B, from both staff and patients, up until this day anyway.

Chapter Eleven

Cruelty For Kindness

The evening was warm and balmy. Annie entered the college gymnasium where the exam was being held. Due to some last minute photocopying, the exam had been slightly delayed. It was very warm in the gym. Annie was prepared for this, in her sports bra and shorts, as well as bringing along a large bottle of cool drinking water. The ceiling fans wafted warm air on high speed, making it a bit more bearable on hot moist skin.

Annie wished the exam would hurry up and be over. All she wanted to do was go home to her nice hot tub and wash away all the negativity from earlier on in the day.

"Hi Annie," a voice called from the other side of the gymnasium.

A lean, toned man with fluffy blond hair approached her as she found herself an empty desk at the back of the exam room. It was Nick, one of the other fitness trainers Annie had been doing her course with.

"How are you," he grinned, flashing his big, white, glossy teeth.

"Oh hi Nick," Annie sighed.

"How are you going?" Nick asked.

"I'm great thanks." Annie didn't sound very convincing.

"How are you?"

Annie tried to conjure up a believable smile.

"I'm great Annie," Nick responded, "But seriously man, you don't seem yourself tonight, are you O.K?"

Annie replied with a true, sweet smile admiring Nicks concern. "Thanks Nick, I'm fine, just had a bit of a ruff, long day at work. The sooner I put it behind me, the better."

The lecturer at the front of the room clapped his hands, getting everyone's attention. He was accustomed to projecting his voice, it was one of the first things you learn as a fitness instructor. If you didn't learn how to project your voice, you'd end up losing it and wrecking your vocal chords.

"Can everyone please find their way to a table. We are about to commence. All your papers should now be placed on the desk in front of you." The lecturer continued, "When you've completed all questions, turn your paper face down. There is to be no talking or conversing of any shape or form through out. If you have any concerns, put your hand up and I will come and speak with you quietly. When you have finished and turned your paper face down, I will come and collect it from you. Once you leave the room, you can not re-enter. Do I make myself clear?"

"Yes Sir," many voices echoed in unison.

"Good luck with your exam Nick," Annie smiled quietly as she rushed to sit down.

"Yeah, you too Annie, thanks," he whispered, rushing across the floor to an available desk and chair on the other side of the gymnasium.

All Annie wanted to do, was to put the silly work incident to the back of her mind and get on with the exam she'd studied so hard for. She'd studied the energy systems over and over. But the only thing going over and over in her head now was Charlie.

As she sat there in the silent room, full of enthusiastic, healthy, glowing instructors, she could not make sense of her answers. It was a though a big dark cloud had come over her and filled her head with emptiness. She realised then and there, as she turned her papers face down, that this was going to be the first exam she was definitely going to fail.

Taking several deep breaths, Annie accepted emotional defeat. She lay her head on the desk and encircled it with her arms. She stayed there, trying to make sense out of the days events.

Annie went home and soaked herself in a long hot bath. She was physically and mentally exhausted and put herself to bed early while Mitch was on afternoon shift. She didn't even hear him crawl into bed. Feeling refreshed after a good nights sleep, Annie was glad that she had the chance to make a new start on the orthopaedics ward, ward 6E. She was looking forward, forward to the challenge of learning more about the medical, surgical world. And to be honest, being away from that dragon lady Charlie.

Annie arrived on ward 6E with plenty of time for the 0700hr hand over from night staff.

"Hey, are you Annie?" one of the nurses called to her down the corridor.

"Yes, good morning."

"Listen sorry to do this to you Annie but they want you back on 2B for today, they're short staffed and they need someone who knows the ward."

"Oh, Oh O.K. Then, I guess I'll see you later then?"

"Guess so."

Annie was not happy to be going back to 2B, not so soon after an unhappy departure. Something just didn't feel right. Getting a rather muddled handover, Annie went out onto the ward 2B hoping it would be for the last time. After all, she didn't know who she could trust to support her now, as a dedicated, caring nurse.

Placing towels and her patients toiletry bag in the shower cubicle, Annie turned on the cold tap and then the hot. She tested the water temperature on her own hand, to make sure it was comfortable. Suddenly Annie was surrounded by three senior sisters, Sister Charlie, Sister Downy and another sister she did not recognise. They shoved her under the water and started tearing at her clothes, scratching her with their short, sharp nails. She was bleeding from their scarring. They were pulling painfully at her hair, clumps of her beautiful, long, dark hair, they were tearing it from her scalp.

Annie screamed in Terror, "No God help me please, help me God, help me." Annie could feel her own screams vibrating through her body. "Someone help me." They slapped at her wet face, it stung with pain under the pouring water. They were pushing her to the floor. She struggled to her feet. She shook her body with every ounce of her being and released herself from their filthy grip.

Running, she wrapped the towels she had collected on the way through, swiftly wrapping them around her naked, scratched, bruised, bloody body. Running frantically into the corridor. Dripping wet, watered down blood, dripping like a path of devastation for her attackers to follow. She tried to wipe the drops from dripping down onto the floor. She ran through corridor, ran through corridor, ran through corridor. She was getting no where fast.

There was not another soul in site. No one to help her at such and early hour of the morning. She was screaming out deathly screams, yet no one could hear her. She found a patient's room but it was empty. She found a telephone in the empty patient's room. She hid down low behind the empty bed, trying to quiet her frantic breaths, breaths of terror. Pulling the phone down from the bedside cabinet. She held the phone to her gut, no dial tone, the phone was dead. "No," she screamed, throwing the phone down. "No God, help me, help me please."

"Annie, Annie," she could hear someone familiar calling her from a distance.

"Annie, Annie Babe, wake up, wake up Babe, you're having a bad dream."

Annie opened her eyes slowly, as she woke up in a daze, feeling like she'd been sobbing for hours.

"Oh my God, thank God that was just a dream, I just had the most real nightmare."

"Your telling me," Mitch comforted Annie, holding her in his strong embrace. "You were actually yelling out in your sleep."

"Really, was I? What was I yelling?"

"Help me, help me God, help me."

"Boy that sure was one real, horrible nightmare. Thank God it was only a nightmare. I felt like I was being spiritually raped." Annie nestled into Mitch's comforting embrace, snuggling in as close as she could get.

Finally Annie got to start work on her new ward 6E and was relieved to know, that she did not have to go relieving to ward 2B in real life. Everything appeared to be running smoothly and she was getting along like a house on fire with the rest of the Orthopod team.

Unfortunately while Annie was looking after one of the larger hip replacement patients, he start e falling to the ground. He grabbed her on the way down with him. At the time, she could feel a pull down her right side, into her lower back. It felt like she'd pulled a muscle or two. Apparently according to the examining doctor, she had torn some muscle and damaged some ligaments.

Annie was so disappointed, this time she had to take a whole month off work. When she returned from leave, she couldn't help but feel, there was one male nurse that took it upon himself to give Annie a hard time. His name was Stan, or Stan the man. He was even more bitchy than some of the female nurses. When it came to the crunch, he could stick his claws in with the best of them.

Everyone was saying, he was trying to claw his way to the top, by dobbing everyone else into the boss, getting in buddy with the seniors. Annie may have been a bit of a goody two shoes, in a lot of respects, especially when it cam to her professionalism and caring for her patients. But if there was one thing she was not, was a brown noser. She expected to gain her respect through sheer hard work. She believed one earned respect and wasn't just given it.

Annie had gained some of her confidence back after ending things on an unhappy note on her previous ward. Her leg had healed extremely well. She'd continued to train as a fitness teacher and was also currently training for state aerobic competitions. She was feeling great again, although her back never felt a hundred percent after her back injury at work but she didn't let it stop her from doing all she loved to do.

Doctors and physiotherapists reassured her that ligament damage took a long time to heal. The doctor never encouraged her to go for any further examination.

She did however, take it upon herself, to manage her own pain, as he did not like pumping her body full of prescription drugs, or any drugs for that matter. Controlling her pain through a lot of deep breathing and relaxation. She continued with her strict fitness regimen, meditation and prayer. Annie felt she would be worse off without these measures and continued to have faith in her higher power, as well as the power of self healing.

Getting back to Satan, oops, I mean Stan the man, most of the time he was nice, to her face, when there wasn't any one else around but as soon as there was an audience, he would embarrass her in front of her other work peers.

During one afternoon shift, five nurses, including Annie, were all sitting on the work benches in the nurses station.

Stan singled her out.

"Get off of the bench Annie," He yelled.

Annie looked at the other nurses as they frowned at Stan.

"Are you serious Stan?" she asked, as he hadn't asked anyone of the other nurses to move from the bench.

"Get down off the bench now," he repeated angrily.

"O.K, O.K," she replied protestingly.

Annie shrugged her shoulders as she looked at the other nurses still sitting on the bench as she climbed down.

They all continued to sit on the bench, while Annie stood there mystified, questioning Stan's motives silently.

Stan took her place on the bench.

"So Annie," Chrystal asked, "are you going to the ward dinner this week end?"

"No," Annie replied I'm rostered on to work."

"How about you?"

'Yeah, absolutely. Thank God I've got the week end to recover," she laughed a loud.

'Stan joined in. "Yeah me too," he laughed.

Chrystal was a very tall, solid built nurse, about twenty eight years of age, with lots of thick, frizzy bleach blond hair. She wore her hair in a pony tail, pulled back at the nape of her neck. She was about four times the size of Annie in width. She wore coloured rimmed glasses, a different colour for each day of the week it seemed. As a matter of observation, many nurses in the LVH appeared to be wearing glasses. Annie thought it was too much sex that sent you blind, not, not having enough.

Chrystal got along extremely well with most of the seniors.

The other nurses rostered on with Annie that week end started discussing what they were going to do for dinner.

"Why don't we order Chinese?" Annie suggested.

"Hey that's a great idea Annie. Maybe if we order a different dish each, we could have our own litle banquet right here," nurse Ally smiled.

Ally was a beautiful nurse, as well as a beautiful human being. All the other nurses agreed on the banquet.

"I'll grab a price list menu from that local Chinese restaurant, The Silver Lake View Dragon, before this Saturday," said Annie. "It's very popular and they deliver."

"Cool," Ally smirked. "Who needs a silly old ward dinner anyway?"

Annie and the remaining nurses laughed as they dispersed from the nurses station to get on with their nursing duties.

Annie was glad to have showed initiative, getting involved with the other nurses, to decide what they were all going to do for dinner, even though the stern look she was getting from Stan, didn't maker her feel very comfortable.

After that weekend, everyone had returned to work. Annie could not help noticing, that other members of nursing staff, that had previously warmed to Annie, were now seemingly giving her the cold shoulder. At first she thought it was her imagination, but then, the ward boss, Sister Fartrol, approached her.

Annie was very much concerned, as she had seen this same woman pulling staff members by the ears and whacking them across the head. She had also had several complaints made against her by patients and their relatives. Most of the staff were so afraid of her, they were not willing to make a complaint. Fearing the consequences.

Many of the staff from the ward ended up resigning from the Lake View Hospital. Some retired from nursing all together, even the younger ones straight out of University. It just wasn't the way they expected to be treated by fellow nurses. Most of them left in shock. Annie thought this extremely sad, as they had done a lot of study, even finalised their Bachelor Of Nursing Degree. It was sad because this was their first taste of real nursing for them, in the real world. It wasn't a very positive first time experience on this ward. If that's the way nurses treated each other, they didn't want any part of it and neither did Annie.

Annie felt somewhat reassured by the fact that she had only just recently finalised a ward report on 6E.

She was given high standards for all her nursing competencies. She was enjoying her work apart from the back pain, considering what a heavy ward it was. Orthopaedics was interesting and Annie found that she was learning about rehabilitation, prosthetics and procedures rather quickly.

Receiving some special thank you cards from her patients, it was something Annie treasured very dearly in her heart. The gratitude from her patient's and their families, was sometimes overwhelming to her, as she was only doing her job.

"Annie," Sister Fartrol called down the hall, "can I see you in the plaster room for a moment?"

"I'll be right there Sister Fartrol."

Annie checked in on all her patient's before heading into the plaster room, on the Orthopaedic Ward.

She met Sister Fartrol at the plaster room door. Chrystal had arrived previously and was sitting, ready with pad and pen in hand. Sister Fartrol waved Annie through the door way, then shut the door behind her. "Why the plaster room, why not the office? or the conference room?" Annie thought to herself.

"Right Chrystal, are you ready to take minutes for this meeting?"

"Yes Sister," Chrystal replied immediately.

"Now Annie, how do you think you are going on this ward?" Was Sister Fartrol's first question.

Annie thought this a reasonable question and replied, "according to my recent ward report and the comments made by my nursing peers, I've appeared to settle in to 6E well Sister."

"That's good then, don't you think so Chrystal?"

"Yes Sister."

Chrystal continued to take minutes and jot down what was said in her little note pad.

"Thanks for your help Chrystal," Sister Fartrol gestured her towards the door. "You can go now Chrystal, shut the door behind you."

Sister Fartrol followed Chrystal to the door and subtly locked the plaster room door behind her.

Glaring at Annie, she came closer and closer towards her. Annie was now standing, pushed up against the wall, Sister Fartrol close up to her face.

Annie could not move back any more, she could smell and feel her boss's stale breath.

"So," Sister Fartrol snapped, you think you're doing well do you?" She looked at Annie with evil in her eyes. "I've heard other stories!" She yelled at the top of her voice, "YOUR OUT OF LINE YOUNG LADY."

Annie tilted her head to one side, trying to avoid the spitting fowl breath.

"You're no nurse," continuing, "nursing's not your niche. Why don't you give up your aerobic instructing and concentrate on your nursing?"

Annie hadn't even told this woman that she was a fitness instructor, she then remembered Sister Charlie had stated something similar to her before she'd hurt her leg.

Annie could not help but feel that there was a little conspiring going on. Annie decided that she'd had enough torment, she had to start sticking up for herself, it was now or never.

"Sister Fartrol," Annie said, with as much bravery as she could possibly muster in this time of feeling extremely vulnerable and intimidated, in a clear loud voice.

"I have been nursing since I left school and up until now, I have had not one honest complaint, not from patients, relatives or nursing staff for that matter. I don't like the way you run your ward, I believe you are inappropriate in your management and I will be going directly to administration to ask for a ward change."

"And you don't stretch on my ward either," Sister Fartrol interrupted.

"I was stretching to try and relieve my back pain, that was caused by an injury on your heavy ward. I am no slacker and I am a great nurse. I work just as hard, if not harder than anyone else. If I need to stretch to relieve my pain, then I will absolutely do so. Good day to you Sister Fartrol and goodbye."

Annie grabbed her belongings and quickly made her way down to administration. Rushing through the grey corridors, trying to make some sense as to why this was happening. Her heart was pounding, BOOM BOOM. She swallowed the lump in her throat, trying to fight back the tears from falling from her eyes. She felt quite stunned and nauseated. Never had she felt so anxious in her entire life. She gave her whole life to caring for others and showing patience and compassion.

Why was this happening?

By the time Annie arrived at the administration office, her head was spinning and her ears were buzzing. Her heart still pounding, she was finding it hard to catch her breath. She hadn't suffered from asthma since she was a bout nine years old, since before she started cross country running.

Katey, the receptionist, looked up in horror. "My goodness Annie, are you O.K?"

"I'm not sure," Annie gasped back tears. Kate stood up from the reception desk.

"Come and take a seat Annie, I'll grab you a glass of water, just keep taking those big breaths. Would you like to speak with someone?" Katey asked as she handed Annie a plastic, disposable cup of spring water from the office dispenser.

Annie now feeling a little more at ease asked, "Is Sister Saij available to speak to?"

"Oh I'm afraid not, it's her programmed day off today but Sister Nat is available."

"I guess she'll have to do then," Annie replied with a quick uneasy smile.

"O.K. Annie, I'll just check to see if she can see you now. Won't be a minute." Katey returned to her desk and promptly rang through to Sister Nat.

"You can go straight in Annie, come this way."

Katey opened the door for her.

"Take a seat Annie, Annie Paggett, is that right?" Sister Nat asked.

"Yes that's right Sister Nat."

"She peered at her computer. "Yes I've just got your record up on screen. What can I dot for you today?

"I'd like to request a ward change if you don't mind, Sister Nat. I'd also like to put in a complaint about the unprofessional treatment experienced by myself and others on my last ward."

"Mmm, I see you've just recently had a ward change." She moved her gaze from the computer screen to to Annie, still peering over her glasses. She screwed up the corner of her mouth, her bright red lips pouting.

"That move was not my choice sister," Annie explained. The ward went Monday to Friday and I am on a seven day roster."

"Oh I see," Sister Nat smiled. "Well that is a different kettle of fish. 8E are quite short staffed, as are most of the wards at the moment. I guess I could put you to good use there?"

"Thank you so much Sister Nat, you don't know how much I appreciate this." Annie smiled, letting out a huge sigh of relief.

"'Don't thank me yet Annie, it's an extremely busy ward." Sister looked at Annie intensely over the rim of her glasses. "You may well go home now, it's nearly time for you to finish anyway. Start on 8E in the morning, they can work out your roster from there."

"Thank you again Sister Nat, busy ward or not, I still really appreciate this. A bit of hard work never killed anyone!"

Annie returned to 6E briefly as in her rush she forgot her lunch box. She tried to make a quiet exit without being noticed but Stan caught up with her.

He took her aside and whispered an apology for being a lager. He said he didn't realise how bad he made it seem, when it really wasn't that much of a big deal, the telling of the sitting on the bench, when everyone else was doing it too.

"Oh well," Annie said to Stan, it certainly snow balled and that snow ball came and bowled me over, but hey, I'm still standing. I guess I'm lucky it wasn't an avalanche, so I guess I'll be seeing you round like a snow ball."

Annie smiled at Stan as she threw her satchel bag over her shoulder. Walking away, she began whistling, walk tall, walk straight and look the world right in the eye. She had great faith and hope, that the next ward would work out better than the last two.

Chapter Twelve

Third Time Lucky?

Finishing her morning work for the day, Annie grabbed a stethoscope from the trolley. Wandering around ward 8E, she asked the other nurses if they needed a hand with their afternoon observations.

There was only a few temperature, pulse and blood pressures to be done, along with a couple of pulse oximetry readings. Oximetry is a machine used for detecting pulse rate or heart rate and oxygen saturation, the amount of oxygen being carried by, or diffused to and transported by the haemoglobin to the tissue. A clever little machine, in basic cases, stopped doctors from having to remove oxygenated blood from the artery, a procedure called a blood gas. Quite a painful procedure for the patient in the past. More often now used in very serious cases of expected cardiac arrest or heart attack victims.

Annie didn't mind doing observations, most nurse put this in the same category as bed making, a tedious task that needed to be done. And most nurses would get out of it if they could. Annie found that this was an opportune time to have a good look at the patient, time to ask how they were feeling, if they were well enough to talk.

Suddenly Annie heard three bells. Cassy one of the other nurses, ran out from Mrs. Espin's room.

"Quick Annie, can you get on the phone and ring 222 CODE BLUE, STAT."

Annie could already feel the adrenaline pumping through the ward. She quickly backtracked to the phone she'd only passed a few second ago and speedily dialled two two two.

"Hello, yes we have a CODE BLUE, eighth floor, Mrs. Espin's room, twenty eight, thank you."

She hurriedly placed the receiver down and grabbed the blue emergency witches hat to place outside room twenty eight, so the resuscitation team would know exactly where to go directly, pushing the emergency trolley along with her, she quickly entered the room.

Cassy stood beside the patient, Mrs. Espin with a ghastly look on her face.

"Annie I couldn't feel a pulse."

"No she's not breathing either," Annie added, "have you ever bagged anyone before?" She quickly checking the airway for any obvious obstruction.

"No, not yet, not in real life, only on a resuscitation dummy." Cassy replied with a quiver in her voice and a worried frown upon her face.

"Well, here's your opportunity," Annie smile at Cassy reassuringly.

They both worked together to slide the resuscitation board underneath the patient's body.

Annie carefully twisted the gadels, adult sized airway down into the patient's mouth and throat.

After turning the oxygen flow up, Annie held the oxygen mask tightly over the patient's mouth and nose and gave full firm pumps with the full span of her hand.

"Do you think you can take over Cassy?"

She handed over to Cassy. "You continue with the breaths and every time I get to the fifth compression, you squeeze the bag O.K."

Climbing up on the bed, Annie knelt as close to the patient as possible. Placing as much strength as possible trough her arms. She plunged all her weight into the patients chest with the heels of her hands, then started counting out loud.

"And one, and two and three and four and five."

Cassy squeezed the bagged oxygen mask, watching Annie intently.

"And one and two and three and four and five."

After the fourth lot of compression, Annie stopped to check for a pulse, first the carotid, then the femoral, still nothing.

"And one and two and three and four and five." She continued desperately. Cassy once again squeezing the bag in rhythm with the fifth compression.

"Don't look so horrified Cassy," Annie quickly jested, "the resus team will be here shortly. They'll take over, or tell us to keep going, if we're doing a good job."

The resuscitation team arrived with the rest of the equipment, gathering quickly around Mrs. Espin's bed. They opened the emergency resus box Annie had grabbed earlier. They placed the monitors on the patient's chest introduced an intravenous access line into Mrs. Espin's right arm.

Once the monitor's sticky dots were in place, it showed that Annie was precise with her compressions.

'Keep those compressions up Annie," Doctor Shoremaker assured her, "your right on target."

"Sister, draw up some IV adrenaline stat," the doctor said confidently, as if he's done it a million times before.

Josephine, a well groomed, attractive blond nurse, with piercing, blue eyes and a sweet sounding voice, replied. "Right away Doctor."

She hurriedly but steadily snapped the top of the glass ampule and place the needle accurately into the tiny glass of clear liquid.

"Stat adrenaline Doctor," Josephine gently handed the syringe filled needle to him.

Calmly taking the needle and syringe from the dish, he began to guide the needle slowly and accurately under the patients chest plate, as close to the heart as possible.

Annie was once again asked to continue with the compressions, Cassy with respirations. It was all happening so quickly, yet in slow motion. Once again after the fourth lot of compression, Annie stopped again, under the direction of the Doctor.

The monitor continued to show a heart beat and pulse. Suddenly Mrs. Espin's chest expanded considerably.

"Oh thank God," Annie let out a big exhausted sigh. "She's breathing on her own."

They all stood around the bed and watched eagerly as Mrs, Espin's chest continued to rise and fall.

"Well her breathing may be a little laboured but at least she's breathing," the doctor commented, "oxygen saturations increasing, blood pressure rising 90 diastolic 25 systolic and rising, pulse 40 and strengthening. He grinned, looks like a job well done then, you've saved a life. And thanks to Annie and Cassy for getting on top of things laterally."

Perspiration had now begun to glisten on Annie's brow. "Well I don't know about you guys but I really need a drink, I'm going to go freshen up a bit.

I'll hand over to afternoon staff now they're here." Annie was confidently reassured now she knew that the resuscitation nurse, Josephine would now stay by the patient's side to continue monitoring her progress.

Annie left the room and made her way to the staff room at the other end of the ward. As she continued down the lengthy ward corridor, she sensed a presence behind her. She turned her head and saw her boss, Benson quickly pulled away, then entered another room. That was weird, he was awfully close. Maybe he was going to ask me something and changed his mind? Annie thought to herself.

She pushed open the big staff room door with two hands, then leaning on it, closed it with her behind. She grabbed her cold water bottle from the staff fridge, thirstily guzzling down quenching that thirst. She could feel the cold liquid burning her now parched throat. She could almost feel her kidneys soaking it up like a sponge. She gazed at the beautiful blue sky, from the huge glass window she could see the lake, glistening and twinkling in the sun light.

"Thank you God," she mouthed in gesture of helping her save a life. Taking several deep breaths

Annie collected herself. At least the views were nice from the Hospital windows. Thank God for small mercies. As she took several more mouth falls of water, she could still feel her kidneys squelching and pulsating. "I really must drink more," she mumbled to herself.

"Yes you must," Cassy said to her, Catching Annie talking to herself. "How about a couple at the Lake View Hotel Resort when we finish?"

"It was actually water I was talking about," Annie giggled.

"Yes I know," Cassy smiled, "but I reckon we deserve a couple of cold ones for our life saving achievement this arvo."

"No look Cas, may be some other time, I'm pretty physically and emotionally drained from the last few days. I'll be in danger of falling asleep at the wheel, even if I don't have a drink."

"Yeah, I guess you're right, I've heard of a few nurses doing that when they are so fatigued, some days are extremely tiring, even when you don't bring someone back to life."

Annie was glad the day was over. She couldn't wait to get home to Mitch. Annie was glad she turned down the drink invitation. Early day shift was always tiring. Up before the birds, once at work it was go, go,go till the minute she knocked off. Most days she'd end up working twenty minutes to a half hour over time. Some days were so hectic, she didn't even get a morning tea or lunch break. She wasn't alone though, every other nurse was in the same boat.

"Oh boy, what a day," Annie sighed, as she slid into her lambswool seat covers of her white Holden Astra convertible. Throwing her satchel over onto the passenger seat. The sun was glaring right in her face, she squinted and flipped both the sun visers down, sliding on her sun glasses.

The car was scorching hot, as it had been in the sun all day. The shade from the big gum tree she had originally parked under, had now moved and was shading someone else's car. Annie's legs were hot from wearing her white nurses stockings all day. She was looking forward to stripping off her uniform when she got home. She wiggled her uniform up to her thighs, to keep her a bit cooler for the time being. Removing the roof, she took a deep breath of mild afternoon breeze. As it gently swept across her face, she closed her eyes for a brief moment. Absorbing the sun's warmth and light, the breeze cooled her flushed cheeks.

Feeling a little more relaxed and focused, Annie began her journey home, it was still a weary one.

She was really looking forward to getting there to run a nice relaxing spa and enjoy a cool glass of Cockatoo Ridge, sparkling white. Warm bubbles on the outside and call bubbles on the inside. Most of all, she looked forward to seeing her husband Mitch.

Walking into the laundry, she stripped naked, throwing all her uniform into the washing machine. She then went to the main bedroom and slid on her translucent, satin, sky blue, long wrap. Just before leaving the room, Annie caught a glimpse of herself in the large mirrored robes that covered one whole wall. Her naked body slightly showing through the translucent fabric. She stood and peered at herself in the mirror, as she pondered for a moment. Reminiscing all the past affections her and Mitch had shared, making love in those mirrors. Oh boy, if only those mirrors could talk, she'd hoped they'd have more to talk about once Mitch got home.

The water was tingling, as Annie poured it over her fatigued, tense body. After only a few minutes, she could feel herself moulding comfortably into the spa bath. After pouring more warm water over her head, she carefully placed the antique, ceramic jug in it's dish. Annie took a long breath., closed her eyes and slid beneath the water. All that she could hear was the sound of her pounding heart, thump, . . . thump, . . . thump . . . , she wondered if this is what babies would here, when in their mother's womb.

As Annie came up for breath, she jumped. "Oh honey, you scared me." Mitch stood in the doorway to the jocose. Smiling down at her adoringly as she lay naked in the spa bath.

"Home already, so glad to see you sweetness. Why don't you grab that bottle of Cockatoo Ridge from the fridge and come and join me." She smiled, raising her eye brows. "I promise you a great foot massage and I won't stop there either." She grinned mischievously, wickedly, gazing into his beautiful, dark, sexy eyes.

"Sounds like an offer too good to refuse." Mitch couldn't move fast enough.

Annie was always amused at his speed, when he was eager, he was always very keen and very eager when it came to their passion for one another. They were so very passionate in their intimacy. They were two human beings that fit each other like a glove, when making love.

So relaxed, she lay in the big bubbly spa bath, even more so now that she knew Mitch was home. She always felt a sense of comfort and safety when he was around. She'd almost drifted off to sleep, when she felt a soft touch on her lips, as soft as a rose petal, she responded by returning the gentle, petal, soft kiss, as Mitch lent over her with his masculine naked body.

As she sat up, Mitch handed her the flute glass full of sparkling golden liquid. The sparkling wine was very refreshing, as its coldness trickled down Annie's throat.

Still holding the bottle, Mitch carefully slid into the spa. Seating himself closely to her, he poured some of the sparkling wine over her breasts. Kissing her lusciously on her lips, he placed the bottle aside. Slowly he began sliding his warm, soft but ruff tongue all over the front of her, sucking and licking at the sweet but sour moisture.

Annie slowly moved around in the water, until she was at Mitch's feet. Placing a small amount of bath oil in her hands, she commenced massaging his right foot and then left. Her hand's still very slippery from the jasmine scented oil, she slowly slid both of them under the water and up the inside of Mitch's thighs. Gently she caressed his now very hot, very erect, very large throbbing penis.

Oiling up his own hands, Mitch placed his big, strong hands around her, she straddled over him, kissing him intensely on the lips as she held his pumping manliness firmly in two hands. He held her tight buttock and firmly rubbed it around and around as if polishing her up, rubbing one way, one way, then the other. He moved in motion, one hand after the other, gently sliding each in time into her throbbing loins. They kissed with soft, gentle, wet open mouths, passion pouring in. Holding lightly in each others hands, fondling, delicately touching each other.

"Oh God, this definitely beats going to the pub with the girls," Annie moaned with extreme pleasure, still hanging onto Mitch's kiss as she groaned.

"And the guys," Mitch growled in Annie's ear, sending shivers up her spine.

They continued to kiss passionately, open mouthed kisses, while they gently but excitedly played with one another.

Mitch gasped Ahhh, as Annie held his hardness in her two hands and slowly sat on top of it. She turned and slowly faced away from him, her legs now straddled wide. Ever so slowly, she began bobbing up and down in the water. As the water gushed in between, it stimulated their senses even further.

Annie couldn't stand facing away from him any longer, while he was still firmly inside of her, she twisted her naked, wet slippery body around once more, until she was face to face with her lover. Sitting tightly on top of him, they kissed uncontrollably. As she held onto his broad, tanned, strong shoulders and pulled him closer to her, her breasts rubbing against his hot, wet, slippery, masculine chest.

Breathing, moaning, expressing heavy sighs. Holding on tight, neither one wanting to let go. Thrusting each other ever so strongly now. Water poring onto the floor. Mitch spun her around on her back, Annie wrapping her legs as tightly as possible around his ruggedly, lean, strong body, pulling him tightly into her, feeling his firmness, tense all over, every muscle hard now . . . . Holding tighter and tighter, bucking, harder and harder, faster and faster, Ah Ah Ah . . . . and then release, silence fell all around, apart from their breathing sounds and the lapping of water settling.

They lay still and quiet, nothing but bubbling water, wrapped up in one another. Annie slowly slithered out from under Mitch, laying beside him, her head on his chest, she looked up at him, he gently stole a kiss on her lips.

"Guess what I did today?" Annie whispered to Mitch, her head still resting peacefully on his chest.

"What did you do today darling?"

"I helped to resuscitate a patient, saved a life. It was quite nerve wracking really."

"Well you can give me mouth to mouth any time you like." Mitch held Annie's chin up and kissed her again, lusciously on her soft, wet lips.

"All I can say," she informed him, "is I'm glad we use bags and masks when we resuscitate at work."

The following morning came around too soon. After a deep night sleep, Annie felt well rested and wonderfully invigorated. Kissing Mitch gently on the cheek, so as not to wake him, she climbed quietly out of bed and made her way to the kitchen.

Entering the kitchen to make their morning coffee, she could already smell the tantalising, delicious aroma of brewing coffee beans. She noticed the full pot of percolated already steaming on it's stand. Next to it a pretty card sat on the bench. Annie smiled as she admired it's pretty, floral rose cover. Opening it she read.

> *"Annie my wife, my best friend, my lover, always stay as beautiful as you are, I love you with all my mind, heart, body and soul. Love Mitch.*
>
> *Xxxxoooollll.*

"Oh what a sweet heart," Annie expressed out loud, pausing for a moment, then placed the card carefully back on the kitchen bench.

After pouring each of them a mug of coffee, she made her way back to their upstairs bedroom. She placed the mugs of steaming, brew gently on Mitch's bedside table. He began to stir.

"MMMMMM," he mumbled sleepily with his eyes still shut, "something smells good."

"Good morning Beautiful," Annie called cheerfully across the room as she pulled back the curtains. The sunlight beamed in through the window, so warm, so brilliant. The strength of it saturating her body.

Mitch opened his eyes slowly, squinting, until he could make out Annie's silhouetted figure against the morning light.

Annie climbed on top of Mitch, cuddling him through the fluffy, quilted cover. They smooched like a couple of teenagers. Mitch wrapped his arms all the way around her firmly, as they began playfully rolling from side to side, from one side of the bed to the other, until, they were both entangled in the twisted bed clothes.

"Ha ha ha," Annie screamed and giggled hard as they both fell to the floor. Laying on the floor, their laughter subsided as they lay gently in each others arms, they softly kissed, in warm sunlight, on top of the big crumpled pile of linen.

"Oh I wish we didn't have to go to work today," Mitch sighed with a subtle frown of disappointment as he looked towards the ceiling.

"Never mind handsome," Annie reassured him, "just a couple more days and we get two glorious days off together. Hey, I've got a great idea," she continued with excitement, "how about we hit the coast, stay in mum and dads shack at Silver Sands, we could spend a couple of nights there. I don't think anyone else in the family is occupying it at the moment!"

"Sounds like a fabulous plan to me Honey." Mitch held Annie tight and gave her a big smacking, smooch on the lips.

"Then that's what we'll do. I'll drop in and grab the keys from mum and dad after work today, I was heading over for a visit anyway."

Chapter Thirteen

The Get Away

"Oh have a look at that, I'm glad we've arrived just in time to see the sun set," Annie beamed with gladness. She glanced over the roof of Mitch's Holden Ute, admiring the view from the gravelled drive way.

As she unlocked the cabin door, she could smell the dusty mustiness and feel the warmth inside. She promptly unlocked all the windows and flung them open, including the double French doors that led out to the decking on the beach.

Mitch stumbled in through the front door, muscles flexed, as he laden himself with what was mostly Annie's luggage.

"How many days did you say we were staying for?" He groaned, bending his knees, he braced himself as he lowered the bags and picnic basket carefully to the floor.

"Well a girl must have a few necessities if she wants to stay looking good for her favourite man. By the time this week end is over, I'm sure you won't have any complaints darling." She winked.

Mitch and Annie met in the middle of the wooden cabin floor, gazing into each others eyes. Clasping his manly hands to the back of her waist, he pulled her into him. She clasped her hands around his neck and looked up into his smiling, sexy, dark hazel, blue green eyes, eyes that appeared to change with the weather. As they held each other tight, Mitch's hands began firmly moving over Annie's body, their gentle kisses becoming hotter and more passionate.

The French doors overlooked the sea shore and the sun slowly lowered down into the ocean. Glowing shades of hot pink and orange illuminated the skyline with a hint of violet sheen. The evening could not have been more romantic. It was like a romantic movie scene, or a chapter from a Mills and Boon romance novel.

They sat out on the decking, on a table for two, enjoying feeding each other local tantalising delicacies Annie had packed for their week end away. The Australian, spicy, sun dried tomatoes and Tasmanian vintage cheese from Mersey Valley, washed down rather well with a glass of Annie's Lane Cabernet Merlot. This fine red wine was always a favourite in the Paggett house hold, smooth on the pallet, not to sweet, with a spicy, fruity flavour, complimenting many dishes, especially rosemary encrusted kangaroo rack. As well as water, Annie also called this wine, Gods medicine.

"A little bit of bread, a little bit of wine to keep you healthy on the inside."

They sat talking for well into the evening.

Mitch picked up Annie's left foot, then right, slowly sliding off her patent red leather slip on heels, placing her feet in his lap, he started to massage her.

"MMM that feels heavenly babe," she sighed as she threw her head gently back.

She sunk into the deck chair and looked up at the clear star filled night sky, the moon shining brightly, big full and glowing a shade of yellow gold.

"Would you like to take a walk along the beach?" Mitch asked with a sparkle in his eyes.

"A walk is just what I had in mind," Annie replied, she smiled serenely, feeling calm after a few wines and a relaxing foot massage.

Moonlight lit their path as they walked arm in arm along the shore, the foam from the waves washing over their bare feet, cold and invigorating. Silver white glistened and danced on the water all the way to the shore, the gentle warm evening breeze swept across their cheeks.

The night was warm, yet so comfortable.

"This is such a perfect evening Mitch," Annie commented. "The sky so clear, you can see every star sparkling, the moon so full, now so crisp and white, high in the sky. I might have to get up and write a poem about this beautiful, inspiring evening."

"How about I get up right now and show you what a great evening it's going to be?" Mitch laughed his deep sexy laugh.

Annie laughed with him, "Oh Mitch you are so funny."

He took her in his arms and swung her around and around, until they were both so dizzy, they flopped onto the sand. Rolling over one another, they wrestled on the ground, giggling and laughing, Annie started to cry.

"What's wrong Honey?"

"Nothings wrong," Annie laughed and cried some more. "I'm crying tears of joy because I couldn't be happier. I'm so full of happiness and joy I feel like I could burst. It feels so good. You know, I hope this never ends, I mean I hope we can keep doing stuff like this for the rest of our lives."

They lay on their backs, holding each others hands, gazing up at the dark, star-filled vastness.

"I don't see why we can't my sweetness, as long as we are able, why don't we make the most of it." He pulled himself up on one elbow, leaning over Annie he kissed her sensuously on her salty, willing and ready lips.

The night had become increasingly hotter. Mitch and Annie wrestled with each others clothing on the secluded beach. Their breathing became heavier and more rapid. Their skin glistening with the moisture in the moonlight. They moved swiftly in animal like passion, eager to get to one another. Laying totally naked, two wet, hot bodies intertwined like snakes on a vine, slithering and sliding all over each other.

Annie opened her eyes fluttering, feeling ecstatic excitement. She rubbed her hands all over his body, as far as she could reach. He lay on her gently, rubbing in and out as his gliding firmness stimulated them simultaneously.

The sound of waves, gently hushing onto the shore. Annie whispered in his ear, with warm sensual breath.

"If this is being closer to nature, then I think we should do this more often. "Oh Mitch, Oh Honey, don't stop, don't stop, Oh yes, Oh yes, Oh yes."

Mitch pulled away and commenced to lick the salty wetness from her neck, as his hot breath tingled her ear. She reached down to feel his hard but smooth erect moist tip. He slid his tongue over her excited erect nipples. She grasped one arm around his strong, broad, tanned shoulders, while she continued to massage his throbbing hardness in her other hand, manipulating, rubbing. She grabbed his firm, gyrating rounded buttocks. He came up and kissed her vigorously and desperately. Holding his hardness along with her, he once again directed it into her tight, wet entrance, moving it in and out, each time entering her a little deeper and deeper inside of her.

Sliding her legs around his waist, she tightly clasped her feet around his back, her hands pulling his chest to her breasts, he entered her even deeper. He could feel every inch inside her now, hitting heights he's never hit before. Slithering in and out, out and in. Wetness trickled and dripped from their hot, pulsating bodies increasing their excitement. They were locked tight in an embrace, lips smothered into moist skin, bodies moving in almost convulsive, rhythmical pulses. Muffled sounds of pleasure echoed in rhythm with gushing waves, as they almost seemed to devour one another.

Mitch stood up from the sand, holding tight to Annie's clinging, naked, wet body as he remain inside of her. He held her in his big, strong, masculine arms and carried her into the moonlit, glistening waters, the water tepidly cool but comfortingly inviting. The water felt like satin sheets brushing against their tightly intertwined torsos.

They continued to thrust harder and harder, as the waves washed up to their bare shoulders. Annie felt ageless and timeless, surrounded by dark blue as far as the eye could see. Deep, sweet moaning, lapping of water, nothing now could come in between them.

Mitch carried Annie back to the sea shore, laying her down closely beside him. He kissed her gently on the cheek and then on the forehead, she kissed him in return.

Lost in the moment as she lay beside her young gorgeous husband on the beach, she looked up to the night sky once more, prayed to God in silence and thanked him for sending her the love of her life. Slowly her eyes began to feel heavier and heavier as she fell asleep in his arms.

"Come on Honey," Mitch spoke softly, "we best get back to the cabin before we both fall asleep." They quickly dressed. He gathered her up in his big, strong, safe embrace as they made their way back.

Annie awoke the next morning to the beautiful bird song and the not so beautiful seagulls squawking loudly. Opening her eyes, she gently kissed Mitch on his resting lips as he lay fast asleep, exhausted from carrying her all the way back to the cabin. She wanted him to have a good rest as he had been working a lot of long hours lately. She slid out of the creaky cabin bed as quietly as she could possibley manage, trying her best not to disturb him.

Annie crept around the cabin organising herself a cup of freshly brewed coffee. She grabbed her pen and note pad and went to sit out on the decking. With pen to paper, she began to write.

Love lullabies

A Perfect Evening
The Moon light shone an endless dream,
It's light on your face surreal moon beam.
Glisten of the sea sparkles in your eyes,
Night bird's song sweet lullabies.
Love Lullabies, Love Lullabies,
Love Lullabies.

Softest touch on the water's edge,
To give our heart's we both do pledge.
Standing as one our spirit and soul,
Passion spiralling out of control.
Love Lullabies, Love Lullabies,
Love Lullabies.

Hands held tight,
Sands sweeping over.
Leave me not,
My life time lover.
Love Lullabies, Love Lullabies
Love Lullabies.

One perfect evening we were walking along the shore,
The sky was pink and the air was warm upon my face.
You took me in your big strong arms,
And you held me in your warm, comforting embrace.

Blood water and spirit, running through our veins,
Blood water and spirit, no more aching no more pain.
Blood water and spirit, flowing through as one,
Flowing on forever, never to come undone.

Hands held tight,
Sands sweeping over.
Leave me not,
My life time lover.
©2000 Copyright All Rights Reserved Annette Evalyn Swain.

Annie could hear foot steps on the decking behind her, warm hands reached around her shoulders. Mitch spoke in his usual croaky morning voice. "Good morning beautiful, what you up to?"

Annie turned her head around and kissed him on the corner of his mouth. "Good morning to you gorgeous, would you like a coffee?"

"It's alright Babe," he screwed up his eyes as he looked out to the glare reflecting off the water. "You stay there, I'll grab one."

For the rest of the day they spent their time relaxing near the water, in front of the cabin. Mitch lay on the beach reading his favourite magazine, Sports illustrated. He looked up and admired Annie's defined figure, in her electric blue, boy leg bikini. She was paddling her feet in some warm puddles that had formed when the tide went out.

"You should be in this magazine," he complimented her, as he held the pages open for her to view.

"In your dreams Buddy," She laughed at his fantasising.

He quickly got to his feet and chased her into the water. He grabbed her around the ribs and started tickling her.

"Mitch, stop," Annie giggled, trying to get away.

"Right, that's it, you've had it now buster," she continued to giggle with a quiver in her voice.

He splashed her, she screamed, as she broke loose and ran out into deeper waters, he chased again, his strong thighs pumping through the depths. This time she used all her might to push him backwards. He fell into the ocean with a huge plonk, cold sea water spraying up all over her, she gasped.

Grabbing one of his legs, she started to tickle his knee caps, she knew he couldn't stand this, it was one of his most sensitive spots. "O.K, O.K.

Annie, stop, alright, you win, you win, ah, ah, ah ha, ha ha, stop it."
Mitch couldn't decide whether to laugh or cry?"

Annie let go of him and started to run away, once more Mitch caught
her and pulled her under the water with him. She screamed again at the
invigorating sensation of crisp, cold water.

Mitch took her by two hands and led her deeper. Shoulders deep in
deep blue, sensuously embracing her, nothing but the calm hush of the
sea and the sounds of their breath. The sun shone down on them, the
warmth of one another touching in between the lapping of the cool
waters.

"Thank you for such a gorgeous week end darling," Annie said softly, as
she cuddled into him in deep water, kissing his wet salty chest.

"No, thank you Babe, I feel totally revitalised," Mitch replied, as he
squeezed her even tighter and kissed her on top of her scruffy, soggy
head full of sea soaked hair. "I Love You Annie."

"Oh I love you to Mitch Darling."

Travelling home along the dry, dusty roads, the state hadn't seen rain
for quite some time, after a long Indian Summer. The silhouette hinting
of Autumn coloured, crispy leaves, complimented the orange glowing
sunset, as it's rays of colour shone through in strong beaming lines
during the twilight hours.

Annie smiled across at Mitch in the drivers seat, "What a fabulous
weekend, hey Honey!"

Mitch reached across with his left hand and placed it affectionately on
her right knee.

"It was the best Babe. I hope we can do it again sometime real soon."
He glanced over at her and smiled, before returning his concentration
quickly back to the road, placing both of his hands safely back on the
steering wheel.

Chapter Fourteen

A Taste Of The Bizarre

The hum of the alarm sliced through Annie's ears, the weekend was over. The time had come to return to work, early morning rise.

"Good morning Darling," Annie softly whispered.

Mitch awoke for his usual stretch in bed. He reached out his arm encircling Annie, pulling her against his still rigid, flexed, stretching body. He kissed her firmly and lingering.

"I'm going to miss you today," he murmured, as he nuzzled into her breasts.

"I've got some lectures tonight for my fitness course," she said, "but I should be back home long before you Baby."

"I'd better get up." She pounced out of bed, "or I might be tempted to linger a little longer and who knows where that may end up?"

"Come here Darling, I'll show you," Mitch smirked, as he tried to pull her back in their bed.

"Sorry darling, duty calls. I'll look forward to having that coffee with you tonight."

Coffee was a code word they used for their rendezvous. If ever Mitch and Annie were at a function or party and wanted to sneak away, they would say to each other, "are you ready to go for coffee?"

"I'll be keen to find out where we will end up then?" Annie stole one more quick kiss before making a swift get away.

She arrived punctually on the ward at 0700hrs. Everyone was sitting around the large, rectangular conference table, waiting for the night senior to come and hand over to the day staff.

In strolled Jorjia, she was always happy to get out of the place, after a long night shift, which most of the nurses were. Especially after a full moon, strange things would happen during the night; some would blame it on tidal changes, others blamed it on the atmospheric pressure that was all controlled by the moon. Some blamed it on unknown phenomena.

"Alright you lot," Jorjia yelled sarcastically. "Shut up and let me get on with it then." She cleared her throat. "I just want to hurry up and get the hell out of here."

Every one around the table fell silent.

"O.K, we've had a few admissions over night, one of them is our regular palliative patients, sweet little Mrs. McFay, you know, the one with nine children, a very supportive family. She's requested that when she was near the end, that she come into hospital, to take the burden off of her children. Even though they insisted on keeping her at home. She has also appreciates the care and support of the nursing staff. She wants her family to have that same comfort and support from us when she passes on. She and her family, have also requested, that Annie look after her where possible."

Annie could feel her cheeks warming, blushing with embarrassment. She remembered back to the first time Mrs. McFay left the Hospital on a stretcher via ambulance service. She was being taken home for her family to care for her, after a lengthy hospital stay, post her initial stroke. All the nurses were standing around her, saying their goodbyes. Mrs.

McFay had grabbed Annie's hand with her one good working hand. In front of all Annie's work peers, she struggled to get words out.

She had only regained partial speech after her massive stroke. It was enough though for Annie to understand and work out what she was trying to say, hence what she wanted.

"Annie, Annie," Mrs. McFay said, "You're the best nurse, you're the best." She smiled as she squeezed Annie's hand in hers.

Annie also remembered blushing that day.

"Do you mind being allocated to the palliative patients Annie?" Jorjia asked her."

"No, not at all," Annie replied, her face still flushed as she shrugged her shoulders." As long as no one else minds," she added.

The nurses around the table mumbled and nodded their heads.

Jorjia continued, "Other than little Mrs. McFay, there has been a few social admission and a couple of chest painers for investigation, they've had to be placed on monitors."

Clouds above grass, smoke above fire and earth in the middle. White, green, black, red, brown. This little verse always helped Annie to remember how to attach the leads for monitors and telemetry.

Annie was privy to verses that helped her to remember things, like during day light savings. When it was time to put the clock forward because we were in Spring time heading in to Summer, you would spring forward, "spring" forward into spring, putting the clock back in Autumn or Fall, "fall" back. "Spring" Forward, "Fall" Back. It just seemed to make life that much easier.

All duties were allocated evenly, six patients to each nurse.

Everyone started up the other end of the ward, sitting patients out of bed for breakfast and making beds. Annie quickly popped her head into the six palliative room to make sure they were all breathing. She grabbed some linen on the trolley and a linen skip, to join the others. Everyone paired up to make beds.

"Good morning gentlemen," Annie smiled cheerfully as she entered the first bay of six male patients. "Let's get some daylight in here shall we?" She drew the curtains back.

"Are you going to be looking after us today Annie?" One of the gentlemen asked.

"No, I'm down the other end of the ward today."

"That's a shame," he sighed, "It's always nice to have someone cheerful around while you're in gloomy hospital."

"Maybe you should put your name down on the Palliative list!" Banina sarcastically commented. The other nurses standing around making beds laughed.

"Pardon?" the patient questioned.

"Don't you worry about it Sir," Annie reassured him. "It's a private joke."

Annie squinted at Banina, "Ha, Ha very funny Banina."

Nursing staff worked their way up to the other end of the ward but by the time Annie had reached her allocated, Palliative patients, all the staff had deserted her and she was left to make all her beds on her own?

She assisted her Palliative patients to sit out of bed for breakfast, if they wanted to. Palliative nursing was always about comfort and choice for the patient.

She entered room one, Mrs. McFay's room, the last bed to make. It was the first room, right at the beginning of the ward. "Good morning Mrs. McFay," Annie said softly.

There was no answer. Annie walked up to the bedside and noted that she was still breathing. She gently brushed her hand over Mrs. McFay's cheek. Oh you poor darling, we'll try and do our best to keep you comfortable."

After reading through the updated notes and care plans. Annie realised that this was going to be this patients last stay in hospital. Saddened, a tear appeared in Annie's eye. A knot in her chest and a lump in her throat. The reality was though, she would no longer be in her physical body of pain. This would be a Godsend. Looking above the bed head, there was a not from her family, it read.

"Dear Nursing Staff, Please shower mum daily, as she is very particular about her hygiene and body odour. Kindest Regards, the McFay Family. :-)

The little smiley face on the note made Annie smile. It was something she liked to do herself, when she was writing a friendly note or letter to someone. "Don't worry Mrs. McFay, we'll keep you smelling like the rose that you are." Annie once again brushed her hand over the patient's forehead and hair.

Mrs. McFay did not respond, she lay peacefully, frail and pale. Annie went to the corridor, to see if anyone was available to help assist her getting Mrs. Mcfay out onto the padded, high back shower chair, no luck. Everyone was busy with their own patients.

Annie decided she would get busy and start her bed sponges and then come back to Mrs. Mcfay when some one was available to help her with the transfer. She could manage her other patients in their beds on her own.

Even though a lot of the time the Palliative care patients were unconscious, or not responding, Annie would always, with out fail, speak to them constantly, as though they were fully alert. She always felt that it would help stimulate their neurological state and helped them remain comfortable with their surroundings. She decided she would start a bed sponge on Mrs. Wisson.

Maintaining Mrs. Wisson's dignity, as she did with all her patients, Annie began organising the bowl for her bed sponge. As she commenced her boss Benson, stood with the door open, peering in whilst she was washing the patient . . . . well what Annie referred to as the nooks and crannies.

The weird thing about her boss was? He just stood there? Watching? Not uttering a word? Just staring? Annie thought it was bad enough, that she had to do the task in the first place, someone had to do it. But the thought of her boss Benson, staring while she washed this female patients genitalia, made her stomach churn.

"Excuse me," Annie asked him, as he stood there still glaring through the ajar doorway he held open with one foot. "Is there something you wanted?"

He continued to stare even more catatonically, as if looking right through her.

"Do you mind, I'm trying to get on with my work," Annie frowned, looking at him with slight agitation. He stared at her directly now, not uttering a word. Then he just shut the door and walked away, only once Annie had pulled the sheet back up to cover Mrs. Wisson.

"That was a bit weird Mrs. Wisson," Mrs. Wisson did not reply, as she lay there in a sleep state. "If he had have asked me if I wanted a hand to turn you or something, it wouldn't have seemed so peculiar. Sorry about that little interruption." Why did this situation leave Annie feeling vulnerable? Almost invaded, if this is how she felt, she hoped the patient didn't feel it?" Taking the bowl over to the sink, after completing the bed sponge, Annie went to pour the remainder of the dirty wash water down the sink. Annie felt distracted, the wash bowl slipping from her hands, she quickly recovered it but not before spilling half of it on the floor.

"Oh bugger, oops, I mean shoot, sorry Mrs. Wisson," Annie said out loud, regardless of whether the patient could hear her or not? Annie quickly grabbed some paper towel to sop up her mess. As she was doing this, Benson re-entered the room, while she was bending down, he held her head down with his hand to his crutch level. Annie rose up in a hurry, almost slipping over on the wet floor.

"What are you doing?" Annie yelled flabbergasted and dumbfound.

"Wow, your hair is really quite soft, I just wanted to see how much hair spray you put in?" He cackled briefly.

"I don't use hairspray," Annie snapped at him.

By the time she had reached the pan room, Annie felt quite unwell. She stood in that little room for a while and took quite a few deep breaths. Trying to regain some composure, trying to think of all the excuses in the world to make sense of her bosses peculiar behaviour. The feeling in the pit of her stomach was telling her something wasn't quite right.

Always go by your gut instinct, rolled through her current, muddled train of thought.

"Don't worry," Annie told herself in her own mind. "It will only be a passing phase, then he'll leave me alone." Besides she did not want to jeopardise, or give up her life's work she loved so much.

To take her mind off of her own stresses, Annie found Banina to double up with. Checking off her D.D.A medication, she also got Banina to help her transfer Mrs. McFay onto a shower chair.

Mrs. McFay let out a quiet moaning noise as the nurse lifted her carefully and as comfortably as possible onto the shower chair. She didn't utter a word in the shower, but when Annie was giving her a standard hand massage, Mrs. McFay looked down at her hand and then gave Annie the biggest, most beautiful smile and squeezed her hands.

When Annie had finished fussing at the bedside she asked, "Are you comfortable enough? Are you warm enough?"

Once again Mrs. McFay opened her eyes wide, lifted her head slightly, she gave Annie another big smile. Annie smiled back a beaming smile. Mrs. McFay did not have to utter a word, Annie knew she'd done a good job.

"You're such a strong old bugger aren't you," Annie smiled, as they both held each others gaze. Mrs. Mcfay smiled back again, this time almost mischievously, giving Annie a little wink, then closed her eyes peacefully continuing to smile gently.

Her daughters arrived arrived for a visit not long after and were amazed to hear mum had responded at all, apparently she hadn't opened her eyes or responded for at least two months,. They said that she was more than ready for the next life.

Annie was so inspired by Mrs. Mcfay's inner strength, that she decided to use her nervous energy positively. She sat down at her morning tea break and wrote an uplifting poem. It was a far away place from worrying about her boss Benson's strange behaviour.

Annie began to write, the words flowed easily. Annie even amazed herself. "That's not a bad poem." She read it through once more in her head.

Power Of An Eye

Sitting there all fragile and torn,
Head hung low as if forlorn.
Withered and broken,
Not a word was spoken,
Child like in some way,
So mild and meek.

Not a muscle to move,
No strength for agility.
Saddened by their lack of ability.
Skin on skeleton, only can I see.

One would think that they're just not there,
As they hang there like that on that chair.
But alas, I feel the eyes physically on me,
As the head lifts ever so slowly.

Taking a hand,
There is no muscle
But power,
As those eyes begin to smile.

There is spirit here in this temple,
There is soul to the end of time.
The eyes are the window to the soul,
So strong yet so sublime.

Never be fooled by an exterior,
A cracked and fragile shell.
Looks can be deceiving,
Even to something you thought,
You knew so well.

Annie felt much more relaxed now she'd refocused on her spirituality. Once again she was comforted by the Higher Power. She spent the rest of her working day staying focused. When she had finished her manual nursing tasks, charting, computing and documentation, she then spent some time talking to and emotionally supporting the patients and their relatives. She thought it best that she stay near company.

Most of the relatives were accepting of the patient's condition, as they had been ill and suffering from terminal illness for quite some time. Their only wish to have them remain as comfortable as possible.

Some of the relatives and even friends of the family, would come in and give hand, arm and foot massages, or gently brush the patient's hair. Sometimes even just hold their hands. It was encouraged that they do this as it made them feel they were helping and gave them some comfort as well.

Chapter Fifteen

Closer Than Comfort

"Don't touch me," Annie said raising her voice assertively. A sickening quiver shivered up her spine. Her neck stiff with fear. Benson ran his fingers through the ringlets on the nape of her neck. He stood right behind her chair. She was concerned. There was no way for her to move away, with out causing an assault to him.

It had been hard for Annie to cope with anyone touching her hair. It was her crowning glory and her neck was one of the most sensitive parts of her body, she only allowed her husband to touch it, in their moments of intimacy. Her boss touching her this way, made her feel invaded.

Annie had loved her long hair as a child and was so devastated at one stage in her life. She had to have her hair all cut short, as she'd contracted head lice at school. It's just what they did in the good old days. It was all cut off really short, even shaved.

Annie sat in the nurses station, still frozen. Benson just standing there now, as he quickly snuck his hand away, hearing multiple foot steps coming up the corridor.

"Thank goodness," Annie looked up to the ceiling, as if to thank God for good timing.

Benson stepped back and swiftly walked away, passing several of his staff members on his way back down the corridor. He didn't say anything to any of them, he just smirked and kept on walking.

Casandra, Tamara, Tamzin, Laurri and Demi approached the nurses station.

"Hi Annie," they all said.

"How are you going up this end of the ward?" Tamzin asked.

"Work wise good," Annie replied quietly, "Otherwise, I'm not sure?" She looked down at the paper work on the nurses desk immediately in front of her.

Tamzin asked, with a curios look on her face. "Are you O.K.? You look like you've seen a ghost." Annie did not want to make mountains out of molehills, so decided to once again keep Bensons bizarre behaviour to herself. Little did she know, male nurse Steven, was watching from a distance.

"Yes," she replied, "you're right, I am not feeling well." She stood. "I'm going to the pantry, to wet my whistle, I won't be long."

As Annie started moving into the hall, Benson moved out from the next lot of rooms along the corridor. He began to pace Annie down the hall. She went to enter the pantry and for some strange reason, she turned around and looked behind her.

She felt a presence close behind, she gasped, there was Benson, right up close, to close for comfort. By this stage Annie's mouth was nervously dry. Her heart pounding, she began to get short of breath. She felt she would gag and began to dry retch, she sipped her water. She had never experienced this sense of helplessness.

Annie arrived late home again that afternoon, feeling more exhausted than usual. Work was always full on but this time Annie felt more mentally drained, she had numbing in her mind, almost to the inner depths of her brain. She felt unfocused, dazed, like she was watching her own life from the outside in.

Mitch was on afternoon shift, so she decided to have an early night and fell asleep quite rapidly, exhausted from the day. Suddenly Annie sat up in bed, gasping for breath, her heart racing. She felt like she'd been asleep for hours. Glancing at the alarm clock, disgruntled that she'd only been asleep for five minutes, it was only seven minutes past ten or 2207 by the 24 hour clock.

Half asleep, walking to the kitchen, still feeling exhausted, she got herself a warm mug of milk. Zapping it in the microwave, it took about a minute and a half on high, just the perfect temperature, she didn't even feel it hit the sides.

Annie flicked through a couple of juicy, gossip magazines and read the latest stars, not that she lived by them but she found the fact that they could mean anything, one way or another, very amusing. She would take all the positives from them and leave the rest behind; she was always a great believer in the power of positive thinking.

Once again, the thought of her darling Mitch came to her thoughts. Oh how I could do with a cuddle right now. He was always so good at a comforting cuddle and a good kisser at that. Just to feel his tender, loving arms around her right now would be enough to take all the days stresses away. It was getting closer to his knock of time and it wouldn't be long before he was home.

Annie jumped with fright, as she woke with a start. Solemnly she took a big breath in, a huge sigh of relief, when she realised it was Mitch. He had just slipped his arm around her waist, as he climbed into bed close behind her. She could smell his aftershave, 'Cool Waters,' it was always such a sensuous fragrance to her, the comforting smell of him. Annie turned to kiss him good night. In silence he slid his hands even more firmly around her waist, as their kisses became more passionate. Annie turned to face him, so she could hold him around his broad strong shoulders.

"I'm so glad you're home handsome," she whispered as they rubbed noses in Eskimo fashion.

"So am I," he replied.

Mitch began running his hands down the curves of Annie's buttock and thighs. Together they lay, gently kissing, touching and caressing, until they were so relaxed. So contently wrapped around one another, they fell asleep.

Annie awoke again later that night, it was about two A.M, 0200hrs. She awoke feeling absolutely miserable, like her best friend had just died. She started gently crying, tears silently running down her cheeks, soaking her satin pillow case. Not wanting to wake Mitch, she took herself to the spare room where the gym and the computer study desk were set up. She sat down on the workout bench and had a quiet sob. Trying to work out why she felt so, not like herself.?

She didn't go back to bed but sat down on the floor beside the gym bench, with her knees drawn up to her chest. She wept and wept uncontrollably, until she could weep no more. Tears streaming down her face, feeling like they were beating down on her heart. The faster she wiped them away, the harder they did fall. Annie always thought crying was a good thing, cleansing the heart and soul. At this moment though, she wasn't so sure. She continued to hug her knees even tighter and rest her head on them. As day light drew near, she began to nod off.

"Oh I really don't feel well, I don't feel well, I feel sick." She held her cramping, nauseated stomach, as she slowly stood upright with what little energy she had. "Must ring work and let them know I'm not feeling too good, time for a day off," she spoke in her own numb mind.

She lent against the wall, as if she would fall any minute. Stumbling for the stair rail, she almost slid down. Her hands grabbed at the furnishings in the dull morning light. Annie had a feeling in the pit of her gut, she really felt like she had lost someone, or something close to her, she just wasn't sure what it was. Lost is how she was feeling, absolutely miserable.

When she finally got through to the LVH on the phone, she was put on hold. She stood there in dullness at the bottom of the stairs, hanging onto the railing, with the phone to her ear. Fifteen to twenty minutes had passed while waiting for the night co-ordinator to get to the other end of the phone.

Annie gathered the night co-ordinator must have been doing her early morning rounds.

"Good morning, nursing co-ordinator, "Sister Savvy speaking."

"Hello Sister Savvy, it's Annie Paggett here, I'm sorry but I'm not well enough to work today, I haven't been well over night. I'll ring and let you know if I'll be well enough to return to work tomorrow."

"O.K. Annie, I'll let the ward know. Thanks for ringing in reasonably early. Hope you feel better, bye bye.

"Bye Sister Savvy, Bye."

Annie was thankful, that she had received one of the nicer nursing co-ordinators. Sister Savvy was always pleasant, even though some of the night staff didn't think so, but maybe, they'd never worked days?

Annie crept slowly back to bed and felt once again the welcoming warmth of Mitch's body. Thank God for small comforts she prayed, as she gently closed her eyes and snuggled down with a big sigh of relief, if not relief then some sense of calm. She knew this was something that she was going to have to deal with herself, well, for today anyway.

Annie smelt Mitch's freshness as he kissed her gently on her cheek, before he left for a day of corporate meetings.

Annie opened her eyes to see her handsome man, standing, looking down at her.

Those gorgeous eyes just melted her soul.

"Are you going to be O.K. Honey?"

"I'll be fine Babe, just a little tummy upset. I'm going to pop in to see the doc today. I know you're keen to start a family and I want to make sure everything is functioning perfectly anyway."

Annie knelt upon the bed and threw her arms around Mitch's strong neck. She kissed him long and gentle.

"You have a great day, you gorgeous hunk, I'll cook up something special for dinner tonight. She looked up gazing into his eyes, her head tilted.

"I might just have you for dinner instead," he mused grabbing her tightly around her waist, he held her close and returned her long, gentle kiss, pulling her even closer to him.

"Oh is that a gun in your pocket, or are you just pleased to see me?"

"Well there is a gun in my pocket and I am please to see you. If you don't let me go now, that gun might go bang and shoot you." Mitch laughed.

"Oh Babe, you're so funny." She slapped him playfully on his chest."

What an amazing man he was, no matter how miserable she was feeling, he always managed to put a smile back on her face. They laughed some more as Mitch left the room.

Annie climbed down from the bed and stood at the window to wave goodbye to him as he drove off in his pride and joy, his black Holden Utility.

She phoned for an early medical appointment with Dr Low, her old family doctor. Shirley his long term receptionist answered the phone.

"Hi Shirley, It's Annie Paggett here."

"Hello Annie, how are you?"

"I'm not to bad thanks, listen would I be able to get in to see Doctor Low as soon as possible please?"

"Actually Annie, we've had a couple of cancellations this morning, ten thirty or twelve?"

"Ten thirty would be great, thanks Shirley, you're a life saver."

Goose bumps came up all over Annie's body as the water gushed down on her. The thought of her boss following her and touching her was giving her shivers. She could feel bad acid churning in her stomach and she felt physically sick to her stomach, to sick to stomach any breakfast.

As she stood under the warm water, tears once again began to stream down her face.

"Snap out of it girl," she told herself. "What on earth has come over you?"

It wasn't a bad thing she was crying, after all she knew there had to be a perfectly good reason she was feeling so out of sorts.

She let the shower run cold while she emptied herself of more tears. She told herself, "O.K. That's enough," Annie believed in her positive self talk. "You're a big strong girl, with the big fella upstairs on your side, just get on with it, you can handle it."

She rubbed her face with the towel and wiped away all the signs of her misery. Looking in the mirror, she smiled at herself. "Smile and the world smiles with you." She was not going to let her boss or anyone for that matter, spoil her happiness, or her smile.

Dressing in casual clothes ready for her doctors appointment, there was still time to hang a load of washing on the line. Mitch had been a darling and threw a load in before he left for work.

"How could I be anything but happy?" Annie encouraged herself. "I have the best husband, such a wonderful husband."

It was a beautiful autumn day out, clouds lightly dusted the sky, the air was warm bit with a touch of gentle, crisp breeze. Some squawking could be heard coming from the big old gum tree at the rear of the back yard. Annie looked up at the tree a little more intently. At the very top of the tree Annie could see. "Oh how pretty," she glance up some more, observing the beautiful Rainbow Lorikeet, its colours brighter than its sweet, sharp tweet.

As she continued to hang out her washing, she found herself constantly fascinated and distracted by this one isolated Lorikeet playing in the gum tree. It was so, so beautiful, bopping up and down and squawking, as if putting on a private performance, just for her.

Securely locking the house, she made her way to her appointment.

"Just in time," Jested Shirley the receptionist.

She new Annie well, Annie always arrived on the dot, never early and occasionally a little late. She also knew Dr Low also ran about half and hour behind schedule with his appointments, so she never stressed herself about it.

"Take a seat Annie," said Shirley, "Doc won't be long."

Sitting there in the quiet area, Annie once again began to think about her work and Benson's behaviour. Putting it once again to the back of her mind. She picked up a magazine and flipped from page to page quickly, trying to absorb every single picture to distract her. She flipped through another and another. She was on the last magazine when the doctor called her.

"Mrs. Annie Paggett," he thought it was funny calling her Mrs. as for so long she had been little Miss Annie. He smiled his usual approachable smile.

"Good morning Doc, how are you?" Annie smiled solemnly.

"I'm fine Annie, come in, take a seat. What can I do for you today?"

145

"Well," Annie began, "I've not been sleeping well, I have never had trouble sleeping before. As you know, I'm really active and normally when I sleep, I sleep like a log."

"Let me just take your blood pressure." He promptly applied the cuff around Annie's arm. He began to pump the cuff up and up and up. He released the valve and the cuff began to deflate.

"It's up a little high Annie. Are you under any stress at the moment, at home at work?"

"Work has been a little full on lately," she replied, "but my home life couldn't be better." Annie not wanting to give away to much information.

"How's that wonderful husband of yours?"

Annie couldn't help but smile, "Still wonderful."

"How is your family Dr Low"?

"They're great, we've actually got our first grandchild on the way."

"Oh how exciting for you, babies are such angelic little bundles. Mitch and I are planning to start our family soon, I can't wait. It might help if I could get back to some kind of sleeping pattern. Perhaps you could give me something?" She frowned and cringed at the same time at the thought of having to take drugs to help her sleep.

"Look Annie, you're probably better off not taking sleeping tablets. I'll prescribe you sinequin, it will help relax you for sleep, slow you down a bit. Just take one for two nights and if that doesn't work, take two for two nights and continue O.K.

"Thank you Doc."

"Is that all I can do for you today Miss, I mean Mrs. Paggett?" He shrugged his shoulders in his big white coat and gave her a genuine smile.

"Oh could you please write out a sickness certificate for work please!"

"I'll give you the next three days off, just until the medication settles in, alright then, sweet dream s my dear."

"Thank you Doc."

He accompanied her to the reception desk.

"Now young lady, you come back and see me in a couple of weeks time, so we can see how you're getting on."

"I'd like to see Annie again in a fortnights time thanks Shirl."

"Certainly Doctor," Shirley confirmed.

When Annie left the surgery, she felt a sudden need to visit her parents. She pulled over to the side of the road to make a call on her mobile phone.

"Hi mum, are you going to be home for a while?"

"Yes Love, why what's up?"

"Oh I'd just like to drop in for a cuppa and a chat, if that's O.K."

"Of course it is dear, is everything alright?"

"Everything is fine mum, it would just be good to see you, that's all, I'll be there in about twenty minutes."

"See you soon, bye, love you, bye." Annie's mum hung up.

It always felt good going back to mum and dad's. It was a blessing that they were still together, after eight children, many trials and tribulations. If ever there were a couple that stuck to there wedding vows, it was mum and dad. They some how battled on through thick and thin, in sickness and in health, definitely for richer for poorer, in good times and bad. Neither of them were fed with a silver spoon but they treated all their children like little princes and princess's.

Annie's mother met her at the front door.

They greeted one another with a loving hug and a warm kiss on the cheek.

"You look pale Annie, are you sure you're O.K? Are you eating right?"

Her mum always worried she wasn't eating enough with all the activity she did.

"Oh I'm just a bit stressed. A little bit of high blood pressure according to the old Doc."

"Well my girl, you had better relax and slow down a bit if you and Mitch want to start a family!"

"I know mum, you know I always do my best where my health is concerned, but I'm afraid I don't have any control over my boss's behaviour."

Annie had to blurt it out to some one sooner or later.

"Why, what's he been up to?"

"I'm not sure, he's been acting a little bizarre actually but I've tried to think nothing of it. I'm hoping if I ignore it, he might stop."

"You make sure you tell someone if he doesn't young lady, won't you?" Her mother looked at her with loving concern.

"It will be fine mum, don't worry, it will all come out in the wash. Now how about a nice cup of tea? Can I get you a cup? Would dad like one? Where is he any way?"

"Oh his out in the back yard, pottering around in his garden as usual, you know how much he loves his garden!"

Annie stuck her head out the back door, "Hi dad."

"Hi Love, how's it going?" Her father called from behind the blue berry bush he'd been watering.

"I'm good thanks dad, would you like a cup of tea?"

"That would be good thanks Love." His voice sounded warn out, I guess after yelling at eight children, whose wouldn't be!"

Annie always felt that when she came home, she was re-establishing, re-stabilising her stability. There was a river not far from here, a river that ran to the sea. Annie grew up here. It was the River Torrens, one of the estuaries from the Great Murray River.

She would run and run along that river, run for kilometres and kilometres, she still did on the odd occasion. Now her and Mitch lived closer to the coast, she spent more time running along the beach path, it was just as tranquil.

"Anyone else dropped in lately Mum?"

"Yes Laura and Mark dropped in on Sunday. They were on their way back from the Central Markets, bought me some lovely melons, you'll have to take one home with you, to many for your father and I, I don't want them going to waste."

Annie stayed for lunch. When she arrived home mid afternoon, she could still hear that beautiful rainbow Lorikeet chirping away and squawking playfully in her big gum tree. She decided to make herself a nice cup of chamomile tea. She sat in the back garden and absorbed the welcoming warmth of the afternoon sunshine. Taking pen in hand she began to write in her note pad. Inspired by that beautiful Rainbow Lorikeet, her words once more began to flow.

©The Rainbow Lorikeet

On the first day of Christmas,
My true love sent to me,
A Rainbow Lorikeet.
Its colours brighter,
Than it's sweet sharp tweet.

Playing amongst the trees,
As they sway,
Colours all so gay.
Being absorbed in such beauty,
Colours all so bold,
Takes away any sign of ugliness,
Darkness or Cold.

There is so much beauty,
In a world that can be so cruel.
Take Gods beauty,
And use it as your fuel.

Always remember that beautiful bird,
The song, the colour, its some what,
Friendly Nature.
Natures beauty can be found,
In any living creature.

So don't be disheartened,
If you feel your world,
Has turned ugly,
As you will see Gods Paradise
Is eternally and internally Lovely.

Annie placed her pen and pad down beside her. She sat back in the high backed garden chair and placed her feet up on the wooden bench seat. Closing her eyes, she could feel the sun warming her face and body. She took several deep breaths, sucking in the air of the universe. She sat peacefully, gently breathing, eyes closed. She pictured herself in her minds eye, sitting in the garden, under the sun and the vast blue sky. Gentle breeze swept across her face. She drifted of into a meditative state.

"Haaaaahhhh," Annie awoke with a gasp, from her state of relaxation. "Oh Mitch you made me jump, I was so far away."

"Am I that scary? And I thought I had a pretty good day at work too," he Joked.

"Oh sweetheart," she screwed her face up at him. 'You look gorgeous as ever, you just startled me, that's all. I didn't sleep that well last night, I'm probably a bit jumpy."

"What did Doc say?" Mitch asked, as he sat on the bench, beside Annie's bare feet.

"Oh just some silly tummy bug, he's given me some silly little tablets to take." Annie was to embarrassed to tell him she'd been put on some relaxation medication, she'd always done well at handling stressful situations on her own

Mitch looked at Annie, "Well, how about I cook dinner tonight and I'll run you a nice warm bath!"

Mitch took Annie by the hand and led her through the garden, to the house, down the hallway and into the bathroom

"But I'm meant to be cooking tonight remember?"

He began running the bath water. He turned to her and placed her hand in his. He placed the other hand on her lower tummy.

152

"Now young lady," he said, "if you're going to carry our beautiful baby in this tummy of yours, you have got to keep yourself in tip top condition. That doesn't mean being run off your feet all day, or working yours and everyone else's butt off at the gym . . ."

"Annie wryly smiled at the seriousness of him. "You know, you are absolutely right for a change."

He smacked her playfully on her bare bottom. "your bottom never wobbles, it's so toned," he observed.

"Well you know one of my favourite sayings," she giggled, "use it or lose it, if it wobbles, then I'm not working hard enough."

"O.K. Then my honey, in you hop, plenty of lavender bubbles in there to help you relax, so lay there and I'll burn some sandalwood oil to help enhance a peaceful atmosphere. I'll go poor us a glass of Annie's Lane."

Annie remembered the medication she had to take, could not be taken with alcohol.

"If you don't mind darling, I'll give my glass of wine a miss tonight, sorry to be a party pooper."

"Boy you really must be feeling pretty crook to turn down a glass of Annie's Lane."

Mitch was busy preparing dinner. There was candles glistening, one at each end of the oval shaped, polished, red cedar dining table. There was calming flute music playing quietly on the stereo CD. The table was set out just as she had done it herself many times before. The wine was breathing and she felt saddened that Mitch would be drinking alone. The aroma of freshly cooked garlic filled the air.

Annie took a breath in through her nose, enjoying the tantalising smell.

"Smells superb gorgeous, what ya cooking?"

153

"Oh it's just tender chicken breast cooked in garlic butter sauce, honey glazed carrot julienne, cauliflower cheese and steamed snow peas."

"Hey, that rhymes," Annie smiles, "I'll make a poet out of you yet. All sounds yum."

"Are you sure you won't join me for a glass of wine?" He asked again.

"No thanks sweety, I'll just stick to spring water for a couple of days and see how my tummy goes. I still feel a bit off colour.

Annie hated the fact that she was telling even the slightest, littlest of white lies to her husband. She didn't want to worry him with such trivial matters. He had enough stress and worry on him being a Police Sergeant. She didn't want him to think she was losing the plot. She's always been so strong willed, independent and determined to handle things on her own.

Explaining to Mitch over dinner, it was a good idea that she cut down her alcohol intake anyway, especially if they were planning on falling pregnant in the near future.

"Just try and eat something at least," Mitch dropped his lips, watching her pick at her plate. "You've hardly touched your dinner?"

"I'm sorry darling," she apologised, feeling awful, especially since Mitch had gone to so much trouble. "I guess I'm still not really feeling the best."

Annie started to feel a little weary and wondered if it was the medication starting to work. She also felt ill at ease knowing deep down, what was really draining her of all her positive energy.

"Are you sure you're alright sweetheart?" Mitch asked, "You're very quiet honey."

"I'm sorry baby but I'm still feeling a little queasy," Annie looked at him sad faced, "I'm so sorry you've gone to so much trouble, I don't thing I can eat any more."

"Don't feel bad," Mitch assured her. "Why don't you go lay down on the lounge."

Annie put her arms around his neck and gave him the biggest hug she could muster.

"Thank you honey for going to all this trouble. I love you and if it's any consolation, you certainly made me feel a whole lot better. I just need a good night sleep. Thank God you're such a wonderful husband."

Tenderly they kissed a lingering kiss. Annie was deep in thought at the time but what she was thinking was of no relative importance to the current situation. She was determined not to let this work oppression interfere with their love making. Besides it was the one thing that relaxed her when she was stressed. After all they were having a baby, and nothing, absolutely nothing would stop her from at least trying to achieve that.

She felt his gentle hands rubbing her back, across her shoulders, up her shirt. Suddenly they were wrapped once again in each others embrace, feeling as smitten as the day they met. Annie took a deep breath and felt all her cares slowly drift by the wayside, as she melted into his arms.

"You sure know how to make a girl feel good, you beautiful thing." She cuddled into him even closer.

"That's because you make me feel good." He asked her again, as he rubbed his hands softly up and down her back, "Are you sure you are going to be O.K?" He held her comfortingly.

"Yes of course. Don't worry your sweet little head about me. All I require is a good nights rest." She yawns, "so tired, sooo sleepy, you have relaxed me to no end. Feel like I'm going to drift off any moment, night, night, sweet dreams," she yawns again. "Thank you again for being so beautiful, I love you."

Her husband gazed down at her, as he watched her drift soundly to sleep in his arms.

"I love you too." He kissed her on the forehead.

Chapter Sixteen

A Wing And A Prayer

Sick leave was over and it was the alarm going off in the early hours of the morning that reminded Annie that she had to go back to work. Oh God please get me through the day I pray, help me to do the job I enjoy and know so well, thank you Lord, Amen.

Crawling out of bed, she kissed Mitch gently on the cheek, as not to wake him. This morning for some reason, she did not feel her enthusiastic self. Getting into the shower felt so good, she didn't want to get out. The thought of her having to go back to work wanted her to stay in there forever. She slid on her bra, G-strings, stocking and white nurses uniform and white lace up shoes.

Suddenly she heard a very loud screaming in her ears. She awoke to find the alarm blaring again. Her neatly pressed uniform, still hanging on its hanger, where she had organised it the day before.

Her sick days were over and it was the alarm, in the early hours of the morning that reminded her, that she had to go back to work. Oh God, please help me through my day I pray, help me to do my job that I know so well, thank you Lord, Amen.

She began to pray as she got in her car that morning. "dear God be my guide oh Holy Spirit, take my hand, oh take my heart, in the light and in the darkness, Holy spirit be my guide, Be my guide oh Holy Spirit, be my comfort strength and shield, through the mountains and the valleys, Holy Spirit be my guide. Be my guide oh Holy Spirit, take my hand oh take my heart and when my work on earth has ended, lead me safely home at last, lead me safely home to God, lead me safely home at last.

Annie pulled up in the work car park, she took a deep breath and adjusted her rear vision mirror to smile at herself.

"Everything will be O.K," she told herself.

Getting out of her car, she straightened her uniform of creases and felt her hair to make sure everything was in place. As she held her head high once again, she approached the building, she felt the familiarity of fear in the pit of her stomach. Her head began to spin internally, as she continued down the morbid, grey corridors, towards the lifts.

The lifts were old and in ill repair. On previous occasions, the door would heavily slam shut. One visitor actually got quite a nasty hip injury when the heavy metal door shut on them. Annie stood there for a moment reading the graffiti on the lift doors.

Jason FUCKED Amy 2000,

"Charming."

"Con was here for a good time, not a long time."

"The smallest of stars shine the brightest in the dark of night."

"Oh that's sweet." Annie thought to herself.

The lifts still not here. She ran for the stair well.

Walking onto the ward, she felt different this morning, after climbing the stairs to her destination, she noticed she was much more breathless than usual. Normally it didn't bother her climbing eight flights of stairs. Her fitness made her feel good and recover quickly. Taking a few more deep breaths helped to relieve the tightness across her chest, making her feel a little more relaxed.

Everyone, as usual, had got there five minutes earlier, all seated with their cups of coffee and tea, ready for hand over. The night staff had already begun hand over. It had been an ultimately busy night. Two patient deaths had occurred and mostly relieving agency staff made things very heavy. Annie thought the agency staff were wonderful, but some of the other regular staff grizzled about the relievers. If it weren't for the agency, they would have been very short staffed. The hospital was renowned for not being able to retain staff.

Some staff were pedantic, if they spent more of their time being productive and less time procrastinating and bitching, then they probably wouldn't need as many agency staff in the first place.

Now Annie thought to herself, "now don't go thinking bitchy like and lowering yourself to everyone else's standards."

Carly, one of the other nurses made a comment. "So you guys had a busy night last night then? What's left to do then, if you've already done all the work?" She laughed along with the other nurses.

"Very funny Carly girl," Jorjia snarled in her comical, cranky morning style. She stuck her determined chin out and laughed. "There's still two bodies to be laid out and sent to the mortuary, once the relatives decide they are ready to depart."

"Oh good, save the best till last then did we?" Tamzin interrupted. "Who's been allocated to lay them out then?"

"You and Annie Actually, well you had to ask." Jorjia confirmed.

"Oh," Tamzin voiced the sound of distaste, "but we always do it!"

"Them's the breaks," Jorjia smiled.

"How much longer do you think the relatives will be?" Annie asked. "I would like to get it done as soon as possible."

Jorjia replied promptly, eager to go home. "They've been standing around in the corridor crying and making cups of tea and coffee for one another, looking very drained. Shouldn't be to much longer!"

"Surely for the love of God, they will be away soon and let these poor souls rest in peace," Annie said anxiously. "Besides I want to get it done as soon as possible, before the boss gets in."

"Miss Goody two shoes, wants to have all the work done before the boss gets in," Banina grinned nastily.

Annie frowned, "no it's not that Banina. Look don't worry, you don't understand."

For such a busy night, hand over was brief, short, sharp and shiny. The night staff were eager to leave the ward for home and get to bed.

"Sweet dreams guys," Annie called after them.

"More like nightmares after the night we've had," Alissa replied.

"Just think of something nice while you're falling asleep, bye guys," Annie smiled.

"Bye Annie."

It wasn't the best start to the day really, having to deal with grieving relatives but Annie hoped to handle it as painlessly as possible and hopefully be able to put it out of her mind in the long term.

"Come on Tamzin," Annie said with a sigh, "I guess we'd better see where these relatives are up to with this lot?"

She and Tamzin entered the last room of the diseased and their families.

"Hello, is there anything we can get you at all?" Annie said, in a soft voice, as not to disturb the calm in the room.

"No thanks Annie, you have done more than enough, taking care of mum through this horrid illness. It's nice to see her lying here looking so peaceful and free of pain. I still can't believe she's gone though. Thank you Annie, for what you've done," the oldest daughter threw her arms around Annie and kissed her affectionately on the cheek.

"You always seem to go that little bit more out of your way to make mum feel comfortable, never rushed or half hearted. Some nurses are born and you are one of them."

"Look after yourselves and one another, don't hesitate to ask if you need anything," Annie replied, blushing from the compliment.

"Goodbye girls," the five daughters thanked the nurses in turn as they left the ward. Walking arm in arm down the ward corridor, they sniffled back tears and occasionally giggled, as they remembered the fond memories of their beautiful mother.

Annie was in a hurry to get these patients laid out, ready for the mortuary and funeral director, as unlike in life, in death she wanted to do it steadfastly but peacefully and before her boss got on the ward. It was as if she knew what was coming.

Tamzin disappeared to the store room to collect the mortuary bundles. Annie started cleaning up the first patient and removing all pain patches and needle sites.

Annie half screamed, half gasped, as she felt a sudden presence directly, close behind her. She turned her head to find Benson, he'd snuck into the decease's room. Annie, the dead patient and Benson, on their own. He was standing to close for comfort once again, he was breathing down her neck and it was sending very bad, chilling shivers down Annie's spine. Pressing herself closer to the decease's bed, she turned and squirmed out of a very difficult, uncomfortable situation. Annie could feel her blood pumping so hard, pulsating through her neck, a lump stuck in her throat, her breaths becoming shallower and shallower with anxiety.

Annie grabbed the bowl of wash water and placed it in front of her, placing a barrier between them. "Is there something I can help you with?" She asked, stuttering with nervousness. He turned and left the room.

"How extraordinarily weird, bizarre even," Annie thought fearfully, trying to make her shallow breathing deeper to calm herself down.

For the rest of the day, Annie did feel quite nauseated, her head spinning from disillusion. Later on in the afternoon, she felt as her worst, sitting down at her usual spot, at the nurses station to write her documentation. She felt a sudden restriction of breath, as though she was suffocating. An aching pain as if someone was standing on her chest, ached up into her jaw and the feeling of nausea was sudden and overwhelming. Her heart began to pound, pound harder and harder, thumping so hard as if it would jump out of her chest at any moment. Her eye sight began to fade, as she felt her head falling into darkness. She lowered her head to the nurses desk.

Moments had passed, woke to find the ward exactly the same. Nina the Ward Clarke, was sitting in her exact same position as before, at her computer. She looked over at Annie.

"Are you O.K. Annie, you look a little green around the gills?" Nina asked, she hadn't seen Annie place her head down on the desk moments before.

Annie concerned about what had just occurred, not knowing what the hell was happening to her body, thought it best to tell Nina about it, just in case something else happened.

"Listen Nina, I just had a funny little turn of some sort, If I stand up and collapse, don't say I didn't warn you. Thank God it's nearly home time." Annie took a big breath and had a big sigh.

"O.K. Is there someone ready to count the drugs," Lauri called, as she came out from the men's bay, she pulled a long red ribbon with a bunch of keys on it from her white, nurses uniform pocket.

"Here, I'll I'll do the drug count with you," Annie offered, eager to get out of the hospital and go home. "Just let me sign off my last bit of documentation, I'll be right with you."

As Annie and Lauri continued the count, Annie was finding it hard to remain focused. Over and over in her head, she tried to think of a reason Benson was singling her out and making her feel intimidated. If that was his aim, he certainly was being successful. She certainly wasn't flirting with him, or by any means encouraging his behaviour. As a matter of fact, she did her best to avoid him on a personal level, to remain professional.

Annie never liked mixing business with pleasure.

She went home from work that afternoon, feeling more than a little off colour. The tablets the doctor had prescribed her didn't seem to help much, so she decided not to take them any more, hiding them away in a high cupboard.

Opening a bottle of Coonawarra Red wine to breath, she slipped of her stockings, shoes and nurses uniform, put her hair down and removed her make up, or as she called it, her polly filler. She slid into the steaming blast of the hot shower spray, letting it flow over her hair, hair clinging to the sides of her face, down onto her neck. Steamy water pounding down hard on her cheeks, nose and lips. She placed both her hands and cupped her face. As the hot water ran over her hands, hot salty tears stung her eyes, running in streams down her face.

Trying to cry silently, she could hold back the fear no more, she began sobbing out loud, sobbing, turned to moaning, uncontrollable, inconsolable moaning.

"Oh God, what is happening to me?" Why is this happening to me? What have I done to deserve this?" She slid down the wall, until she was crouched on the floor. "Why is my boss treating me this way?

Be my guide Oh Holy Spirit, take my hand, oh take my heart, through the . . . . the, through the mountains and the valleys, Holy Spirit be my guide."

She sat there on the floor, water pounding down. She wanted that water to wash away all her troubles and fears but she knew it wasn't going to be that easy. Annie sat there for a very long time, singing, praying and chanting, until the higher power takes hold of her.

"Be my guide oh Holy Spirit, take my hand, oh take my heart, in the light and in the darkness, Holy Spirit be my guide. Be my guide oh Holy Spirit, be my comfort strength and shield and when my work on earth has ended, lead me safely home at last, lead me safely home to God, lead me safely home at last."

Funnily enough after a really good cry and a very long praying session, she knew she was going to get through this, come hell or high water.

"Where are you?" Mitch called from the front door, thinking it strange that Annie wasn't there to greet him.

"Annie coughed to clear her throat. "In the bathroom baby."

He brushed her cheek with the back of his hand. "What's wrong beautiful, your eyes look extremely red?"

"Oh it's some silly irritation, something I came in contact with at work!" Well it wasn't all together an untruth, she thought to herself. "I feel much better though, after a long hot shower."

"That's a relief hun, I see you've cracked a bottle of red. What say we have a night off from cooking and we'll order a gourmet pizza in." Mitch gave her a big cuddle as she stood there in the bathroom, wrapped in her towelling robe.

"That sounds like a grand plan. You must have read my mind, I really don't feel like cooking tonight anyway," she replied, trying to sound enthusiastic. Annie drank more glasses of wine that night, than she ate pieces of pizza. She fell asleep early that evening that she rarely did.

The alarm screamed and Annie flopped her hand over the snooze button, usually she was up and about after the initial alarm. It went off once, twice, three, four times this morning, before she could gathered the energy to get out of bed. She lent over and flopped her other arm over Mitch, nuzzling into his back. He grabbed her arm and wrapped it in his, holding upon his strong chest.

"You piked out a little early last night," he whispered to her in the darkness.

"Sorry babe," she softly replied, feeling a little guilty once again, for keeping her secret from him. "I've been a bit tired lately, I have no idea what's come over me?"

"You wouldn't be pregnant would you?" he whispered again, this time his sexy tone of voice breaking through.

"Afraid not handsome," she said sadly, holding Mitch to her. "Unfortunately I only had the nasties last week."

"Well we better work on that hadn't we!" he replied, stroking her cheek and kissing her soft morning lips ever so gently. Annie responded, gently kissing him back, nibbling his top lip. Mitch continued holding her in hid strong, masculine embrace. She could feel his hard, hot manly anatomy against her, stimulating her warm womanhood. She gently licked his lips, before kissing him again.

Annie snuck under the doona and licked aaaaaaand flicked her tongue over both his hard nipples, before ever so slowly kissing his body, while moving further down under the covers. She came to his strong,firm, erect penis and continued to kiss and lick him up and down his very hard, throbbing shaft. Every so often she licked it's full length, before placing it fully, deep in her mouth.

"MMMMMMMMMMM," Mitch moaned with pleasure. Annie loved that sound, she loved to please him as he pleased ands pleasured her, oh so many times. She then wrapped her lips around the end of his hard masculinity and thanked God it wasn't any larger, flicking her tongue over and around its tip.

Mitch moaned with more and more intensity, she continued to lick and flick her tongue as she fed him deeper into her mouth. She was feeling so aroused just listening to Mitch's satisfaction. She could feel the moist, pulsating parts of her body now as her heart pumped full of excitement. Mitch began to gently thrust his body, his hips slowly moving, assisting her to slip him in and out of her mouth. His hardness penetrating the whole length now. Mitch stopped and held her head in his two hands for a moment. He grabbed her under her arm and pulled her up onto him.

"Come up here beautiful, you know I love it when you do that but it's no way to get pregnant." he smiled a smouldering smile, with his sexy bedroom eyes.

Annie straddled his firm thighs, she grabbed his firm large erection with both hands, glancing down upon him passionately. She lent over and kissed him wantonly, as she placed him inside her very wet, well lubricated vagina. She wiggled in small, gentle circular motion. Manoeuvring herself around and back and up and down, holding his waist firmly in her hands.

She flung her head back in divine ecstasy, thrusting her pelvis in strong, controlled motion.

"Oh God, you feel so good baby, I don't want this to end, slowing herself down, she held back the temptation to finalise this loving, passionate entanglement."

She lay on him now, kissing his moist, soft lips, him kissing hers. She could feel his bulging, hard erection, fitting deep inside of her so sensitively. His manly chest rubbing against her erect nipple breasts. She place her arm down to the side of his thighs and cupped his firm, masculine buttock cheeks in her hands, holding him firmly. She sucked on the side of his neck as the thrusting became more and more erratic.

"Oh my God, oh God Mitch," Annie whispered in his ear, with hot breath, "I'm going to come baby, oh God, oh God, Ahhh, Ahhhh."

"Come baby, come." Mitch groaned as he held her tight and thrust. her deeper and deeper inside. Thrusting and pulsating, moans of pleasure and fulfilment taking each other there. Nothing else mattered when they were lost in this moment together, their private, passionate performance.

Exploding together, they lay there in a pool of love and serenity.

After that blissful morning awakening, it was time to get back to reality, at least Annie was on afternoon shift, so it gave her plenty of time to warm to the idea of going to work, at least it was some relief knowing Benson was only there until 1700hrs. Then she would be able to enjoy the rest of her shift which finished at 2300hrs.

Annie arrived at work at approximately 1500hrs.

"You have to go relieving to ward 6E," Benson told her, even before she had a chance to put her bag away in her locker.

"I'm sorry," Annie replied, "I asked to be removed from that ward for a reason and I was told I had the right to do so!"

"No wonder you got kicked off of that ward with that attitude," he yelled in front of everyone.

Annie was extremely intimidated and embarrassed.

"I'm sorry sir," she explained, "I did not get kicked off of that ward, 6E, I asked to leave for good reason. The ward was very inappropriately managed and extremely unprofessional."

Her boss asked her to come with him to the office. He closed the door behind her but she opened it again, he tried to shut it. She said, "I'm sorry sir but what ever you have got to say, is good enough for everyone to hear, as I have done nothing wrong and am stating my rights for my own safety." She stood in the doorway so he couldn't close it.

"You are going to ward 6E, he demanded.

"I'm sorry sir, I'm really not feeling well. I'll be going to the nurse coordinators office and letting them know, I'll be going home now." She clasped her chest as she left the ward.

She could feel her head thumping, dizziness had taken over. She felt extremely sick in the stomach and it had nothing to do with the red wine she'd drank the night before. Short of breath her heart pounding, her chest tight.

Approaching the coordinator, she informed them that she was going off duty, as she had become suddenly unwell when arriving to work. She drove straight to Doctor Lows Surgery.

Annie stumbled, fumbling her bag, as she came through the doorway.

"Annie have you finished work?" Shirley asked, "what brings you here today?"

"No I just started work actually Shirl, but I'm feeling a little peculiar, so I thought I'd better come and have the good Doc check me out."

"well you have perfect timing, there has been a cancellation for half past three. Do you mind waiting ten minutes? He's running a few minutes behind as usual." She smiled.

"No of course not, thank you." Annie was relieved she wouldn't have to wait to long. Sitting on the patients waiting bench, Annie picked up a magazine, this time she didn't even look at the pictures. She sat there staring and staring in a big blurb, feeling very numb and trying to understand why she had to deal with these awful people? Was there a lesson to be learnt here? She also felt her stomach upset turn to nausea. Sitting breathing deeply, Annie attempted getting in to a more relaxed state.

She could not stop thinking about the time she had spent on this ward, it had been almost two years, a lot of staff had moved on, changed wards, resigned, or gone to permanent night shift. She was still trying to deal with the strange behaviours of her Boss Benson, then before that, Sister Fartrol, then Charlie. All the negative treatment began saturating Annie's concious mind, she hadn't realised how much she'd bottled up inside her.

She just continued putting it to her subconscious mind, trying to get on with her work. No one saw what her boss got up to, not that she knew of, he always seemed to wait for the opportune moment, when she was alone, seated, or bent over, or even worse, when she was laying out the dead.

"Annie, come right in." Doctor Low called from his office door,. "Come in and take a seat. What can we do for you today?"

"Bring back my serenity, would be a good start," she continued with sadness and sorrow in her voice. "The last time I came to see you Doc, I wasn't completely honest with you, it wasn't just work stress and sleepless nights, I've been having some trouble with my boss. He's been acting peculiar, well I will tell you and you can decide for your self. I believe his behaviour has been inappropriate!"

She went on to tell him all that had occurred since working at the Lake View Hospital, making it as brief as possible. From the behaviour of her two female seniors on the first two wards. The following, the touching, the watching, the sneaking up behind her. She told how she would yell out to Benson, "DON'T TOUCH ME," yet he still continued to intimidate her, even after her expressing her disapproval. She told the Doc, how it made her feel quite unwell, anxious, feelings of tightness in her chest, the blacking out on the desk, shortness of breath. She also told him, she'd tried those relaxant tablets he'd prescribed for her and how they had no affect, so she stopped taking them. Explaining to the Doc, the real reason for all those sleepless and restless nights.

Dr Low took Annie's blood pressure.

"It's not good news Annie," he said looking at her with honest concern. "For the sake of your health, I will have to give you a certificate for stress leave. Your blood pressure is even higher than it was last visit and that's no good, considering you've had nice healthy blood pressure your whole life. Your calm disposition has also been affected. I've never known you to be such a bundle of nerves."

"Oh please Doc" she sighed, "Isn't there something else we can do?"

"No," he said insistently, "this has obviously gone on long enough. It's classed as bullying and sexual harassment and they just can't get away with that sort of behaviour. They're abusing their position of authority, abusing the power, harassing and bullying you like that, It's appalling."

"But Doc, I don't want to make a fuss about this, I just want to do what I have always done and get back to enjoying my nursing, without being watched and touched and yelled at all the time, without defamation to my character."

"Well then Annie, perhaps once I've filled out these incident reports and medical certificates, you get on to your union representative and make an appointment to put in an internal complaint. While you're at it, make an appointment to put in an internal complaint. While your at it, make sure you make an appointment to speak with your hospital counsellor."

She left the surgery feeling quite devastated. She looked up at the sky and once again talked to her higher power quietly in her mind. "What's going on God? I love my nursing but I just don't want to do this any more. If only I could look after my patients without all this extra stress. I want to enjoy my life's work, not give it up."

Annie could not understand, nor make heads nor tails of why she was going through all this. She glanced up at the sky again.

"Dear God, is there something I'm supposed to learn from all this Lord? Please hear me, please help me Lord, show me the way I pray."

Once again, she felt protected and reassured, as the higher power placed a feeling of shielded strength and protection all around her. It gave her the confidence to deal with the situation that had been placed upon her.

Chapter Seventeen

To Believe Or Not To Believe

Pulling up in the driveway of their suburban home, Annie noticed that Mitch was already home. He normally had cricket training when she was on afternoons, then went to the Police Club for a few drinks with the boys.

MMMMMM He must have finished early this evening? He was lucky to be home by midnight on normal training nights. At the front door, Mitch stood with his arms wide open, ready to give her a big cuddle.

"Hi Baby, what are you doing home so early? What happened to cricket training?"

"I rang work to say hello and to see how you were going, they told me you weren't feeling well and you'd gone home. I was worried about you, so I'm giving cricket training a miss tonight, so I can stay home and look after my beautiful wife."

"Oh Sweetheart, you are so gorgeous, you don't have to do that. I'm a big girl, I'll be fine," she reassured him. She reached up, kissing him affectionately upon his cheek.

"I know I don't have to," he said, "but I want to." He cuddled her inside the doorway, holding her head to his strong broad chest. "Come on

171

then, get out of that uniform, into something a little more comfortable and put your feet up, I'll make us a nice cup of tea."

She was really glad Mitch was home. She didn't want to be sitting on her own this time, even though she was a little more relaxed now she'd left work. She still felt an uneasiness about something, still anxious, tightness across her chest still present, feeling like something bad was about to happen. But she didn't know what!"

As she prepared some finger food, she tried to distract her mind from the strange events at work. Eating dinner in the lounge, huddled up to Mitch, with her head in his lap. She and Mitch were having a quiet night watching some of their favourite comedians on T.V. At the Annual Comedy Festival in Melbourne. She rarely missed it and hoped one day to get over to Melbourne to see it live.

"Do you mind if I turn in early this evening Baby? The Doc has given me three days off, so I want to catch up on some rest." She yawned, as she put her hand over her mouth.

"Of course I don't mind Honey," Mitch replied, "I'll just finish watching the comedy and I'll be right behind you."

Annie got up slowly, almost half asleep already. She kissed her husband gently on the lips twice, three times, gave him a cuddle and retired to their bedroom.

She slipped out of her house clothes, into her purple, satin pyjamas. Loving the feeling of the satin against her bare skin, she rubbed herself all over, holding herself within her own arms. Climbing into bed she turned off the main light and flicked on the lamp light at the bedside table. Nestling down into the white, silky smooth bed sheets. She pulled her pocket bible from beneath her pillow.

She always found strength and comfort in the verses from her bible, it some times brought tears to her eyes because of the wisdom it expressed. It wasn't long before she felt herself drifting off into a deep slumber. The bible still in one hand, resting upon her left breast. It only seemed like a moment of sleep had passed, when she lay there wide awake, someone whispering her name. The quiet murmur of the television could still be heard in the lounge room, living area.

"Annie," the voice whispered again.

She lay very still in her bed, alone, feeling calm, unafraid. Suddenly a shadow appeared, looking down over her, as if protecting her. It had a beautiful warm, soft glow around it, showing the figure of a man. It wasn't talking to her as if out loud but in spirit. Feeling this strong presence in the room with her, it gave her a feeling of strength, to help her through whatever it was she was going through.

The spirit continued to hover over her.

"Don't let them knock you down Annie, keep fighting for what is right and just. You can do this Annie, you have the strength to carry on, what ever they may do, you will get through this, you have many innocent good spirited souls fighting for you and your cause. You must not let them win, they have oppressed and destroyed one too many innocent souls. Don't let them shoot you down."

Annie heard Mitch turn the T.V. off in the living area. As he entered the bedroom, he yawned.

"Ah your still awake Babe."

Then the glowing shadow was gone.

"I dropped off for a little while," she smiled, closing her eyes and falling back to sleep almost instantly.

Mitch watched his wife sleeping soundly and soon fell asleep with his arms and legs wrapped around hers.

Annie awoke in the early morning, feeling quite alert and refreshed. It was still dark outside. She glanced over at the clock, 0500hrs.

"Oh goodness," she thought, the annual City to Bay fun run was coming up in a couple of months. No better time than the present to start training.

She threw herself out of bed and grabbed all her jogging gear, placing it all on swiftly and quietly, not to wake Mitch. Starting with a warm up, she used the same techniques she taught her fitness clients. It was an all over body work out, warm up and stretch, using full range of motion, or as she called it Fromotion Fitness. Annie always believed you should practice what you preached. The warm up gave her strength in feeling all of her muscles controlling and supporting her while she ran.

Before heading out the door, Annie drank two glasses of water and one glass of orange juice with her women's multivitamin, two cod-liver oil capsules and three vitamin C tablets. She hadn't had a cold or influenza for about seven years and hadn't had to take antibiotics for over fifteen, so she thought it must be all doing her justice. At least something was! She felt younger and healthier now than when she was eighteen, although she didn't know if she was all the wiser?

Outside she took a few deep breaths of crisp morning air. It was quite cold, as the winter mornings had already started to creep in before Autumn was over. Sometimes at this time of the day, it would be two degrees below zero. Annie was absolutely freezing.

"Time to get moving, the quicker you go, the warmer you get." (Annie self talked.)

Starting a rhythmical pace, her breathing in time with her steps, breathing faster as her pace increased. The bike path along the river was covered in Autumn leaves. The mildewy, damp earth smell was prominent in Annie's nostrils and the birds had only just begun their early morning chatter.

It was still quite dark, fog hovering just above the wet ground. The moisture of the crisp air stung her now warming face. Cutting through the fog, she left the path and jogged cross country, as she had done since she was a child.

Annie jumped as she heard a gunshot like sounds ringing through her ears. At first she thought it was a car back firing from the main road. Again, BANG, she was deafened by the blast as she felt something swiftly sweep past her hair. She ran further into the overgrowth, trying to escape the direction of the terrorising blasts coming from behind her.

Suddenly she felt a sharp pain, stinging sensation in her legs. She was being shot at, like a moving target. Loud shots rang through her ears. She ran for her life. Tripping and falling to the damp muddy ground. Struggling to her feet, she continued running away from the blasts direction but she couldn't get away. Running and running, no where to hide, she fell to the ground again and again struggling to her blood soaked feet. Running, running,BANG BANG, two more loud blasts rang out, this time even closer, one of her arms was blown off, AAAAAAAAAAAAAAAAAAA, AAAAAAAAAAAAA. She screamed and cried out in excruciating pain as she felt her other arm hanging, dangling by a thread at the side of her body. Once more she fell, this time slipping to the ground repeatedly and frantically on the moist, cold, muddy, slippery, bloodied ground. The pain in her legs was unbearable but she picked herself up and kept on running. Again the shots rang out, this time blowing off her remaining arm, blood spraying everywhere but still she did not stop.

Time and time again, the shots plummeted to the depths of her shattering bones, no arms, just bludgeoned legs carrying her, screaming out in pain, running and running, a shot blew away chunk of her thigh, she fell to the ground again. The morning cold and dark, the ground wet, bloodstained and muddy, she struggled to her feet for the second and third time, telling herself, keep going Annie, keep going, you can survive this.

"AAAAAAHHHHHHHHHHHHHHHHHHHHHH," she screamed again, her other leg went from beneath her, slipping from under her body. She got up again. This time her bones were pierced through her skin, broken from the blow of shots. She managed once again to struggle to her feet, both of her legs damaged beyond repair. She collapsed heavily to the ground, to the ground, to the ground. Her heart still beating, racing against time. She could still feel the strength of her spirit from with in, as if not attached to her bloodied flesh.

She could see a bright light shining, glowing through her now closed eye lids. The light was warm and welcoming, she felt no more pain. She lay still, calm and peaceful, her breathing slow and relaxed, her heart beating strongly from within. She could feel it thumping with strength and vigour. She lay there, eyes still closed. Silence fell all around, not even a bird sound. With that soft welcoming light still warmly glowing through her eyelids and she was afraid but excited to open them at the sight of what was about to be revealed.

Annie didn't know where she was, as it certainly felt like a lifetime away from what she had just experienced.

She slowly opened opened her eyes. There she lay in her bed where she had been all night. Her pocket book Bible still resting upon her left chest. Focused as never before, on the strength of her spirituality. She believed this nightmare, dream, what ever it was called, was a lesson in the power of strength of the divine spirit world.

After that experience, she slept so soundly. In a weird way, it gave her more strength and hope. What ever was going on, she was determined to hold her head up high and never let anyone shoot her down. Not to let them get the better of her, under any circumstances.

Screaming and blaring, the alarm awoke her in the early hours of the morning. It was time to get up and get on with her life. This time she jumped straight out of bed, not forgetting her kiss on Mitch's cheek.

In the shower, she felt the water tingling her skin, it felt good. Placing the cleansing soap in her hand, she began to rub it all over her body, massaging all the way from her face, to her breasts, down the body, massaging her womanly, soft skin gently, she stayed there for a while as the warm water ran over her. Moving her hands to the back and front, feeling more relaxed and more comfortable than she had for some time. She felt a new lease on life. Placing one hand on each buttock cheek, softly rubbing herself in around and back. Raising up one leg at a time, she lathered up the soap and rubbed her legs up and down, right into her crotch. Cleansing and breathing, so relaxed now. Everything is going to be alright, today will be a brighter day.

When Annie returned to work after having her sick leave, she felt like she had been given the power to deal with the situation. She was determined to deal with her problems head on, she felt like nothing could knock her down or intimidate her.

As she entered the building, she stood taller and prouder than ever before. She could hear the song her mother sang to her when she was just a child, walk tall walk straight and look the world right in the eye and that's exactly what Annie decided she would do.

Along the way down the corridor, she passed several patients and nurses, she greeted them with a smile and a good morning, it was good to see them smiling back. This was going to be a, as well as a lot of hard work but . . . . for the first time in twelve months Annie felt her fighting spirit return, it was guiding her, protecting her; some how, it all started to make sense.

"Good morning," she smiled, as she walked energetically through he conference room door. For some reason, the climbing of eight flights of stairs this day was a breeze.

"What's up with you?" Jorjia smiled, "You're bright and bubbly today, did you get a bit last night?"

The whole room broke into laughter. Annie waltzed up to her and bent over and whispered to her.

"I get a bit every night." She bragged this quietly but so everyone could hear.

Jorjia pulled a face and laughed, "half your luck, you lucky cow." Everyone seated around the hand over table burst into laughter and chuckled.

"O.K. Enough discussing of my sex life guys. Are we going to get on with hand over?"

"No," Jorjia replied, "Your sex life sounds much more exciting."

Annie gave Jorjia a playful, gentle slap across the arm, as she took a seat beside her.

"Annie I forgot," Jorjia said, "you are specialling, one on one, with the MVA, intubated, male patient in side room seven. He's got a tracheotomy and the third degree burns. So you will have to go down and get hand over from the night special.

"No worries, thanks Jorjia, I'll head down there straight away. When one of you guys gets a spare five minutes some time this morning, could you please come and give me a hand to wash and reposition him? Thanks guys, have a good morning. And sweet dreams Jorjia."

"Thanks Annie, hope you have a pleasant shift." Jorjia stated as Annie left the conference room.

Annie knew once she started with this patient, the day would go quickly, as there would be drugs to give, a machine and pump to check, suctioning to be done to keep the airway clear and free from obstruction and most of all, constant observations for any changes with vital sign and monitoring. Not to mention redressing all the burn wounds after taking down dressings for the doctors to review and for her to redo.

Hand over from the night special was nothing significant. Still sedated over night, keeping him pumped up with pain relief. His burns from the accident would cause him to be in way to much pain without drugs at the moment. His dressings were to remain in-situ until doctor ordered them to come down for review.

Leaving the dressings in place would not be a problem, as the less pain Annie caused the patient, the better. Even though the burns victims always had a lot of pain relief medication to help numb their pain, they still felt a lot of discomfort during wound dressing procedures.

Before Annie sat down to study the patients progress notes, she made sure she had everything she needed. All of the equipment she would require for the shift for the best care of her patient. Sterile bed linen, towels and face washers, check. Mouth swabs, mouth wash, lanolin, check. Saline, check, naso specs, check, oxygen mask, yanka sucker, Y-suction catheter, sealed emergency box, check.

Everything seemed to be in order.

She sat down and began to read about her patient for today. As she read further about him, she felt quite sad. A young man age twenty five, comes from interstate, to visit his girlfriend for the first time in six months. He had a head on with a semi trailer after the truck driver had fallen asleep at the wheel. Apparently the driver had been a manic depressive, or bipolar, who hadn't slept for weeks and he'd taken himself of his medications. It was a miracle they weren't both blown away, as the truck was a fuel carrier.

I guess even in this young man's condition he was lucky to be alive at all. And even though he had been unconscious, it was a blessing he did not have any brain damage, or head injuries. After his scars had healed and his tracheotomy hole closes over, he would be able to get on with his relatively normal lifestyle. The emotional scarring would be another challenge but from reading his notes he had many supportive family and friends, not to mention his girlfriend, who was happy to see him alive. She would come in every day, after finishing work and sat with him until midnight every night. Until his condition stabilised, she would also sleep at the hospital overnight.

His family made up a roster system and they would sit with him around the clock and he was improving every day. On the patient's walls were pictures of his family and friends, with well wishes and get well cards around the boarder of his room. Annie stood there and felt a sense of calm surrounding this young man; she had a good feeling that he would make a speedy recovery. He certainly had plenty of love and encouragement surrounding him.

She sat and documented the handover from the night nurse at the chair and table next to the patient's room. Suddenly a chilling tingle went up her back and goose bumps appeared all over her body.

"DON'T TOUCH ME," Annie yelled, oh God his at it again.

Benson disappeared down the corridor before any of the busy morning nurses could see what he was doing. Placing her head in both hands, Annie held them there for a while. She could never tolerate anyone touching her hair, apart from Mitch. This time, once again, Benson picked up the ringlets at the back of her neck and started twirling them in his fingers. Before Annie had realised what was going on, she'd screamed, "DON'T TOUCH ME," and once again he just walked away. Annie's hair was a very intimate thing to her. When she was making love to her husband, he would run his fingers through her hair, she found it very arousing but her boss made her feel sick to the stomach, she felt violated from these unwanted touches.

Benson knew she felt uncomfortable with it; he certainly knew when she yelled out, "DON'T TOUCH ME," that she meant it. Once again, once may have been a joke but this had gone too far.

She sat for a moment longer, then got up and shut herself in the patient's room for a few minutes, breathing deeply.

"You can stick this out Annie," she reassured herself. "Don't let him get the better of you."

"That's right Annie, don't let them drag you down," a voice came from the cupboard in the corner of the room.

The patient continue to lay unconscious in his hospital bed. Once again Annie did not feel fearful of this spiritual presence that appeared to solidify as it emerged through the cupboard in the corner of the room.

Her jaw dropped as her mouth dropped open, "Oh my God Demi, is that you?" Annie pinched herself, to make sure she wasn't dreaming again.

"Don't be afraid Annie, you are protected by the Holy One. He is the one who sent me."

"Oh God Demi, you were always so kind, so gentle and such a beautiful nurse, what did you do to yourself? I can't believe you've gone. When someone told me what you had done, I didn't believe it, I thought it was just a nasty rumour. I couldn't understand why someone as nice and as kind as you, would want to go and do something like that to yourself? You always seemed so cheerful and happy."

"It's true Annie, I really did do it, I committed sui . . . . suicide, I was provoked for a very long time. I couldn't understand how either, until it was to late, I cried and cried and cried and I couldn't see any way out."

"I wasn't sure if it was true but I prayed for you Demi and I cried for you, I'm so sorry. So sorry."

"Demi continued. "Be strong Annie, for the Holy One has sent me as a messenger, for I am unable to lay to rest until the ones that have damaged the spirits of many have been brought to justice."

"Annie questioned the good spirit of Demi, "the ones who have damaged the Spirits of many?"

Demi spoke in an Angelic, soft echoing voice. "What you are going through now and have been going through for quite some time now, almost since your very first ward placement here, it is no coincidence, you have survived longer than any of us. Do you remember hearing any awful rumours about me Annie?"

"Yes Demi I did, but I didn't believe them." Annie knew that all the reassurance in the world was not going to help Demi now. "People can be so malicious, gossiping is such an evil trait."

"Yes that is true, because of gossip, I gradually lost all my self esteem and my confidence was blatantly abused. I could no longer see the light at the end of the tunnel, then the day I got called into the nursing co-ordinators office and they handed me a news paper, telling me to look for another job, I became absolutely devastated. This happened all without warning.

They started rumours that I was drunk, a drug addict in rehab, they said my husband beat me up because I came to work with bruises on my legs. Annie I was having treatment for leukaemia, I was bruising easily and in actual fact, my husband was being extremely supportive, he wanted me to do something about the harassment before it got so bad. But it's to late for me Annie, they'd already destroyed me.

The day they called me into the office, they said I'd been washing patients twice. I was putting more hot water in the wash bowl because I had been called away to help someone else with a lift, the water had gone cold."

"Yes Demi, I remember that day. You know I stuck up for you when that happened, it was absolutely ridiculous," Annie reminded her.

"Yes I know now," Demi replied, "you know we've been watching you!"

"We . . . .?" Annie frowned.

"Yes, you do remember the spirit that came to visit you at your bedside at home last night?"

"You mean I wasn't just dreaming?"

"No Annie, That was Andy."

"Andy, not Andy the theatre Nurse? He committed suicide seven months ago."

"Yes, that's right Annie, he was happily married, with two beautiful children. He'd pleaded with management to have more flexible working hours with his roster, so they went out of their way, to make his life a misery. Apart from spreading nasty rumours that he was gay and that his wife was having an affair and their marriage was on the rocks. They took it upon themselves to give him the worst possible roster they could muster up between them. Lots of split days off, seven days straight, not filling roster requests, many quick changes, late, early. We all know how that can cause sleep deprivation and disturbance, it's enough to drive anyone mad. Even if he was gay or his marriage was on the rocks, doesn't give those evil people the right to treat us as they have."

"When you say they, I know exactly who you mean, Annie agreed, why you don't even have to mention their names, as a matter of fact, I suspect that is why my boss Benson thinks he can get away with murder. I believe his wife was in training with one of them."

"It's not the first time he's got away with it Annie!"

"You mean there has been others?" Annie asked.

"Yes and management are well aware of it. He has had many complaints but most of the nurses just resign from their jobs, change wards, leave nursing all together and the worst thing is some of them leave the earth all together and commit suicide. The management try and blame it on the nurses social lives, even though they spend seventy percent of their waking hours at work and the last place these poor nurses are seen alive is leaving a boss's office."

"Yes, most of the time on these rosters, you feel like you're doing all work and no sleep. Rest, work, no time for play makes for a very long day without being tormented as well." Annie sighed one big long sigh.

"Annie," Demi said as she looked intently into her eyes, "you do know there is more of us, don't you?"

"More of you? You have to be joking with me now right? Please don't tell me that Demi. What is wrong with this place?" Annie started to feel rather angry.

"Yes, in the last ten years of down sizing, especially in 1995 in a space of two months, there were eight suicides and at least forty resignations of nursing staff alone in this very hospital, the good old Lake View."

"Oh no," Annie gasped, "Oh my God . . . ." a few more seconds of silence passed. "I'm almost afraid to ask who they were. Annie looked extremely sorrowful.

"Don't be afraid Annie, the Lord has great works for you. There are many trials for you to go through but eventually it will all make sense, you'll see."

Demi almost gone from view, Annie called to her. "So will I know what to expect?"

"No Annie, like I said, things will happen but you will not know why. You should remain as strong in your faith as you can. There will be irony, you will be confused but just stay strong in your faith, you have faith, hope and love, hold onto that love."

"I have had faith and hope all my life. I can't say I have made all the right decisions and am by no means perfect."

"No one is perfect Annie and one thing you shouldn't do, is let them make you feel guilty about your past. They will try and use it against your good nature. Remember what they are doing is not just and it certainly isn't fair."

The door opened and Tamzin entered. Annie quickly turned her head back to where Demi first appeared but she had gone, vanished as if she had known someone was approaching.

"Is now a good time to give you a hand with that sponge?" Tamzin grinned eager to help Annie.

Tamzin was always happy to help, a hard working girl with a kind heart. Beautiful looking, with the biggest brown eyes, olive skin and dark brown glossy hair, a picture of health.

"Thanks Tamzin, that would be great. How are you going with your lot?" Annie asked, still a little distracted from her previous visitor.

"Oh quite good actually," she replied enthusiastically. "I've got all the bay of men today, up the end of the ward there. They're asking where you are today. We told them you're in solitary confinement, only joking of course. Anyway they are mostly independent. My morning rush is over, so I'm free to make myself useful to you."

Annie grinned, "I've taught you well, and thank you, I'm very grateful, it's always a pain when you have to go chasing people to help you, especially when you know everyone is so busy."

"Annie, are you all right?" Tamzin asked with concern. "I haven't been here that long but I've noticed that you get a little jumpy when he's around, you know, Benson."

"I'm O.K, I can handle it. Nothing for you to worry about."

"How are you enjoying the ward so far Tamzin?" Annie asked, trying to open up communication with the young nurse.

Tamzin frowned, "not bad, but I'm finding the late early shifts a little exhausting." A furrow formed in her forehead.

"Yes I know, I can't understand why, when they have that many relieving nurses, they still keep on insisting on giving us late early shifts. I mean it's not like there is any continuity of care with such a big staff turnover."

"Well that's true I guess, but if it doesn't improve by the time I finalise my general nursing practice certificate, I won't be returning here to work. As a matter of fact because of these awful boss's and their horrible rosters, I might consider retiring from nursing all together."

"Don't do that Tamzin, you're such a great nurse, born not made." Annie gave her an encouraging smile.

"What do you mean born, not made?" Tamzin asked.

"Good nurses are born kind, compassionate and caring. They are real people pleases who go out of their way, give up their own time, to make you feel more secure and comfortable."

"A bit like Angels," Tamzin laughed.

"Yes, that's what people say," Annie smiled, secretively aware of that fact, in more ways than one.

"There are some nurses out there, who couldn't be bothered giving you the time of day; They'd bite your head off if you asked them for anything."

"Made not born!" Tamzin said with a giggle.

"That's correct," Annie smiled and laughed along with Tamzin. "You learn fast."

"What do you think Darren?" Annie tried to include the unconscious patient in their conversation.

"You've had your share of nurses since you've been in here Darren, you'll be able to write a book on the good, the bad and the ugly."

A slight smirk appeared on Darren's face

"Oh my goodness Tamzin, did you see that?" Annie amazed as she stood there with her jaw dropped open. "Did you see him smile?"

"Yes I did, Darren, Darren can you here us, Darren," Tamzin kept calling his name.

Squealing, popping and vibrating came from beneath Darren's bed linen. A very smelly gas filled the room.

"Phew, Darren, you stinker," Annie and Tamzin immediately looked at one another and burst into belly laughter.

Darren's eyes remained closed but the smile on his face became bigger.

"O.K, the jokes on us, lets get you washed and changed. If Doc wants to re-do your dressings today, we're going to have to pump your drugs up matey, because I think you, being so alert and all this morning, you will feel fart to much pain."

"Very funny," Tamzin said, "everybody wants to be a comedian, don't they. There is one in every crowd, isn't there Darren!"

Annie and Tamzin continue giggling as Darren lay there the whole time looking the happiest they'd seen him to this day.

"Do you know Darren?" Annie quizzed, "that scientists say, that if they could create the hormone you release when you laugh and bottle it, that it would probably cure many diseases including cancer but they apparently haven't been able to duplicate it synthetically yet?"

"Wow, that's amazing," said Tamzin, as she laughed her face lighting up like a mad laughing clown, "we better do more laughing then."

There was a knock at the door.

"Come in," Annie called, placing a towel over Darren's body to keep him looking respectable.

"Oh good morning Dr Athinasia, would you like Darren's dressings down today so you can see his wounds?"

"Yes please Annie, take them down after you've administered plenty of that morphine I've ordered for him. I've still got my ward round to do yet, so I'll be back in about half an hour. Give you plenty of time to top up that pain relief and get it taking affect."

"Thank you Dr Athinasia."

"Be back soon Darren, O.K?" Dr Athinasia left the room as quickly as he'd entered it.

"It's such a shame we have to dope you up again Darren," Annie said sadly, "It's nice to see you responding with a smile. Oh well, I guess it is just another step in the right direction, hey Tamzin!"

Chapter Eighteen

Planting The Seed

The time seemed to be spinning faster and faster, it was already June again, the month of Mitch and Annie's wedding anniversary. Two years had passed since she started at the Lake View Hospital.

Where did the time go? Every year seemed to fly by, though Annie and Mitch trying to become pregnant seemed to take forever. Every month they would wait patiently Annie's nasties (Monthly's) wouldn't turn up. Every month it didn't happen.

Now everything was prepared and set out, Annie went to the bedroom to decide what to wear, or what not to wear, to be precise. She had a good feeling about this evening. Would this be the recipe for the ripe time to conceive? After all, she was feeling rather amorous.

This month, their anniversary month, would be different. Annie felt in such a positive mood, that she decided to put on all the frills for a an extra special candle lit dinner and made it as romantic as possible. Candle light, romance blend of oils burning, soft sensual music playing, flute recorded with the sounds of the North Queensland rain Forest, it was magic. She made Mitch's favourite meal, her families secret recipe of traditional Pasta Bolognese. Mitch would never eat bolognese out at an Italian restaurant because he said he never really enjoyed it after trying Annie's old family favourite. With that there was home made garlic bread and for his favourite desert, home made lemon cheese cake with strawberries and whipped cream, mmmmm strawberries and whipped cream, always reminded her of their beautiful wedding night . . . . She also made a platter of great Australian cheeses and fruits but hoped they'd get way too busy to even worry about those.

Oh yes, I think this little black dress will do the trick, G-string, mmmmmaybe not, no, no knickers, that should get him going. No knickers, suspenders, stockings and black stilettos. He was always a sucker for a woman in stilettos. She was getting so excited thinking about Mitch, she wasn't even sure she would be able to get him in the door with out jumping on him, let alone eat dinner and the rest.

In the shower she could hardly contain herself but she did because she wanted to make sure she saved all the excitement for her husband. Before drying herself off, she lathered her whole body with baby oil, making her skin so soft and silky smooth.

"Right now," Annie took a breath, Mitch would be home soon from work in about forty minutes, plenty of time to do her hair, just as he liked it. Soft, natural, wavy ringlets fell around her face and neck, hair half up and half down. Just a little bit of polly filler to add a little extra colour to her already glowing complexion. A little lip balm under the lippy, to make the lips soft and extremely kissable, slither and sensuous, sort of like the sensation one gets when eating oysters. Annie smiled at herself in the mirror, won't be needing any of those tonight.

"Looking pretty damned fine girl, if I do say so my self."

She gave a little chuckle, turning around to flip the back of her little black dress up, revealing what she hoped would get Mitch turned on, so they can make wild passionate love, making their dream of having a baby come true. She finished off with a touch of his and her favourite musk perfume and a little dab of musk oil.

Soon Mitch would be home and Annie would have to hold herself back to get through dinner.

The keys rattled at the front door. Whipping into the bedroom, she took one more quick glance over her appearance, to make sure she looked perfect, or as close to perfect as she could possibly get. Carefully she took each one of the stairs in her black stilettos and made it to the bottom to greet her husband coming through the front door. She made it to the bottom with out a falter.

"Good evening handsome man," she smiled as Mitch reached for her at the bottom of the stair case.

"WOW, look at you and what's that great smell?" He pulled a bunch of a dozen red roses from behind his back. "Happy Anniversary my beautiful wife, I love you so dearly."

Mitch grinned from ear to ear as he grabbed her firmly around her waist and planted a big firm smooch upon her moist lips. "MMMMM You smell so good as well." He sighed.

"You're so beautiful," Annie giggled. "I love you too babe and while you go upstairs and have yourself a nice relaxing hot shower, I'll go and get dinner served and open a bottle of our favourite wine."

"Annie's Lane?" Mitch queried.

"That' the one, Cabernet Merlot," she confirmed.

He kissed her again gently and quickly on the lips. "No worries Honey."

Lighting the candles and dimming the lights, Annie could see her reflection in the polished wine glasses. She smiled a she noticed her lips shimmering in the romantic candle light. This night, this night feels right. She polished the silver wear some more.

Pouring herself a glass of Annie's Lane from the bottle after it had been sitting breathing for a while, she turned her nose up to smell, ahhhhh smells divine, nothing like a good drop of fine red wine. This one had won a gold medal. It was a sweet but dry combination, very smooth on the palate, quite soft, she took another small sip and licked the residue from her lips. It was quite robust with a full bodied fruity flavour, it clung to the glass as she whirled it around. There were minimal tastes of taninns, enabling it to be a little too easy to drink.

She felt Mitch's strong arms sliding around her waist from behind. He kissed her neck, it sent tingles all over her. His warm breath on her ear made her melt. She spun around to face him. Placing her arms around his neck, she licked his lips playfully.

They were going to require plenty of lasting energy, if they were going to get through this special evening, no better dish to do that with than the good family recipe.

"Have a seat Babe and I'll serve up your favourite dish," she gave him a soft kiss on the cheek.

"Pasta Bolognese?" Mitch asked, raising his eyebrows.

"Yes, how ever did you guess?" Annie called as she headed into the kitchen.

They both grinned at each other as they sat across at the table, their eyes were glistening. This recipe was very special, handed down from generation to generation, each one adding another secret little ingredient to add their own personal touch. Annie had added a few secret ingredient's of her own over the years.

Anne placed the salad and garlic bread on the table, then went back for the pasta plates.

"MMM, smells great," Mitch commented in his deep manly voice.

She loved his voice, matter of fact, she loved everything about him, his smell, his touch, his looks, his mannerisms, his sense of humour, his personality, everything, which was just as well, considering she wanted to make that all important step and have his baby.

"Two, four, six eight, bog in don't wait," Annie laughed with extreme happiness, "and thank you God for this meal before us. Amen"

Sitting directly across from him, Annie was looking straight into his gorgeous, sexy eyes.

"So how was your day baby?" Annie asked as she continued. "As you can see, I've been extremely busy."

"Yes, I can see that, everything looks and smell incredible, including you." Mitch winked cutely at her as he paid the compliment. "I've had a pretty busy day at work, a bit of a drag really, lots of paper work and you know how much I hate paper work! I was so looking forward to just getting home to you."

"Hopefully everything will taste better than expected." Annie smiled wryly, wondering what Mitch would think about her wearing no knickers. She wasn't really very hungry, well not for food anyway. She picked at her salad and had a reasonable amount of Pasta Bolognes.

"Are you O.K. Hun?" Mitch asked. "You've hardly eaten a thing."

"I am perfectly fine Sweetheart," she assured him, "I'm just sitting here admiring the view."

"Well, I must say, as usual, you have once again excelled yourself with this delicious sauce and must I add, your looking pretty damned saucy yourself this evening."

"Ditto Darling, but that is nothing unusual, you always look good enough to eat." Annie savoured the thought as they both sat there laughing together. She continued to ask Mitch, "Darling, can I ask you something?"

"Sure, ask away."

"Well, I just want to make sure one final time," she hesitated for a moment, at the importance of the matter. "Do you really want me to have your child because if there is any doubt in your mind, what so ever, I don't want to push you into something your not quite ready for. I want you to be with me 100%."

"Absolutely Honey, I love you and you have my 100% enthusiasm and support."

"I'm so glad because I couldn't pray for anything more beautiful, than to have your baby." She looked at him with such adoration.

As they ate their meal and gazed lovingly at one another, the chemistry between them became intensely electric. Annie elevated her leg under the table to brush against his. She slowly and gently slid her foot into his groin. Slipping off her stiletto. Annie flung her tongue to suck up the pasta, then caressed his groin with her silk, stockinged foot, as she looked deeply into those eyes.

"Give me your foot," she whispered to him across the table."

He responded immediately. Sliding off this comfy boat shoe, she slid his bare foot under her little black dress.

"What are you wearing under there?" He asked.

"What do you feel?" Annie Asked, smiling at him sexily.

"MMMMMMMMM nothing, absolutely nothing, nothing at all!"

Annie smiled the most irresistible smile. "Must be absolutely nothing then."

They sat there for a short time, sipping red wine, feeling fine and looking into each others eyes as the fondled each other gently with their feet. For some reason, Mitch was in a hurry to finish his meal?

"I can't stand this a moment longer," Mitch took a quick mouthful of red wine as he looked even deeper into Annie's hazel, green eyes. He got up swiftly from the table and then disappeared underneath.

"But babe" Annie laughed, "what about the cheesecake?"

"Oh my God," she gasped.

Mitch had nuzzled between her thighs and began kissing her softly, it sent shivers of pleasure quivering to every nerve ending and neuron surrounding the atmosphere. He slowly slid his hands up, gently rubbing her delicate, short labia with his thumb as he continued to lick her closer and closer.

"Oh God!" she moaned.

He was brushing his tongue over her little hard clitoris.

"Oh Baby," she continued to moan with pleasure.

This was not going to get her pregnant but it felt so overwhelmingly satisfying, she was now in a place that was not of this earth.

He slowly pushed her chair away from the dining table, sliding himself up on her body, caressing every inch of her body with his strong manly hands. He placed a hand on her mount of women, looking into her eyes, once again their spirits intertwining in time and space.

"Annie my darling wife, you are so beautiful, and you are so wet." He kissed her neck, as his hot breath brushed her ear, he continued to fondle her. If she wasn't melting before, she was definitely melting now.

"Oh Mitch, you always make me feel so beautiful, so good, more than I ever could have imagined. You are my prince, my one and only. I've never felt so fulfilled in every way in all my life." She whispered these words of sincerity in his ear as she tried to control her gasps of enjoyment.

She ran her fingers through his short, sexy, soft hair, cupped her hands around his face and kissed him long and warm, moist and passionate. Mitch pulled her up from the chair and took her into his arms, his hands firmly holding her slim waist, a hand sliding down her tight, petite buttock, their sensuous kisses lingering.

Removing herself from his lips, she kissed his neck and began rubbing his large firmness with one hand, his buttock with the other. Unbuttoning his shirt, she slowly kissed his neck again and then his lips, neck and chest. She kissed his nipples before moving down the centre of his tight, tidy abdomen. She loved the fine line of sexy, dark hair that ran all the way to his warm, throbbing, hard, wonderful manhood, that's exactly where she wanted to be at this moment.

Placing her hands around his hot shaft, she gently rubbed him with both her hands, down on her knees. Slowly she slid his trousers down over his thighs and pushed them all the way down to his ankles. She lifted her head gently to glance up at him as he stood looking down at her, rubbing her neck and jawline, he groaned deeply, wanting more.

"Oh Annie, Baby, I am such a lucky man." Then he closed his eyes as her warm lips and moist mouth sensitively kissed the tip of his extremely, firm, hot, throbbing wand. Yes, a wand, for this was going to be the night they created magic. She took this wand fully into her mouth and sucked it savouring and wanting.

Mitch removed her mouth from his manhood and pulled her up under her arms, pulling her up towards his broad, tight chest and kissed her madly. He picked her up, knowing she had nothing on under that little black dress. Her warm, moist place, his hard, hot throbbing place sitting on top of one another's. She wrapped her legs tightly around his hips, her arms around his neck, firmly connected lips, sucking and slithering frantically with huge open mouthed kisses.

They stayed there for a long while, lost in this moment. Annie could feel herself getting hotter and hotter and wetter and wetter, as those moments passed, wonderful, timeless moments, that only two could share.

Shuffling his feet, Mitch finally made it up the stairs to their bedroom, Annie clinging enthusiastic body with him. Her legs astride, he lay her on their marital bed. He assisted her to remove her little black dress, leaving her in her black suspenders, stockings and stilettos.

He slid down on her, placing a single finger inside her very wet, lubricated vagina and licked at it, tasting her womanly juices as he gently moved his finger delicately around and around. He kissed her legs, placing his firm hand on her lower toned tummy, he continue to kiss her womanly place as he twirled his other hands finger inside her.

Placing one of each of his hands on each of her breasts, he manipulated her erect nipples as he continued to drink from her juices. He had his mouth firmly but delicately over all of her womanly parts now, as he sucked on her gently, every now and then his tongue entering her. Slowly, ever so slowly, he kissed her and licked his way up to her slender neck, kissing her until he reached her lips. Then they both gasped, humming in ecstasy, pleasurably moaning as he placed himself deeper and deeper, finally entering her, hard and fitting, deeper, harder, firmer.

She could feel herself welcoming him, as the moist, warmness clasped him firmly and tightly inside of her. Slowly they moved, in and out of one another, not a word was spoken, spirits once again awoken, breathing, gasping in harmony as he pulled her tightly into him, into her.

"Oh Mitch you are amazing," she sighed, as she threw her head back, pushing herself up on her arm, arms behind her, she arched her back, her long, dark, flowing hair cascading down to her bottom.

"Then we must make a perfect match, Oh Babe, you are so amazing," Mitch responded, as he continued to move that hard wand in and out of her swelling tightening vagina. He kissed her firmly on the lips, as his hardness was as tightly fitting as it could be now.

"Oh Baby, Oh God, are you going to come? I'm going to come." He groaned and gasped and moaned with her.

"Oh yes Mitch, I'm coming, come with me Baby, Oh God, Oh God, Oh Mitch, don't stop, don't stop,come Baby, come."

"Oh yes Baby, Oh yes, that's it, your amazing, come baby, come. Your hips are amazing, how do you move like that, I can't hold myself back," Mitch's body hard and ridged, he pressed Annie even tighter to him, her vagina wet, hot and clasping his erection with throbbing, pulsating orgasmic motion. Mitch paned as he reached his peak.

They both breathed a sigh of relief as they flopped in each others arms.

"You're such a turn on when you reach orgasm Babe, I find it impossible not to come with you. I can't hold back," Mitch gasped breathlessly. "By the way, how do you do that thing with your pelvis?"

"Strong pelvic floors? I guess," Annie replied, as she breathed deeply to try and slow her heart rate down. "The thought of you coming makes me want to orgasm Babe, it pleases me, to please you, you're such a turn on." She lay fully on top of him, legs astride.

Breathless, they lay together, holding one another, hearts still pounding.

"You know something Mitch?"

Mitch kissed her cheek, "What's that sweetheart?"

"Well, I love the way we can talk to each other about anything and that includes what we do in the bedroom!"

"Yeah, it's great, isn't it Gorgeous." He kissed her again.

"I love you so much Mitch," she stretched her head up from his chest and pecked him on his lips as she looked into his eyes.

"Oh you just love me cos I'm good in bed," Mitch laughed out loud.

Annie laughed with him, "I love everything about you Babe, including that and what a bone-us that is, ha ha ha," she laughed with him some more.

"I do love you to Hun." He pecked her in return on her now salty lips as he gazed down at her.

They kissed each other gently on the lips; he kissed her on the for head. Annie slid down beside him, where she wrapped her legs around his and he his arm around her. When they were together, they were lost in one another. It didn't take long before they were g fast asleep.

Annie awoke at 0200hrs. She carefully climbed out of bed, to avoid waking Mitch. He had an early start in the morning. As she pulled gently away from him, he groaned.

"Where are you going baby?"

"Just to have a pee Sweet," she whispered. Sorry to wake you."

MMM that's O.K," he mumbled as he fell back into a deep sleep.

Approaching the bathroom, Annie could hear something shuffling and rustling about down stairs.

"Those damned mice at it again," she thought to herself. "I thought the mice plague was over."

She' had trouble with mice earlier in the year, they appeared to like eating her wheat pack she used for her pain, when she left it sitting on top of the microwave.

She decided to go to the toilet before checking it out.

Heading quietly down stairs, she became a little concerned because the quiet shuffling had now become quite loud thumping. It was then that Annie realised there was someone knocking on the sliding glass doors in the living room. She pulled the curtain back, she gasped. A figure of a young woman, in the same nurses uniform as she wore, stood there in terror, blood streaming from her wrists.

"My God, Susie, not you too? What happened to you?" Annie asked as she stood there in a funny sort of calm shock, trying to keep herself together.

She opened the glass sliding door enough to slide out under the pergola, it was a mild night for the month of June and the stars were sparkling in the early hours.

"It's too late for me Annie," Susie cried with the look of sheer terror still showing all over her face and deep in her eyes.

"What do you mean it's to late?" Annie's eyes became glassy with tear now welling in her eyes. She shut them tight, squeezing the hot tear drops onto her high cheek bones. She wanted this to be all gone, she was hoping when she opened them again that she would be safely back in her nice warm bed with her beloved husband and this was just one of those horrible dream, nightmare things she'd been having a few of lately!

When she opened them, Susie wasn't gone but her wounds to her wrists had disappeared. Susie stood there, a glowing image of her former self.

She told Annie of how she couldn't do a thing right and just when she thought that things had been going along nicely, the boss would again call her into the office to tell her how useless she was. How she would never make a good nurse, that she would never get another job as a nurse, that no other hospital would employ her.

She said she couldn't understand what was happening. All her ward reports were excellent and she'd never received any complaints from her patients or the staff she'd worked with on the ward, aswell as the ones that did her appraisal on her ward reports. For some reason, Annie knew that all of this was sounding a little too familiar.

Susie continued to say that she had never been given anything in writing to say that she was a bad nurse.

"I loved my job Annie," Susie said, "but it's too, too late now, too, too late, everything has gone, I've lost my soul and I'll never have a chance to save myself. They really made me believe I was a bad person, a bad nurse. Now that I've passed over, I see the truth Annie."

"It's up to you now Annie, your the only one that can save us." As she spoke, so, so sorrowfully, the white glow surrounding her became stronger and stronger, brighter and brighter, as if protecting her. The strong white light almost blinding Annie from view. Protecting Susie from any more harm.

"I couldn't see my future any more, then my boyfriend left me because I'd gotten so irritable and depressing. I don't think he could stand the sight of me any more. I'd changed, I'd become a whole different person.

Annie gave her a compassionate smile, "I'm sure that's not true Susie, he was probably just as freaked out as you. God I wish you could have come to me sooner." Annie caringly lifted her hands towards her, wanting to bring her back from where ever it was she was going.

There was a rustling coming from the bushes, at the rear of the back yard.

"Don't be afraid Annie," Susie smiled serenely. "On my way through I met some one else, you see I'm not alone, none of us are ever alone, not in passing."

"Passing?" Annie frowned.

"Yes, It's Lindsy, do you remember Lindsy?"

"Lindsy is one of my closest friends, she's having a baby. We were going to have a baby together. She's on maternity leave soon to have her baby," . . . . Annie paused as she heard more rustling coming from the back bush, "A baby, baby... a baby girl."

With a look of empathy, Susie bit down on her immortal lip. She sadly responded to Annie that all was not well, the bright glow around her strengthening once again.

"And the baby? What about the baby? Oh God, not Lindsy too? Please don't tell me her as well? Let me wake up Lord, please let me wake up, this is just a bad dream, a very bad nightmare."

She immediately turned again to the rustling bushes, she couldn't believe her eyes, she turned away and then looked back again, not wanting to believe what she was seeing.

Annie closed her eyes tightly again hoping that when she opened them, that she would be in a place she would not see her best friend Lindsy, a dead friend walking towards her also in glowing form. "A bad dream, a very bad dream."

Annie opened her eyes again, this time very slowly. She knew in her heart and soul that she would still be seeing the female figure approaching her in full bloom.

"Oh Lindsy girl," Annie looked at her through teary, sad eyes, as she gasped back anguish and despair, sobbing to catch her breath. "What has become of you?"

"Have you got a few hours Annie? I could probably tell you the whole story from beginning to dismal end."

Annie stood there in total disbelief.

Lindsy told me how she went to her boss in radiology several times at the beginning of her pregnancy, to let her know that she was unable to work with the radioactive machines and contrast dyes. As her tummy grew, she went to work each day And sat down beside Sister Pillowy, asking her,

"Sister, where would you like me to work today?"

And each day Sister Pillowy would sit there ignoring her, continuing her crossword, without a word. Lindsy would check the roster. Her name was down to work but her name would not be allocated anywhere. Every day the same thing would happen. She would go to work, check her allocation, ask Sister Pillowy politely where she wanted her to work and every day she was ignored, like she was invisible, like she didn't exist, like she was nothing.

Then one faithful day, Lindsy came to work on an afternoon shift that she had been rostered on to work, for the final time she was ignored. Lindsy had become quite distressed by her boss's silent treatment, so she decided to go seek some advice from the Occupational Health and Safety Nurse, a Registered Nurse with in the Radiology and Emergency departments. The OHSN informed her, that, she was right not to be working with the radioactive treatments and should have been allocated to the waiting bay only.

Lindsy had also explained that she had asked her boss on many occasions, about where she had wanted her to work, only to be ignored, so Lindsy spent most of her time assisting patients in the waiting bay anyway.

The other nurses she worked with, didn't mind and knew Sister Pillowy was giving her a difficult time because she was pregnant, apparently she wasn't the first pregnant nurse to be ignored, most left the department and the hospital for good. There's also been a formal complaint about her professional conduct from the Radiographers and the Radiologists themselves.

So then the OHSN herself, decided it was time to intervene, to go and have a chat to Sister Pillowy.

She told Lindsy, not to worry, everything would sort itself out.

"I came to work the next day," Lindsy said, "I was on an afternoon shift. I still hadn't been allocated anywhere but I knew I was going to Emergency Radiology that evening and wouldn't have to be near the radiation, just assisting the radiographer to adjust patients for their X-rays."

"The next thing I know, I'm being asked by Sister Pillowy to go to the office of the Director of Nursing. When I got there, Sister Pillowy followed me in behind and shut the door. Ms Ratman the D.O.N. Was sitting behind the desk."

"Sternly she looked at me, down at me over the rim of her glasses." "Sit down Lindsy."

"She was a very hard faced women, with black high hair, almost as high as Marj Simpson but this is no joking matter as you can see. I'm sure though, that hives been there since the nineteen sixties."

"Sister Pillowy told Ms Ratman, that I had gone over her head to the OHSN, Occupational Health and Safety Nurse, without acknowledging her first. As everyone knew, this was not true. I'd approached her countless amounts of times, more than a reasonable amount of times. I'd approached her every day off my pregnancy, until I felt I'd be safer to seek more professional advice."

"It was then Ms Ratman told me," "If you want to go bucking around with horses and getting yourself pregnant, then you deserve to put up with bad treatment and suffer the consequences." "In other words, If I want to go fucking around and fall pregnant, then I deserve to be treated badly?"

"My God Annie," Lindsay continued to explain, "I'd been married for over five years and this was our second planned child. I felt so violated by these women, so emotionally raped. Suddenly I felt extremely ill, I held my stomach, I could feel it pulsating inside of me. My head was throbbing hard. After being allowed to leave the D.O.N's office, I went down to emergency/radiology where I was meant to be working that evening. Nurse Laurie took my blood pressure, it was two hundred and thirty over one hundred and seventy."

"The throbbing in my head just kept getting worse, the thumping louder and louder. I started to feel very nauseous. I couldn't stop thinking or feeling the filth Ms Ratman had said. To me having a child is a treasured gift from God. Then in my worst nightmare, I could feel a hot warm gush trickle down between my legs, it was blood, I'd started bleeding, Laurie asked me if I was O.K. But she couldn't understand what I was saying, I was a babbling mess. I couldn't even speak to answer her. Everything started going blurry. I started falling into a big black empty hole, I just kept falling and falling, that's all I remember."

"There was nothing that could have prepared me for what happened next."

"Within what seemed like seconds, I was watching myself being transported to the CT room."

"She's still breathing," one of the younger Doctors said.

"I just took her blood pressure and it was extremely high, critically high for a pregnant women." Laurie confirmed.

"How high was it?" the Doctor called across the barouche.

"Two Hundred and thirty over one hundred and seventy." Laurie replied loudly.

"Oh shit, she's probably stroked." The Doctor frowned angrily as he struggled to take a palpable blood pressure.

"What about the baby, is the baby going to be O.K?" Laurie queried.

Before the Doctor had a chance to answer, Laurie screamed, "Oh no Doctor, Lindsy's stopped breathing." Laurie screamed again, this time to everyone. "Quick get her to RED DOORS, she, she's going to need resuscitation."

"They tilted me on my side, as I watched over me, I couldn't feel a thing, is was like I'd already gone. I wanted to tell them not to waste their energies, as I knew it was to late. I knew that my baby had died, as her spirit was still within me, warm and safe in my soul. In all the commotion, I couldn't tell if she had passed physically before me or after me? At least I can be assured, that she is still with me, her little spirit safe within mine."

"Annie . . . ." Lindsay spoke with a solemn, glowing smile, the one who has sent us to you, is protecting us on our travels. He knows of your spiritual beliefs and your understanding of love, hope and faith. He knows you will not fail because he is guiding you. Have faith in God as you have always done. What ever you do, keep believing, we will be right beside you. The ones that harm the Angel Spirits will be brought to justice."

Mitch called out.

"Annie, Honey, where are you?"

Her Spirit nursing friends defused into the surroundings, the bushes and the trees.

Mitch let out a sigh of relief as he located her.

"Good early morning Gorgeous, are you alright Baby, you look like you've been crying?" Mitch was concerned about her.

"Yes Darling, I'm perfectly fine, I just thought I heard a noise, thought it was those damned mice again, I'm obviously hearing things." She frowned secretively as she took Mitch by the arm, looking over her shoulder as they squeezed in through the double glass sliding doorway.

Annie slept soundly, weirdly enough after all that had happened, but when she awoke later at 0545hrs, she felt quite whoozy in the tummy. After a big drink and a bowl of musili for breakfast, she felt much better. She showered and left for work at 0625hrs.

When she arrived the lifts were busy, so she once again for the umpteenth time, she raced up the stairs. She arrived in handover puffing and panting right on 0700hrs.

"Looking a little flushed aren't we!" nurse Tamzin commented.

"Am I," Annie took a gasp of air, still trying to get her breath.

"MMM a little rosy around the cheeks this morning, eyes sparkling with it." Cassandra smiled from ear to ear.

"Oh go on," Annie said blushing even more.

As she sat down, she thought, surely it couldn't happen that quickly? Could it? Even though she did feel rather unusual this morning. Mind you, she had witnessed a pretty frightening event overnight. Throughout hand over, she sat with a little cheeky grin, hoping it was going to be a pregnancy side affect, rather than anxiety. Hand over was a little mundane this morning, especially after all the excitement the previous evening, the evening fantastic, the night not good at all. She tried to keep her mind on the positive.

Throughout her day at work, Annie felt a little nauseous, on a couple of occasions, she thought of what it would be like to be pregnant. On the other hand, she felt she was getting a little to excited about the whole getting pregnant thing, with all that was going on around her at this early stage.

She and Tamzin worked in pairs to help some of the older, not so agile patients to get up out of bed ready for breakfast.

"Annie, would you like me to sit Mr. Antonio up?" Tamzin asked.

"No, I can manage Mr. Antonio on my own thanks Tam."

"Buongiorno Mr. Antonio, Annie smiled as she did at all her patients.

"Buonjiorno Annie," he smiled, "Comestai?"

"Bene gratzia, etu?"

"Bravo, bene, bene, gratzi Bella." Mr Antonio replied with a shrug of his shoulders and raising of the palms of his hands in the air.

The patient wiggled around a little in bed, before placing his legs down the side, sitting right on the edge, he then stood straight up.

Annie commented, "I had no idea you were so tall Mr. Antonio."

She guided him to his chair and as he turned to sit, he grabbed her left arm and flopped down, falling to the ground. Annie cringed and bit her lip as she felt an excruciating pain go down her right side of her spine. She realised she had pulled some muscles, the pain didn't subside.

Tamzin looked at her with concern, "Annie, are you O.K?"

"Sorry Bella, stupid old fool," Mr Antonio grumbled to himself as he picked himself up and got itno his chair."

"I think I've pulled some muscles, I'll be O.K."

"Are you sure you're alright?" Tamzin asked again.

"I'll be fine, no fuss." Annie said.

She stood throughout the morning, dosing medication, feeding patients their breakfast, assisting them with their morning activities and making beds. It was time for morning tea at 1000hrs and as usual it came around very quickly.

Tamzin called out from the nurses station, "are you ready for morning tea Annie?"

"Anyone left on the floor if we go now?" Annie called in return.

"Yes, four nurses, we're going two at a time this morning."

"Great," Annie sighed, "let's go then."

They sat down together in the staffroom.

"Oh God," Annie screwed up her face in agony.

"What's wrong? What have you done?" Tamzin's expression was almost as painful looking as Annie's.

"It's my back, and I just felt this electric volt like feeling go down my right leg!"

Annie's eyes began to well with tears as the severe pain overwhelmed her. She took several big breaths in and out and held firmly to her right side of her lower back, trying to ease the pain.

"Oh dear," She took another breath. "I think I've done more than just pull a muscle. I don't think I'm going to be able to get up!"

"Looks like I'd better call for the orderlies to take you down to the E.R. To have you checked out!" Tamzin responded concernedly.

"Oh no Tamzin, I'm so embarrassed, I don't want all those goofy orderlies gawking at me, especially, especially when I'm lying flat on my back."

"I can understand where you're coming from, I wouldn't want those dorks gawking at me either. Orderlies have a bit of a reputation as gawking dorks," she giggled at the sound of it.

"Ouch, don't make me laugh Tamzin, it hurts, stop with the wise cracks already, ahh ha ha owe."

"Now sorry Annie," Tamzin said in a more serious tone of voice, "I guess I really don't have a choice, I'm going to have to call on the boys."

Annie attempted to get up from her chair one last time, trying to avoid looking like a complete invalid in front of her work mates.

"Oh God, I can't get up from this damned chair."

When the orderlies heard that Annie was hurt, they all came running. They were always very friendly to her and she, polite to them. One of them, Andrew, was tall, lean and quite nice looking. He would go quiet whenever Annie was around. According to his work buddies, he had quite a crush on her. Annie already being married thought it was sweet and took it as a compliment. She's always remembered her Grandma's saying, "Accept compliments graciously my dear." Of course Andrew the orderly was the first orderly on the seen to aide Annie.

Andrew said softly and sympathetically, "What on earth have you done to yourself?"

"Oh I'm O.K. just a little pulled muscle to my back, it's nothing really, this was all Tamzin's idea."

"Well come on then, let's get you up, up you get." Andrew started to take her arm.

"That's the problem, I can't stand up."

Before Annie knew it, the staffroom was full of orderlies and nurses, assisting her to get onto the stretcher, to transfer her down to the E.R.

"Look guys, if you bring the stretcher a little closer," Annie said, not wanting to cause anyone bother, "I should be able to at least try and climb onto it myself."

"Annie," Tamzin reminded her, "you have to be very careful or you could do more damage to your spine, if you move the wrong way!"

"Yes, you are right but if you help me onto the stretcher," Annie replied, "I should be able to lie flat on my back."

She managed to sit herself up in a sitting position and sat across the stretcher.

"You're so far down," Andrew the orderly noted. "Here we'll lift you back a bit further."

All six orderlies stood evenly, three on each side, Tamzin at her head and Cassandra at her feet.

"Ready everyone," Andrew made the call, "On the count of three, one, two, three lift."

"Oops, nearly threw you off the stretcher, you're lighter than you look."

"Hey, what are you saying? Thanks very much," Annie smirked as she looked at Tamzin.

"You're right about those orderlies Tamzin."

"What's that? Andrew asked. "Right about what?"

As they wheeled her down the corridor to the lifts to the E.R. She called out.

"Never mind and don't worry, it's all good."

Chapter Nineteen

Never Broken

It was a whole month before Annie was cleared to go back to work after her little back injury. For four weeks she had regular visits with her Doctor and every second day she would be treated by her physiotherapist. She had massage and electrode treatment to the muscles in her lower back. It was still very tender after all that time but she was told that sometimes ligaments and muscles can take a long time to heal, sometime longer than bones. It almost killed Annie not being able to be productive or being able to stick to her rigorous fitness routine.

Spending most of her time laying flat on her back. Sitting and standing too long was extremely painful. She was keen to go back to work but the physiotherapist said she wasn't ready. The good old Doc said she couldn't return until she was physically well enough to perform her full nursing duties.

There was no light duties according to her boss Benson, who took it upon himself to call her at home, just to let her know. He also told her that she was being watched by work cover investigator, so she had better be genuine about her injury.

Annie once again felt very personally violated when she received his call at her home. She felt it was very inappropriate, no need for such an unusual call. He didn't even enquire about how her injury was going.

She began to feel paranoid about the fact that he said someone was watching her, who wouldn't?

Across the street one night, while Mitch was on afternoon shift, she swore she could see a parked car, two men watching her, one with a video camera facing her home. So scared was she in fact, that she decided to get one of Mitch's life size cardboard cut outs of Damon Hill, the formula one driver, to make it look like there was a man at home. She placed it in the upstairs bedroom window as a deterrent, made her feel a bit like McCauley Caulkin from home alone.

During the day, Alice was coming over to help her hang her washing on the line and assist her with house hold chores. Alice had been a long time nursing friend. She worked for a nursing agency now, after having enough of the political shenanigans and goings on at the Lake View Hospital.

Annie heard a bang at the door and even though she'd expected Alice, she still near jumped out of her skin with nervous tension.

"Oh Alice, how are you?" Annie spoke relieved at the sight of a friendly face at the front door.

"I'm great, how are you going, how is your back?" Alice asked in her so kind sounding voice.

Annie shrugged, "I've been lying on my back a lot, quite a bit actually, to get relief. That's about how I feel at the most comfortable, it's improving slowly."

Alice was always able to put a smile on Annie's face.

"Flat on your back hey?" she said nudging Annie, "I bet Mitch is loving that, hey, hey, hey?"

"Yeah, Yeah, very funny, don't even mention it. It's been a bit of a drought around here where that's concerned, he'll be lucky to get a leg over!"

"The physiotherapy stretches tend to ease the pain a bit as well, so I've been told to continue those indefinitely. Most of the pain is down my right side, so my right hamstring gets very tight as well as my hip flexors. I can tell you now," Annie laughed, "There ain't much gyrating going on around here."

Annie bent over to show Alice one of her hamstring stretches. "It doesn't fix the pain up all together but it does help."

"If it's any constellation Annie, your looking fabulous as usual, bitch," Alice smiled and grumbled all at once.

"Yes, well, thanks for that, I think, it makes me feel so much better, you certainly have a way with words." They both broke into laughter.

Alice let out a loud cheeky laugh, "you know me." Alice said with a smile.

"Yes, all to well I'm afraid." Annie smirked with her dimples showing through.

Alice and Annie enjoyed a lovely afternoon cup of tea out in the garden, while she helped her hang the washing on the line.

"Oh God Alice, I feel such an invalid. Apart from a broken wrist as a child, I've never felt so useless."

"Are you still going to work at the gym when you get better?" Alice asked.

"God, I hope so. Don't know if I'll be able to teach everything I have in the past though. I may have to compromise a little bit, until I'm back on track." I'll try and work out a routine that will help rehabilitate me while teaching everyone else."

Annie's eyes welled up with tears as she spoke. "God it's not fair, I've always been so careful. How did this happen? How was I supposed to stop that elderly gentleman from pulling me down with him like that? It was totally unexpected."

"Shhh Shhh, come on Annie, it was an accident, not all work cover injuries can be avoided. Human beings are always going to make human errors, that's why we're human beings, that's why they invented work cover in the first place, to look after the injured worker. You can't blame yourself."

Alice put her arms around Annie and gave her a comforting hug.

"Sorry Alice, I'm just not myself at the moment," Annie sobbed, "I feel like a big sooky la la," She giggled and sobbed some more as she grabbed a tissue from her pocket to dry her eyes.

"Don't you be sorry, it must be very frustrating, especially after all, you have always been so capable, you can't be super nurse, super instructor, aerobic queen, super daughter, super wife and super friend all the god damn time you know."

"Why the hell not?" Annie let out a half sob, half chuckle as she took a gasp for breath.

Alice squeezed her again gently before releasing her, "time for you to look after you for a change."

"You're such a great friend Alice. I thank God for you."

"I'm just returning the favours," Alice smiled.

Annie and Alice sat quietly pondering, reminiscing, as they sat together in the tranquil garden.

"Do you remember the time I was pregnant with Josh?" Alice reminded her.

"Yes, Annie beamed. "How could I forget, I think I was as excited as you were."

"Well do you remember the time you called in and I was so miserable, I sat at home sipping on good old Ozzy bubbly. Who should rock up on my doorstep with many encouraging words and enthusiasm for life. It was like you always knew when I needed someone to talk to and you always rang or dropped in to see me at the perfect moment," Alice completed.

"What else are friends for? Thank you Alice, I feel one hundred percent better already. (Annie gave Alice another brief cuddle.)

Annie also recalled the spirits that had been communicating with her over the past few months. Maybe this is what they were talking about? They said that things were going to happen that were out of her control but to have faith because it was all happening for a reason, a greater good.

Taking a few deep breaths of the garden fresh air, Annie did feel much better again. Over and over in her mind she kept telling herself that everything was going to be fine.

"You'll come out of it on top Annie!" Alice reassured her.

"I hope so." Annie looked towards the vast blue sky, feeling the higher power protecting her.

Alice rubbed Annie's arm and smiled at her comfortingly once more, "Are you going to be O.K. Now if I leave? I have to pick Josh up from day care. I can come back if you like?"

"No don't be silly Alice, I'll be fine. Mitch will be home in an hour. Thank you so much for dropping in, I really appreciate your support."

"My pleasure, my friend."

Annie waved her good friend goodbye as she drove off around the corner. She always waved people off until she could see them no more.

Mitch arrived home as expected at 1600hrs. He poured the both of them a nice glass of Coonawarra Red Wine.

"I want you to relax," He said, you are in for a night of pampering. Sip your wine, while I get the spar tub ready, then you are going to jump in with me for a nice long soak."

"All sounds wonderful honey, except for that jumping bit," Annie frowned.

"Bad choice of words, I'll help you ease into the spa, don't you worry about a thing," Mitch winked before giving her a quick peck on her lips.

Annie slowly slipped out of her casual clothes. She hadn't worn stockings for quite some time, but she had difficulty even putting on her little bobby socks. Bending to touch her toes in any shape or form was really quite a challenge. She caught the edge of each sock with her big toes and dragged them off, not wanting to bend down in fear of increasing her pain.

Frustrated she was unable to quite remove the second sock. "For God sake, I'm a joke."

"Here darling, let me help you with that, lie down on the bed." Mitch gently eased her back and ever so gently removed the last little bobby sock. Using his big strong hands, he began to massage her leg in circular motion. As he rubbed her higher and higher, he was now at Annie's thighs. He rubbed her hips, then worked his way up to her abdomen, where he gently caressed her silky, soft flesh. Annie lay there more relaxed than she had felt since the beginning of her unusual work experiences and her injuries. She wondered if all those crazy endorphins were running around, with the feel good sensation she was feeling and accepted her own explanation was easing her pain.

"Oh Mitch, that feels wonderful," Annie sighed in her sexy, breathy voice he hadn't heard for a while.

Mitch then placed his hands on the warmth of her softest spot without saying a word he rubbed it up and down and side to side.

"Oh Baby, that definitely feels so good." She began to feel very warm and very moist as he continues to rub and fondle her gently. While soft kissing the lower part of her abdomen and then her pelvis, as he licked her gently, he played her with one finger and she became extremely moist. She became overwhelmed at how amazing she was feeling at this very moment.

At this point the pain in her back had faded into the background. She began to feel herself tighten around his finger as he played with her.

She began to moan, "Oh Mitch! Oh God!" She drew a big gasping breath as she bit down on her lip.

He could feel her throbbing around his fingers, he had two of them inside her hot, moist, vagina now. He placed her hand on his hard, burning penis and began moving it up and down in his hand, holding it tight. He began moaning along with her.

"Oh Annie! Oh God!"

Annie felt a warm spray up the middle of her body, it was hottest in the middle of her abdomen.

Mitch, who had just previously been up on one elbow, fell limply beside her.

"Wow," Annie commented, "this is the most relaxed I've felt for some time, thanks Baby."

"MMMMM," Mitch agreed, "And that was one of the best synchronised orgasmic love making sessions I've actually had with you, without actually making love." He laughed. "You know with out the full thing going in."

Mitch and Annie lay floating on their backs in the spa, turning their heads facing one another.

"You spoil me Mitch," Annie whispered."

"No baby, you spoil me, just by being here." He lent over and kissed her softly on her lips and she kissed him back eagerly.

The very next morning, Annie awoke feeling quite nauseous but with a strange ravenous hunger for vegemite toast. "Nauseous but hungry," Annie thought to herself, "now there's a combinations of sensations that I've never had before."

She let Mitch sleep in as he had been on lots of early day shifts lately and this was his first day off in a week.

Feeling reasonably pain free, she climbed out of bed. The first thing she did, was make herself some vegemite toast, it was the best vegemite toast Annie had ever tasted.

Putting on her bonds sportswear, she decide to go for a walk along the beach. It was a magnificent day. Mitch still fast asleep, she quietly placed a note upon the bedside table.

The sun was shining, the sky clear blue and the see view a site for saw eyes, she hadn't got down here enough for her tranquil fix lately. Just one big breath in and out and she already felt more serene. She gazed out over the crystal, blue waters that continued with that vast blue sky, you could barely make the sky out from the sea. She talked to the Lord and he in turn, helped her to sort out her troubles. And of course she found inspiration for another loving poem.

Spirit Of Australia

Sitting by the waters edge, It brings me back to calm.
Thinking of my Lover, His strong comforting arms.
Looking out to sea, I feel the tension go.
Breathing in the sea fresh air, Brings back an afterglow.

Serenity is something, Money just can't buy.
With love, laughter, Tears of joy, Help the spirit cry.
The spirit of the sea, Is in the spirit of me.
Not attached to my mind,But to the very soul,
You see!

I take not for granted, This spirit that I feel.
For this spirit is far beyond, Any explanation,
That all humans feel.

Science knows how we eat, Walk talk and breath.
It can tell when we are stressed, Or happy with glee.
But the strength of ones spirit, Can be felt all around.
Change your thought process, In an instant, Pick you up,
When you're feeling down.

Never let anyone or anything, Take your spirit away.
Exercise it daily, In every possible way.
Show some one else your spirit, With a smile or a joke.
Teach someone else your spirit, Especially the younger folk.

Lead them to the waters edge, Show them Mother Earth.
Give them all the encouragement, Show them what they're worth.
For everyone is individually unique, In some special way.
I felt all this in my spirit, As I sat by the sea today.

For my spirit is my Lover, And one must learn to love themselves,
Before they can truly love another.
Against all suicide, The spirit is so.
Spirit of Australia, Let our children grow.
©2007Copyright Annette Evalyn Swain All Rights Reserved.
Performed In The South Australian Poetry State Final 2007.

Give me strength Lord and help me get over this back injury, there is still so much work to be done, so much for me to achieve. Lord I hope soon, I will be able to get back to my life's work as you have planned.

She remembered the poem that she had recited at her late Mother in-law, Marie's funeral. She'd see it all over the place, especially on hospital and hospice walls. She hoped and prayed her poetry would not end in the same fate!

"AUTHOR UNKNOWN, "FOOTPRINTS IN THE SAND"

I walk along the shore and the Lord walks beside me, Guiding me, I see two sets of footprints in the sand. But why Oh Lord, When it seems I need you most, Do you desert me? I see only one set of foot prints in the sand? The Lord replied, Have Faith my child, For when you need me most, I do not desert you. But I share your burden. You only see one set of foot prints in the sand for . . . .

Annie continued reciting the poem to herself out loud, as she got to the last verse, a sweet familiar voice joined in beside her . . . . ,

"FOR I AM CARRYING YOU."

The voice echoed in unison.

"Mum, mum" . . . . Annie said exasperated with a surprised, shocked but happy look upon her face.

Her mother-in-law Marie, had appeared out of nowhere. It wasn't the first time Annie had spiritual contact with her. Marie had come to her seven days after her passing from breast cancer. They walked together in the most beautiful place, while Annie was in a transit sleep state. It was like visiting Paradise or Heaven. Annie had written another poem about that previous meeting and it was given to the wife of her brother in-law, who was her husband Mitch's brother, also Marie's son. He had died in a tragic trucking accident. It was a family business, he had wanted to give it up, just a few short months before the tragic accident happened. Annie believed she was meant to pass this poem onto the brother in-laws wife, to comfort her, also a message from Marie. Annie ended up calling the poem, "WALK BESIDE ME", initially titled "WARRENS POEM" in memory of her brother-in-law.

As they once again walked side by side, this time along the sea shore, Marie said that she had been watching over the family and Warren was safe with her once again. Annie told her of how she could feel her presents. Marie explained how she had been in touch with all the lost spirits, the ones who were visiting Annie.

"You do realise my girl," Marie said, "you have got quite a task ahead of you."

"The games have only just begun."

"What does that all mean mum?" Annie asked, totally absorbed.

"You will be aware of it all when it happens Annie and you will also know how to deal with it. The greater one who also watches over you, is guiding you. Annie you will be sent back to work soon by the Doctor. Just go about your business to the best of your ability, just as you have always done. You will get a lot of support and encouragement along the way, you will not, will not give up. You will fight for what is right because we all know you have great faith my dear."

Suddenly Marie was gone, she was gone as quickly as she had appeared, diffusing as it were, into the tranquil surroundings, the sun, the sky, the sand and the deep blue sea.

"What an absolutely glorious day Lord."

The warm rays of sun on Annie's back felt very therapeutic, her pain now a dull ache. She stood tall, stretching through the crown of her head to the tip of her toes. She started to take strong, controlled strides, as she strutted with a bit more pace. Her back hadn't felt this good in weeks.

Exhausted after her walk, she never told Mitch about the visit from his mum. He of course would think she was absolutely insane. From the time

Annie had met Marie, they had formed a special bond. She reminded her a lot of herself, even though she was over sixty, she portrayed this child like innocence. They had laughed for hours when they used to get together and there were many happy memories. Marie put great trust in her. After all, she was married to her baby boy, she knew Annie would always take good care of him.

When Annie arrived home from her walk, Mitch was mowing the lawns.

"Hi Darling," she called above the grinding of the mower blades, as she stole a kiss on his cheek."

"Been for a walk? How are you today?"

"Yes good actually, magnificent day, isn't it baby," she grinned, "how long before you finish mowing the lawns?" She asked.

"Hey," he yelled.

"How long before you finish mowing the lawns?" Annie mouthed the words loud and clear.

"About ten minutes," Mitch mouthed back laughing.

Annie giggled, O.K, I'll get us some lunch."

"O.K.," he smiled and winked at her as he pushed the mower in the opposite direction.

Annie admired his backside as he walked away, "God he's so cute," she thought on her way into the house to prepare their lunch.

Sitting in the garden, eating lunch, the smell of freshly cut grass always made Annie feel at home.

"My back feels much better today Mitch," Annie said seriously. I might drop in and see the Doc this afternoon. Maybe if he gives me clearance? I will be able to return to work after your days off?"

"Are you sure you are up to it Annie? You know you can still hurt your back if you don't let it heal completely!"

"I'll be fine, just wait and see, I'll be running rings around you in no time, after all they've said that there will be no long term damage. I'll be back to my old self as quick as you can say pubar!"

"Pubar! What the hell is pubar?" Mitch laughed inquisitively.

"P.U.B.A.R, PRAYING UPWARDS BEYOND ALL RELIGION!"

"Oh right, O.K. Then," Mitch frowned.

"Well, I just made it up off the top of my head." she replied.

"Ha HA Ha," Mitch cracked up laughing. "You sure are one crazy lady and I love ya, come give us a hug."

He pulled her towards him and kissed her adoringly on the cheek, lips and forehead.

"There is also something else I've been wanting to tell you," Annie spoke as they cuddled closer into each other in the garden. "I wanted to wait a little longer because I wanted to be sure it wasn't just a tummy bug," she said with a grin.

"What's that baby? Mitch asked wide eyed. "Are you telling me you've got morning sickness?"

As she spoke tears began to well in Mitch's eyes. "What are you waiting for, let's go get a pregnancy test."

"I don't know if that's such a good idea?" she said quietly.

"Why not?" Mitch gave Annie a look of concern as he always did when he wanted to get his own way.

"Well it may be to soon to show in a pregnancy, urine test and I don't want to be disappointed by seeing a negative or a minus instead of a positive or a plus."

"Come on Annie," Mitch said excitedly, "if it doesn't show this time, we'll wait a bit longer and try again." He was like a kid in a candy shop, or more like a man in a prestige car yard. Or maybe he was just a daddy in waiting?

"O.K, O.K," she weakened, "let's go get the pregnancy kit then Gorgeous, let's do it."

"Great," Mitch said eagerly, "I'll grab the car and we'll zip down and get a test right now."

"You're so funny Honey," Annie laughed, "God I love you so much. I couldn't think of anything more wonderful, than sharing this child with you."

"So you're pretty sure then? About being pregnant and all?" Mitch put his arm around her shoulders and guided her to his black Holden Utility, "I might have to trade this one in for a Holden, family wagon," he said with a cheesy grin.

"Now, don't go getting to carried away baby, I'd hate for you to be disappointed. I've felt different for the last couple of months, even before I hurt my back, that's why I've hesitated to take any pain relief. The thing that did worry me how ever, is that I'd had that X-ray done before I knew I'd missed a period and before feeling sick in the morning before breakfast.

I hope that hasn't done any harm?"

Mitch took Annie by the hand and almost pulled her into the local pharmacy. "I'm sure everything is going to just fine Honey."

She rushed by his side, she was so happy and knew that as soon as she saw the result the definitely positive of the pregnancy test, that she wouldn't be able to contain her joy any longer. She was trying to be so cool about the whole thing.

They stood in their bathroom, watching, waiting, both staring at the little dish on the corner of the spa bath, watching and waiting, it wouldn't be long now.

"Come on," Mitch grizzled impatiently, "what's taking so long? I thought this modern technology was meant to be quick?"

"Patience Sweetheart, it only takes a couple of minutes, then you should be able to see a pink stripe or a pink cross," Annie informed him, feeling a little nervously excited about it herself.

Standing there a little longer, staring at that dish, staring at one another, watching and waiting as a pink stripe began to appear. Mitch was looking at Annie with a furrowed brow, when another faint line began to strengthen to form a cross. Mitch's jaw dropped open. Annie covered her mouth as tears filled her eyes, tears of absolute joy.

"Oh my God," Annie squealed with excitement, her hand still covering her mouth, "I'm now officially pregnant."

Mitch had tears running down his cheeks and a big grin on his face, baring all his white Hollywood smile.

"Come and give us a hug mummy," he sniffled joyfully.

"You are going to be a daddy at last," Happy tears streamed down both their faces as Mitch held on to her tight.

They had been trying to conceive for about six month and every month Annie got her nasty monthlies (Periods). It had been the longest six months of her life. Finally she could see a joyous light at the end of that long, dark tunnel she'd been dealing with at work. An escape if you like, a distraction from all things negative of late, things Annie found so hard just to forget.

Chapter twenty

Priceless Friendships

"You look fantastic Annie," Cassy complimented her as they went strutting down the pathway along the beach front together, "From behind, you wouldn't even know you were pregnant."

Another car tooted on it's way past. "God Annie, I don't even get tooted at and I'm not even pregnant," Cassy laughed.

"They're tooting at you," Annie replied, "they wouldn't be tooting at me."

"Oh you're so modest Annie, you deserve it, you really work hard to look after yourself. Not long now before you go on maternity leave is it?" Cassy asked.

"Only about four weeks to go. I can't wait to get out of having to put on those nursing support hose every morning. I'm having to get up ten minutes earlier every morning, just to struggle putting on those silly stockings. I can hardly touch my toes with this huge belly."

How are you going with old touchy feely?" Cassy inquired about their boss Benson.

"Oh he's still grossing me out but he will start picking on someone else now I'm gross, Ha Ha.

"Oh Annie, you are not gross," Cassy reassured her, "glowing but not gross, not in the slightest.

"For some reason," Annie told Cassy, as they continued walking, "he did comment the other day though, of how I remind him of his wife, when she was pregnant. The weird thing is, his children are in their mid teens now, so that would have been an awful long time ago. He's still spooking me out, touching me and sneaking up behind me. In fact, I feel quite ill with it especially now I'm pregnant, maybe it's a primitive, protective mechanism or something? Alert, Alert! Mr Touchy feely approaching, ready to invade, Alert, Danger, Danger!" Annie tried to laugh it off as she chased Cassy down the beach path, grabbing her playfully around the neck.

"Yuck Annie," Cassy said, "that's gross, you poor thing."

They walked for miles along pleasant scenic, coastal pathways, then diverted onto the sand and returned on their walk along the water. It was a relief to laugh at life and relieve some of that built up tension. Annie knew that soon she would have at least six months or more off of work, a break from it all and she was so much, looking forward to starting a family with the love of her life. Cassy and Annie walked their usual approximate ten kilometres. As they neared the end, Annie turned to Cassy and said,

"Cassy, do you believe in life after death? You know, spirits and all that?"

"Yes Annie, absolutely, I do believe there is more than just flesh and blood, I believe this because I know my own spirit and I can feel it within myself, as something that is neither attached nor detached from my body and mind."

"What do you think happens to people that don't die of natural causes? Like if they had a premature death?"

"You mean like suicide or murder? Or something?"

"Yeah, that's right," Annie looked at Cassy with a seriousness.

"Are you sure you're alright Annie, you look a little pale. Here, let's sit down for a few minutes."

They found the nearest bench seat, there were many of them a hundred metres apart along the beach path. They were all named after and dedicated to locals loved ones that had passed away. Each with their own little remembrance plaques.

"Cassy, can I trust you, If I tell you something that is probably going to sound really far out? You'll probably think I'm a pregnant, kooky, crazy woman."

"I've always thought that anyway Annie," Cassy chuckles.

"No Cassy, I'm serious about this, I haven't mentioned this to anyone, not even my mum."

"Not even Mitch?" Cassy looked intrigued. "Not even Mitch."

"No Cassy, not even Mitch."

"This must be serious then. You know you can trust me with your life, so what's up girlfriend?"

"Well I've sighted a few strange things lately," she said in a quiet voice so other path walkers wouldn't over hear her.

"You too?" Cassy smiled.

"As a matter of fact, I've had quite a few visitors Cassy."

"Yes I know Annie."

"You know?"

"Yes I'm here to help you and the lost spirits, to save their soul, so they may be free from the ones who oppressed them and terrorised them.

I'm here for you to bare witness to the terrible behaviours you've had to endure."

"I'm hoping it will improve once I've had this little Munchkin." Annie rubbed her belly, as she smiled down on it, then serenely gazing out to sea in a day dream.

"Annie," Cassy regained Annie's attention.

"Sorry Cassy," Annie apologised. "I slipped into La La Land there for a moment, I've been doing a bit of that lately. I guess I do have an excuse though. Did you know that it's scientific fact, that pregnant women actually get a fluid shift from their brain and it takes about six months after the birth to go back to normal, what ever normal is? A bit like the word perfect really? Anyway, apparently, that's why us women get a little vague when we are pregnant. Vague mentally but more physically and spiritually sensitive."

"Annie this is the reason you have been chosen to go through all this," Cassy explained.

Annie crinkled up her forehead and raised her eyebrows in concern. "You mean there is more to come?"

"You're going to be fine Annie." Cassy smiled care and compassion. "You have a lot of good spirits guiding you, protecting you, you must not worry O.K."

"I feel safe," Annie replied, "I'm just not sure what to expect next?"

"All in good time Annie, all in good time." Cassy grabbed Annie's hands and shook them, swinging them in and out, like two young school children.

They walked home arm in arm, like a couple of old ladies, silently watching the scenery of the seascape.

Annie was so grateful for her long time friends, they were like gaurdian Angels in Annie's heart, Angels sent from heaven.

Cassy was on afternoon shift, so she left as soon as they got back from their walk. Annie was inspired by the fact that Cassy took the time to walk with her while she was pregnant. Even when she had to work, she was there without fail.

Annie had the day off, so she decided to sit quietly that afternoon and write some poetry about her special friendships, her Angels.

"Unforbidden Love," the kind that is true love, not at all sexual, love that comes in pure form, purely from the the heart. Not forbidden but unforbidden.

©Unforbidden Love

I see my angels through your eyes,
Fly over seas and drift through the skies.
You touch my spirit with the power above,
You fill my heart with such unconditional love.

I a life of love, one can not ignore,
the feeling to cherish, love and adore.
Admiration from some one,
That cares from their heart.
UnconditionaL, unforbidden love,
We'll never part.

Unforbidden Love does shine through the skin,
Unforbidden love does shine from with in.
No Money no gold, not a half penny old,
Unforbidden Love can never be sold.

Unforbidden Love comes from deep down in your soul,
Unforbidden Love your life takes control.
Don't ignore it, express it, every single day,
Let it show you life's lessons, let it show you the way.

"Unforbidden, unconditional love,
has no colour shape or creed.
Unforbidden, unconditional love has no conditions,
limits or greed."

The true purpose in life is to know how to love,
Not to stand first in line, or to push or to shove.
Unfortunately for many, this lesson comes too late,
Without it, your life will always be second rate.

She whispered, "I see my Angels through your eyes, fly over seas and drift through the skies

Annie read through her poem several times, she was quite please with this one.

"Time for a rest baby." she rubbed her tummy.

She often spoke out loud, especially now baby was growing. She went into the living room and dimmed the light. She put some relaxation music on the CD player, a CD titled, Gentle Island Surf.

Annie lay there, in the recliner chair, breathing in and exhaling as much as she could before breathing in again. She raised the footrest of the recliner. Continuing to breath in, she flexed her feet up, breathing out as she relaxed them down. She took another deep breath in, flexing her feet and this time clenching her calf muscles, breathing out she let them flop down on the leg rest. She let her feet and lower legs relax. The music of the waves washing on the shore and soft island breeze made Annie's mind drift off to a deserted island, with palm trees, warm white silicon sand and the suns rays warming her whole mind, heart, body and soul.

She continued her deep breathing and relaxation, as she let her mind bask in the sun, on that tropical island. Flexing and clenching her whole legs with her feet flexed now, she lifted her calves off of the leg rest. She locked her knees and clenched her quadriceps muscles, also squeezing her gluteal muscles in her bottom, breathing in deeply and relaxing as she exhaled. She pulled her belly button into her back bone as much as she could. She felt baby wiggle inside her and let out a quiet chuckle as she lay there peacefully with her eyes closed.

With her legs floppy and relaxed now, she braced her abdominal muscles, pulling her tummy in once more, then filled her lungs with air expanding her rib cage as she could, then she let her whole self flop on exhalation.

Breathing in again, she shrugged her shoulders up to her ears, squeezing them as close as she could as she breathed in, then relaxed them down, she exhaled. Once again she let her whole mind, heart, body and soul relax as she sunk into the recliner chair. She took another big breath in, as big as she could, she stretched up through her neck and shoulders, through to the crown of her head. She exhaled as she flopped her whole body again into the chair. Gently now, she took breaths in and out, in and out.

Quietly she took a breath in and let her head fall gently to the right and exhaled as her head relaxed gently down to the left. Again she inhaled and let her head fall gently forward as she relaxed and exhaled, gently taking her head back. As she went into her last little postural deep breathing and relaxation stretch, her eyes still closed, a little smirk appeared on her face. She recalled momentarily, how she told all her fitness clients to pucker up during this stretch that she had taught them. "Pucker Up," she would say, "and give everyone a kiss good day." She insisted they didn't take their heads back too far. One last little exercise Annie performed in her deep breathing and relaxation routine, while gently breathing, was to raise her eye brows and make the biggest possible grin on her face, when teaching clients, she encouraged them to do the same, she called this her Jack Nicholson grin, this helped stretch and relax all the facial muscles. It also got her whole class cackling at one another.

Annie could feel her heart beating quietly, softly, relaxing, breathing, in and out, in and out. Laying in that warm tropical breeze. Water lapping at her feet. She had removed herself from all place and time. Drifting into a relaxation of weightlessness, nothingness, sleepiness.

Suddenly she awoke with pain, terrible pain in her stomach. The pains in her tummy were unreal. The sounds of waves still lapping on the shore. She got up quickly from the chair, holding onto her lower abdomen, an immense pressure bearing down on her pelvic area.

She made her way to the bathroom as quickly as she possibly could. Something had started to come away from her. Looking down, she could see globules of blood running down the inside of her legs and onto the floor.

"Oh God," Annie gasped, "Oh my God, I can't have this baby now, it's not time yet."

As she felt more and more pressure bearing down on her, the blood and more liquid flooded from her body.

"Oh my God my waters breaking," Suddenly something huge was passing from her, slithering out of her, this long slithery thing. She felt like all her insides were dropping out of her, onto the bathroom floor.

"What is this?" She screamed, looking down at the floor in horror.

How bizarre, a little monkey, looking chimp like creature was wiggling around. She bent down to pick him up and before she knew it, this little monkey climbed all over the place. It climbed onto her breast and bit her on the nipple.

"Ouch, you little begger," she yelled.

As she felt the pain of her crippled nipple, she gasped for breath.

She awoke from her meditative rest. "Oh thank God, that was really just a dream," she said to herself as she began to open her eyes, realising thank goodness, she was still in her recliner chair. "What a bizarre, weird dream, a little monkey, ha, ha quite funny" she giggles and rubs her belly.

"Are you alright baby? Maybe something is tying to tell me you're going to be a cheeky little monkey." Annie had been warned by several experienced mums, that you have some strange dreams when you're pregnant. But Annie had already been prepared with weird dreams before she even got pregnant, well nightmares anyway.

That night as her and Mitch lay in bed. She told him about her bizarre dream of the monkey. He was quite amused. He said if it was any constellation, that monkeys were meant to be highly intelligent, the missing link, he gestured as Mitch rubbed Annie's belly. "Hey champion," he said to Annie's belly. She smacked his hand away playfully. They lay there laughing.

"How are you going in there Champ?" Mitch asked baby. "How about daddy read you a little bed time story?"

Mitch smiled as Annie allowed him to put his hand back on her belly. He smiled at her, and her at him, as she passed him a Mr. Men book from the bedside table, he kissed her tenderly on the lips. Mitch had been buying these books since Annie's tummy had began to show.

At this moment, Annie could feel their baby wiggling around inside of her. "Mitch, Mitch, have a look at this!"

As Mitch began to speak, baby began to recognise his fathers voice. The more Mitch spoke, the closer baby swooned towards him. Annie's belly was actually moving towards her husband. It was quite an amazing sight to see. From then on, Mitch and Annie realised that this child was born, before he was born.

Annie talked and sang to baby constantly. Two of her favourite songs were, Unforgettable by Nat King Cole and the other was a song called, Loving you, is easy cos you're beautiful. She loved singing these songs to her husband and her baby.

She remembered the song Loving You, from when she was a very little girl. She remembered seeing this pretty young African lady on T.V. With lots of big curly hair, apparently her name was Minnie Ripiton. Annie only remembered hearing the song that once but through her whole life, the words and that beautiful girl and her beautiful voice remained with her.

As Annie grew up, she was saddened to find out that some people said she died from a drug over dose and others said she died of cancer, either way Annie thought she was an Angel. She remembered sitting there, eyes glued to the T.V. Screen when she was about seven years old, the words etched into her heart and her minds soul memory.

"Loving you, is easy cause your beautiful and every day of my life, I'm more in love with you. LA LA LA LA LA, LA LA LA LA LA, LA LA LA LA LA LA LA LA, Do IN DOODINDOOODINDOOOOODOOOOO AAAH AAAH AAAH AAAH AAAH AAAH."

Annie had arrived back at work, it was a cold and wet day. She loved the smell of damp soil, it smelt so new, a real clean, earthy smell. She hoped her garden was getting a good soaking, as she watched the rain pouring down from the Lake View Hospital window. She felt in quite bright spirits, after spending days off with family and close friends. She felt very blessed to have such wonderful people in her life.

As she walked up the corridor, she didn't bother taking the lifts. The old rickety things always took forever anyway. Even though she was nine months pregnant, with a bad back, she still beat the the other nurses up the eight flights of stairs. She did not see pregnancy as an illness or a good excuse to over eat, or eat for two. Apart from her back pain, she felt healthier than ever.

Usually after handover, Annie would go around the ward and help everyone sit their patient's out of bed for breakfast. Of course after her back injury, she was extra cautious, especially with the patients that needed more assistance, being pregnant and all.

Annie started up one end of the ward and always helped everyone with their bed making before doing her own. For the first time, one of the seniors, Banina, came in to help Annie with the remainder of her beds.

"Thanks for your help," Annie said to Banina, "That's O.K." Banina replied.

But Annie became extremely upset when she overheard Banina complain to her Boss Benson.

"She shouldn't be at work in her condition," Banina continued bitching to Benson.

As if Annie needed to give Benson any more ammunition for giving her more of a difficult time.

"She's always the last nurse to finish making her beds." Banina completed.

Annie tried not to let Banina's snide remarks bother her. After all everyone knew she'd helped make all of their beds first. How was Banina supposed to know that, she didn't start work until 0800hrs, an hour after everyone else.

Helping everyone make beds was Annie's way of making sure everyone had a reasonably easy, pleasant start to their day and the ward always looked more organised when the beds were all made.

There were many patients for Annie to discharge this morning. There were also cardiac examinations being admitted this afternoon for angiograms the following morning. Annie wanted to get her discharge patients organised as soon as possible.

Mr Brebener, one of the discharges, was almost ready to go, his wife was patiently waiting by his side ready to transport him home.

Annie entered the six bed bay. "Happy to be going home Mr Brebener?" Annie asked her patient.

"Certainly am love, no place like home!"

"That's for sure." Annie briefly interrupted.

"Thank you so much for taking good care of him, I hope his not expecting the same treatment at home," Mrs. Brebener smiled.

Annie laughed. "We aim to please. I've rang the hospital pharmacy." Annie informed the couple. "The hospital courier is delivering the D/C discharge medication as we speak. Once you've collected those, you will be free to go. I've got your chariot waiting." (Annie pointed to the wheel chair.)

There was a lot of activity going on in the nurses station. Nurses, doctors, therapists.

Benson started yelling at Annie in front of all the staff. She stood there stunned for a few seconds, wondering what the hell was happening. Everyone looked at him, then stared at Annie.

"ANNIE," he screamed at her, "PULL YOUR FINGER OUT AND GET ON THE DAMN PHONE NOW, RING PHARMACY SO THOSE PEOPLE CAN GO HOME, MOVE IT, HURRY UP."

Annie felt very nervous and intimidated, at the same time extremely embarrassed, being yelled at like a child in front of all her work colleagues. And just as Annie was about to explain that she had already rang pharmacy, the courier's trolley entered the nurses station.

She approached the trolley and asked for Mr. Brebener's discharge medications.

Benson watched Annie like a hawk awaiting to devour his prey. She approached Mr. and Mrs.Brebener to explain his discharge medication to them.

"What's that blokes problem?" Mr. Brebener asked, having witnessed the commotion in the nurses station. "You shouldn't have to put up with that rubbish."

"It's O.K." Annie shrugged, "Don't let it worry you, here you go, come in and sit in your chariot and we'll take you down stairs."

"Well," Mr. Brebener continued, "I can tell you, if you were my daughter, I wouldn't want my girl to be spoken to like that, boss or no boss, especially if she was a good nurse like you."

"Thank you for your encouraging word Mr. Brebener."

Annie put two and two together and obviously the little chat the senior Banina had with Benson earlier about her slow bed making, had given him the ammunition that Annie wasn't pulling her weight, just a slack, pregnant bludger. How wrong they were.

Annie worked harder than ever because she knew she was getting hassled. She even did more than her share. Such as making everyone else's beds, emptying everyone else's dirty linen skips, cleaning every one else's dirty bed pans, urinals and bowels.

This was the first morning anyone had helped her make her beds and she was paying for it. The tongue can be a wicked thing, so nasty and untrue.

As Annie tried to remain focused, she organised the rest of her day. She tried to forget about the mornings little set backs. At least she had a lot to keep herself occupied. Before she knew it, it was time for lunch. She went to lunch with Jorjia, one of her closest nursing peers and friends. Annie had actually set her up with one of Mitch's police buddies and now they were engaged to be married, Annie was so happy for them.

Jorjia was a little concerned with the way Benson had come down on Annie that morning. They decided to have a break from the ward and headed down to the Lake View Cafe' for lunch. Annie ordered her usual chicken salad role and orange juice.

"You're way to healthy for me today," Jorjia told her, "I'm going to grab a Balfour's Pasty, with lots of dead horse and a big fattening chocolate milk. Then I'm going out for a breath or two or three or four cigarettes." She laughed.

"You know Jorjia, I had the occasional cigarette but I haven't touched one of those things since I found out I was pregnant, not even a social smoke. No tea, no coffee, no alcohol of any sort. Once I found out I was responsible for this little miracle growing inside me, it was easy to go cold turkey on all things toxic.

Jorjia rubbed Annie's belly. "How you going, beautiful little baby?" She chuckled. "Oh," she said, "I just felt him kick my hand."

"Yes I felt it to believe it or not." Annie said cheekily, rolling her eyes.

"He's been a little restless all morning, probably due to my upset, especially when Benson embarrassed me in front of everyone."

"Yeah, that was bullshit, I can't believe he did that, pardon my French," Jorjia Frowned. Understandable you'd be upset, you poor thing, I felt embarrassed as well and I wasn't even the one being yelled at."

"Is he still following you Annie?"

"Yes, but luckily for me, we haven't been rostered on to many shifts since I've come back from my work injury. I've had a bit of a break from him lately. I think it's because the boss's aren't aloud to work week ends any more, it's costing the system too much money."

"Yeah, maybe that's why he's been in more of a foul mood lately, he's probably down on the bucks, not getting any penalty rates."

"Oh," Annie said sarcastically, "I guess that gives him the right to give me an extra hard time then." Annie pulled a long face, they both laughed it off.

When they returned to the ward from lunch, Benson approached them in the corridor.

"Annie, I want to see you in my office when you finish at 1530hrs today," he mumbled something neither Jorjia or Annie could understand as he walked away. He did not even give Annie any time to respond.

Annie looked upset and worried. "Looks like I'm going to see the boss after work then."

"You O.K. Annie?" Jorjia asked.

"I'll guess I'll have to wait and see?" Annie started walking into her bay of patients to get on with her nursing duties.

Jorjia called out, "I'll wait for you after work, O.K."

"Thanks Jorjia," Annie called from the six bed patient's bay.

Chapter Twenty One

Love Conquers All

She stood at the door of Benson office

"Come in and sit down Annie." Benson mumbled.

"I'd rather stand if you don't mind," Annie did not want to put herself in a compromising position. She was already feeling a little squeamish and uncomfortable. Benson shut the door.

Annie opened the door. "If you don't mind sir, I'd rather leave the door open please."

Benson tried to shut the door again but Annie stood right in the door way, she had been shut and locked in one office too many, with one too many boss's, one too many times, with them telling one to many lies in this place. She was feeling quite ill and very anxious about the over all situation.

"I've heard you've had a few complaints," he said to her. "Not that I'm aware of sir."

"Someone told me you were doing stretches on the ward the other evening when you were on afternoon shift, hamstring stretches."

"Yes I was sir."

"Well he said, raising his voice a little more, "that is a bit unprofessional and inappropriate don't you think? This is a hospital, not your gym."

"That's not fair, the pain in my lower back was getting worse as the evening progressed," Annie replied, so I had to do some stretching to try and relieve my pain sir. As you are well a ware, I am carrying a baby and I do not take pain killers for my work back injury."

"NO WONDER YOU GOT KICKED OFF OF THOSE OTHER WARDS," Benson screamed at her.

"Excuse me sir, I told you last time, I did not get kicked off the other wards, I asked management to be removed from them. I was locked in a plaster room and abused about nothing, none of their business, nothing to do with my nursing, just like this."

As Annie recalled the plaster room incident, she began to have flash backs.

"Someone told me you used an incorrect dressing technique too, when you were bandaging," he went on.

Annie started to feel her heart beating in her throat. "Sorry sir, I haven't done any bandaging since I've been on this ward.'

"What about that young lad, Darren, the one that had the MVA with the burns, in the side room?"

"Yes I took his dressing down sir, for the doctors rounds but the burns unit nurse came up and dressed them all."

She realised, he was trying his hardest to pick fault.

Annie had been working so hard and tried to be the best nurse she could be. She was absolutely exhausted from her boss Benson's weird idiosyncrasies.

Feeling quite breathless, Annie's chest started to tighten, her upper abdomen began pulsating, like she had really bad hunger pains but she knew it wasn't hunger. Her throat filled with acid juices as her blood pressure rose. She was so dizzy, her head spinning, holding her tummy, she could feel herself falling, falling into a deep, dark, bottomless pit, spinning and falling, it was so dark.

Benson started slapping Annie around the face as she lay motionless on the floor. Another staff member Kane, one of the male nurses was passing by.

"Oh my God sir, what is wrong with Annie? She looks like she's turned blue."

"She's alright," Benson replied. "She's just fainted-it happens all the time in her condition."

"NO SIR," Kane yelled at him,Her lips are blue and she's not breathing."

Kane ran and called CODE BLUE 222, yelling at other staff members to get the portable oxygen and the emergency trolley.

"Down to the boss's office stat."

CODE BLUE EIGHTH FLOOR, CODE BLUE EIGHTH FLOOR, blared out over the intercom system.

Suddenly Annie was there, watching over the whole commotion, as if watching a scene from a dream, she felt nothing.

People were rushing about with I.V. Trolleys and oxygen bottles, defibrillator, stretchers. Sticking I.V. Needles in her arms, needles in her neck, tubes down her throat, oxygen mask on her face. She felt nothing. They were bagging her and she couldn't feel a thing, not even the beat of her heart or the sound of her breath.

She lay flat out on the floor now, with a wedge under her left side. They gave her cardio pulmonary resuscitation. She stood there watching over them, over herself, watching them trying so hard to get her back. To bring her back to life.

Annie did not feel distressed any more, nor did any feelings of anxiety still fill her being. As a white light encapsulated her and her unborn child, she felt warm and comforted, protected. Her soul was in that meditative state, where she had been many times before. She knew that warm, white, glowing light that surround her, was the Lord protecting her.

As she stood beside her earthly body, she knew that the other Spirits, Lindsy, Demi, Andy, Cassy and Marie, were there watching with her, all standing as one strong soul.

Lindsy spoke first.

"You are going back Annie, you and your beautiful baby."

"Yes, I know," Annie replied. "I know when the time is right, I will be returning to my earthly body. I realise now, why I've been through all this, this trial. You all need this case to be put to rest. I know what you have been through. I will fight for your dignity, I will fight for every last one of you. I too have forte strong feelings of suicide, at the height of my harassment, I had no self esteem and felt I was not worthy of being treated any differently. I couldn't understand how I became so weak, as I had always been a battler and soldiered on, the one who others came to for advise, when their hearts were breaking. There were days that I just wanted to curl up on my bed and die, leave this world that I had once thrived in. Now my heart is broken and I must protect my spirit and save our souls."

"You have a very strong spiritual sense and a very great faith in the Lord." Andy said. "We connected with you from the very first time you were taken into the office, after your leg operation. Everything you have been through, we have witnessed and understand that you almost ended up in our place but your strength in your faith, it pulled you through and that is certainly admirable."

245

"Yes, that's for sure," Cassy added. "You just got straight back out on the wards again and got on with everything so religiously and so thoroughly."

"That's because I truly love my work," said Annie. "Yes I still do love my work. All of the harassment and they couldn't say one bad thing about my work. Each time I was taken into an office and abused, I felt like I had to work harder and harder, time and time again, to keep proving myself. But all along it had nothing to do with my work. It was all about the POWER. I have nothing to prove, this isn't about me, it's about them, their behaviour. "I am" a competent, confident nurse with a good attitude and there is nothing wrong with that."

"Here, here," all the spirits agreed. "Now Annie, it's time."

Her mother in-law Marie touched her with strong, warm, comforting, glowing strength of the light. "Be happy Annie, everything is going to turn out wonderfully, so beautifully."

As a ball of white light, glowing energy started to retract, Annie could feel the spiritual hand pulling away from her, letting her go, as earth's gravitational pull started sending her heavenly, energised, spiritual body, back to her earthly body.

"You are of a select few Annie," the spiritual souls called. "A select few who put on the earth to care for other's mind's, heart's bodies and souls. You maybe human on the outside but on the inside, we are all Angels, with hope, faith and love, yes, most of all love."

"Lindsy spoke again. "You see Annie, if we can not be released from this evil oppression, we will remain in limbo forever with our aggressors. It is up to you to seek justice. You have been chosen to walk the path that we walked but also to return to your mortal life, to bring it to the attention of others. So the Angels, good hearted spirits, just like us, won't lose their spirits and get lost in limbo for ever, lost souls, instead of getting our Angels wings and having our spirited souls remain. So much pain and heart ache. To break a bone is one thing, to break a spirit and taint the soul of another for ever is another. We are all tired, we need to be put to rest from this limbo. You have broken your back and dealt with that, don't let them break your spirit Annie. Please don't make a fool of our souls."

As the warm, white light surrounded Annie stronger than ever, she felt herself being lifted and transported back to her place, her earthly body on the floor. Like the sinking, falling motion when she fell, getting back into her earthly body was quite the opposite. She was given back, light and life, yet a priceless task lay before her, she could not deny.

Slowly Annie could feel her eye lids begin to flutter, she could feel herself choking, as a plastic tube was being removed, drawn out of her fleshy throat.

"It's alright Annie," the nurse spoke with care, "we're keeping an eye on you, that's it, your breathing all on your own now. Don't want that horrible tube down your throat any more do you!"

Her eyelids twitched and then fluttered some more, this time opening just for a flicker. Then again, open for a bit longer, everything appeared blurry. She blinked and blinked again until things became a little clearer in her sight.

She felt very groggy, blinking again, everything started to come into focus. She looked to the right, recognising Geoff, the critical care nurse, from the intensive care unit, he was a gorgeous nurse. She looked to the left where there was someone holding her hand, she looked a little more intently, her vision cleared.

"Mitch, Mitch," she whispered, with a husky voice, her throat extremely sore and so dry. She felt so dazed and so weak.

"Don't talk Baby," Mitch spoke softly and sweetly, he gently squeezed her hand. "Just rest and concentrate on your breathing, you're doing great Honey."

"The baby Mitch, is the baby?" Annie stumbled over her words. "Is the baby, the baby." She didn't have the energy to finish the sentence.

"The baby is going great Honey, look at his little heart beating away on the monitor. The more you relax and just breath, the better it will be for the both of you."

Annie closed her eyes, "thank God." She used all her strength to try and lift her other hand up onto her swollen belly. Mitch could see she was struggling, he took her hand in his and placed it on top of hers. Tears and emotions filled their hearts, spirits and eyes. Mitch gently cupped her hand in his and caressed it on top of her baby tummy.

Annie managed a smile as Mitch watched her curl up the corners of her mouth, she fell into a deep sleep.

"Is she alright?" He asked the nurse.

"She's doing well," Geoff replied. "She'll be a bit groggy for a few days. She's had a lot of medication over the last twenty four hours. Once she is more alert, it won't take long for the sedative drugs to wear off. It's quite exhausting dealing with cardiac arrest, she'll need plenty of bed rest from now until junior is born."

Mitch looked at Geoff curiously.

"Do you know what actually caused the cardiac arrest? I mean, she'd had such a healthy life style and pregnancy, I don't understand how this could have happened?"

"We won't be one hundred percent sure until we run a few more tests and examine the current test results." Geoff replied. "We have reason to believe Annie's blood pressure was extremely high at the time of her collapse but we can't say for sure, if that was the only cause for cardiac arrest."

Mitch looked even more puzzled. "High blood pressure? I can't believe that."

"I've been to every one of her anti-natal appointments with her and it hasn't been high at all since the very beginning. Is there something else besides pregnancy that could cause your blood pressure to rise that much it could cause damage?"

Sometimes at the end of pregnancy, there is a medical term for it, they call it pre-eclampsia," Geoff explained. "It happens mainly in the final trimester of pregnancy and is normally due to fluid retention, which I must say, Annie doesn't appear to have a lot of. This fluid of course is what causes the blood pressure to rise most of the time. Mind you, other things can cause high blood pressure, like stress, anxiety, pain and illness."

Mitch frowned a little. "No, Annie's always so calm, she's fit and healthy, she's always doing that, you know, meditation or reiki stuff. She knows how to relax. She even teaches the stuff."

"I'm sure time will tell." Geoff smiled as he turned to dispose of some needles and syringes in the sharps container.

Mitch sat by Annie's bedside for the whole week she was in intensive care. He watched the staff come and go. He noticed how one younger lad was getting a difficult time from his senior nurse. Mitch could see through the glass windows of the nurse managers office, in the ICU unit. The young male nurse was Adam, he had looked after Annie on a couple of occasions in the past week. He appeared to be a fine upstanding young man, with a good head on his shoulders. He appeared to do a fine nursing job looking after Annie, Mitch certainly had no complaints.

The young male nurse came out of the office, his face was red and he looked as though he would burst into tears at any moment. He sat at the nurses desk for a short time with his elbows on his knees and his head in his hands. He took a deep breath and had a large sigh, then he got up and disappeared for about ten minutes. When he came back, he looked as though he had calmed down considerably. Mitch felt for him, as he remembered being reprimanded a few times as a young probationary police officer.

Adam came over to the monitors and recorded Annie and the babies vital signs and observations on the special hourly charts.

"Everything O.K. Buddy?" Mitch asked Adam, concerned for the young man.

"Yeah, yeah I'm fine," Adam smiled an almost sadly, worried smile. "Just a little disagreement between me and the boss, seems to be a frequent occurrence, nothing uncommon in this place."

He spoke quietly as he put his head down to continue writing on Annie's medical charts. "I'll get over it. On a happier not, Annie's doing great. I was very sad when I saw her first come in but she has now picked up amazingly well."

"Yes, I can't tell you how happy I am about that," Mitch replied with a huge smile.

"Excuse me," Annie suddenly opened her eyes, she seemed bright eyed and bushy tailed. "You wouldn't happen to be talking about me now would you?"

"Yes well we are actually talking about you, to be honest," Adam answered.

"That's O.K." Annie said pleasantly. "I'll let you off this once, only because I know what a wonderful nurse you are. Talking from personal experience, you really know your stuff."

"Thank you," Adam beamed. "Thank you, I've really been enjoying my work, it's a pity the boss couldn't say the same. It's nice to get recognition from someone, I guess when it boils down to it, it's the patients opinion that truly counts."

Annie playfully tapped Adam on the hand, "and don't you forget it." Annie turned to face her husband, She looked at him adoringly.

"Oh Babe, you look so exhausted. Why don't you go home and get a good nights sleep tonight in our comfy bed? I'm out of danger, besides, I'll get the hospital to ring you if I have any doubt about me or the baby.

I'm sure they'll be moving into the general wards tomorrow anyway, then home in a few days."

Annie knew Mitch would have a thousand questions when she was well enough. She also knew that he would be very angry when he found out the trigger for her collapse that day.

"Are you sure you'll be O.K. If I go? It will only be overnight, I'll be back first thing in the morning Honey," he smiled reassuringly.

"I'm in good hands. The staff here have been great. I'm just glad that old cow hasn't had to take care of me," Annie whispered, so only Adam and Mitch could hear. She winked towards The direction of the nurses office.

Adam laughed. "Thanks Annie, I thought I was on my own there."

Mitch kissed Annie gently on the forehead, lips and then the belly. Mitch left her bedside shortly after sundown. She lay in a deep, deep sleep. She looked restful so restful now, unlike the previous days he'd spent sitting by her side, gurgled breathing, in distress, chest rising and falling under duress.

"I Love you Baby," he whispered, as he kissed her once more on the forehead. He lay his hand gently on her abdomen. "Goodnight Champ," he softly whispered to his unborn child. He looked at Annie's serene face once more before walking away. He smiled subtly, he could see the corners of Annie's mouth curling up just a little, in an ever slight, cheeky smile. He always wondered what she was dreaming about when she did that.

Annie was awoken suddenly from a dee sleep. Adam stood over her.

"Not observation time again already?" She grinned at him. Adam are you O.K?" He didn't answer her. She looked around the intensive care unit. She looked over at the clock, 0230hrs. She looked over at the nurses station. All the nurses were sitting at the station as they usually did that hour of the early morning. All that could be heard was the intubated patient in the bed next to her. Air pumping in and out of the respirator and beeping of the heart monitor on her unborn child.

"Adam, what are you still doing here? You should have gone home hours ago." Adam looked down at Annie with cold, lifeless eyes, looking lost and lonely. He turned and looked at the night staff sitting at the nurses station.

"Oh God Adam," she gasped. As he turned around, she could see a big bloody dent in the back of his skull. Blood was seeping out of the raw fleshy wound and oozing down his back.

"Oh God not you too?" She was talking to him out loud but her mouth wasn't moving. She was talking and no one else in the ICU room could hear her.

"Adam, what have you done?"

"Annie, my time walking on this earth is finally over. The boss asked me to see her in the office when I finished work, she knows I have agreed to bare witness to someone else's sexual harassment that's been going on here in the hospital. She has made my job unbearable and unenjoyable. She's actually good friend with this man's wife and she has made things very difficult for me. I've been under a lot of pressure from work, earning my degree. My young wife has just had our first and now last baby. Apart from settling in with the little one, I've had a few problems at home as well but when the boss threatened me with the possibility of losing my nursing certificate, I flipped out, walked out of here half numb and confused. I didn't really know where to go, or who to talk to. The weird thing was, I wanted to do what was best for my family and that was to support them. How was I going to do that without a job?"

"Oh God Adam, I am so sorry," Annie could feel the tears welling in her eyes, her heart still beating steadily within her chest. It was at this moment she decided that her heart was going to go on beating for as long as possible.

Adam continued, "I was so numb by the time I finished work, I couldn't even think about going to see the boss again, not after she had threatened my position. I had put blood, sweat and tears into my training and getting a nursing job, to take care of my young family."

"What happened to your head? Adam, who did this to you?"

"I couldn't think straight," Adam replied, "I had to air my mind. In previous stressful times, I would go for a walk in the Kypoe Forest, you know, to meditate, to sort my head out. This time I just couldn't get my mind around the problems, I couldn't see the forest through the trees, so to speak. I couldn't see that light at the end of the tunnel. I'd achieved so much, yet my superior made me feel like I was a huge failure, a worthless piece of shit. I kept thinking of how I would support my wife and baby, without a job, without money? As I stood there with negativity spinning around in my head, I wanted it to stop, I just wanted to get off of the world for a little while. I lost my energy inside. I had nothing else to give and nothing left to replenish me. I started running, running frustratedly through the forest. I kept hearing my boss's voice in my head, over and over again."

"NURSING IS NOT YOUR NICHE, YOU SHOULD NEVER HAVE BOTHERED DOING YOUR TRAINING, YOU'LL BE LUCKY TO MAKE IT THROUGH YOUR FIRST YEAR HERE, NO ONE ELSE WILL WANT TO EMPLOY YOU, I'LL HAVE YOUR CERTIFICATE REMOVED FOR GIVING THAT WRONG MEDICATION LAST WEEK, I'VE SEEN SOME ERRORS IN MY TIME BUT IT WON'T BE THE LAST ONE YOU MAKE, YOU'RE HOPELESS."

Adam went on as he stood there with no life light in his eyes.

"As I stood with my mind spinning, my heart aching, my spirit breaking, a big black whole appeared in front of me, a mine shaft, before I had time to stop and think, within a matter of a split second, I jumped off the embankment. As my feet hit the bottom, I got caught up in an over hanging rock ledge and crack-one blow to the back of my head and it was all over."

A night nurse came over to check on Annie's hourly observations, she lay there, her eyes closed, as if nothing was amiss. As she opened them again, Adam had gone. Annie knew that she would never rest until these poor souls of these poor, beautiful nurses had been released.

The only way she could do this, was to bring these awful, bitter, vindictive, evil bullies to justice.

Chapter Twenty Two

Lead Me To Paradise

It wouldn't be long before the baby was due. Annie was happy to be home from hospital, on early maternity leave. She prayed every night and thanked God for saving her and her baby. She prayed and thanked God for keeping them safe, prayed for her wonderful husband, family and friends. She thanked God for all their support.

She was home and Mitch was happy to have her there. Of course, after such a close call and because Annie was now suffering from a heart condition, she had to go for regular check ups at her doctors. Mitch had not yet questioned why she had collapsed that day but she knew that when he felt she was up to it, that she would tell him.

Before Annie went to see her regular family doctor, Dr Low, she was referred to the cardiac specialist by the name of Dr Whitewhore. He made Annie feel very intimidated. He was apparently on the hospital board of the Lake View Hospital. He told her that just because she thought that she was healthy in body, didn't mean she was healthy in mind. He also said that he had met women like her before? He handled her very roughly, even in her pregnant state. Annie was extremely concerned because he told her that her test results, being her ECG's and her ECHO—heart ultra sound, showed signs of a myocardial infarct, but he said he couldn't be sure if it was an old one or a fresh one. The strange thing was, he never sent her for any further investigation, so

Annie thought it wasn't necessary for her to have ongoing cardiac investigation or treatment. Dr. Whitewhore didn't seem very concerned about Annie at all and appeared to brush her off.

He said the only way he could properly examine her was to cut her heart out and cut it up into little pieces and examine it.

By the time Annie had finished being examined, by this so called doctor, with an extremely bad bedside manner, she was quite shaken and exhausted. She couldn't understand how a doctor could be so unprofessional and so non compassionate, even to a pregnant women that had had a major collapse, whether that be physical or emotional. This so called heart doctor, she believed, didn't have a heart.

Maybe he had been a physician too long, or should she be a little wiser to not just brush off this man's interrogation style?

Mitch had a programmed day off work when Annie's next appointment was due. He decided he would tag along with her and then take her somewhere special for lunch.

Annie put all her trust in her family doctor, Doc Low. She felt quite comfortable and open discussing things with him. Mitch said he would wait while she went in for her appointment.

"Don't be silly darling," Annie told him. "I've got nothing to hide. Besides, you've just about seen and heard it all with the Obstetrician Doctor Larvay, remember?"

Mitch agreed. "Alright, if you don't really mind, I'd like to hear what he's got to say."

"Come in folks, come in. Doc Low waved them in, "have a seat." As usual they were greeted with a friendly smile. "I've received your results and your reports from the LVH Annie. My goodness you have been on a bit of an emotional roller coaster ride, haven't you. Is your boss still giving you a hard time?" The rush up?"

"Rush up?" Mitch looked at Annie with a worried furrow in his forehead. "What is that supposed to mean?"

"Well not at the moment, I've taken early maternity leave because of my little heart incident, which according to Dr Whitewhore was maybe a myocardial infarct, maybe old maybe new."

"Really, that is not the report he sent me. He said most of your problems were probably anxiety related. But don't worry Annie, we'll be sure to look into that for you."

Annie sat there, knowing that crunch time, time to spill the beans, time to get her husband involved in her healing process. "Because of the circumstances, I need to take is easy from now until baby id born."

"Exactly what the doctors ordered," Doc Low said with another pleasant smile upon his face.

"Annie," Mitch interrupted, "what's been going on with your boss?"

"He's been giving me a bit of a hard time at work."

"Why haven't you told me about this before Annie?" Mitch asked with deep concern in his voice.

"You have enough to worry about, you have enough on your plate with your job baby, I didn't want you stressing out about it."

"Oh Annie!"

"Annie," Doctor Low asked, "What happened the day you collapsed?"

"The boss asked me to see him in his office after he had been picking on me throughout the day, but it wasn't just him another senior nurse helped it along too. He wanted to shut me in his office but I insisted the door be left open. When he almost forced the door shut after making untruthful accusations about my work, I said I had nothing to hide and wanted the door left open."

257

"It's then I began to feel terribly unwell and collapsed."

"Did you put an internal complaint in about what had been going on Annie?"

Mitch raised his voice angrily, not at Annie but at the situation.

"Babe, why didn't you tell me you were unsafe at work? Annie, how long has this been going on?"

"On this ward, about two and a half years," she replied with some hesitation, hoping he wouldn't become more upset.

"My God Annie, he almost kills you, not to mention our baby and you haven't even told me anything."

"Please don't be angry with me Mitch. I thought I could handle it, just not very well at the moment. I'm just exhausted with it all. I'm glad to be away from him and that hospital and I guess I better let you know about the body they're going to find in the mind shaft in the Kypoe Forest."

"What body? What mine shaft?" Mitch's expression was getting more and more concerned and confused.

"I know that another nurse jumped to his death down a mine shaft because he was also bullied in the LVH. He left the intensive care unit very upset a few days ago, you know, the one you saw in the office with that senior nurse, the day you were visiting me."

"Young Adam? How do you know?"

"I just know, I dreamt it when I was there in the ICU, he never came back to work after that night."

Annie did not want to tell them all she knew as they probably would lock her up and throw away the key, they would have thought she was mad, not just crazy.

Taking a really deep breath, Annie sighed a loud forceful sigh, relieved she was getting this last few years stress out of her system, she was a ticking time bomb, a bubble ready to burst, explode more like it.

Mitch, who was also ready to explode continued. "You didn't have to handle any of this on your own. God Annie, I wished you had have told me about this earlier. I nearly lost you Baby, do you know how I felt, when I saw you, my beautiful pregnant wife lying limp, in a hospital bed, connected up along with our little Champ, to all those life lines? Surely Doc, there must be something that can be done about these peoples unprofessional behaviours?"

"I asked Annie if she wanted to go on stress leave and she said that it was the last thing she had wanted, In the end, she had taken a few days sick leave, just to recuperate."

"I also suggested that it would be a good idea to at least put in an internal complaint. This male nursing boss has a power problem and it's obvious that the LVH has a major problem with its management professionalism in general. This bloke in particular is obviously not good for running a busy ward. But they've probably given him the job cos no one else will have it, but that's beside the point. Annie actually came into see me long before she was pregnant, as she was concerned something was wrong as she wasn't sleeping well."

"O.K. I think I've heard enough to know I'm not happy about this. Doctor Low is right," Mitch agreed. "You need to at least put in an internal complaint. You need to document everything that has happened."

"I've already kept a few notes of some of the bizarre treatment because I just didn't feel right about it. I felt it was extremely unprofessional and inappropriate behaviour. Even stuff that happened to other nurses, not just me," Annie explained.

"That was probably a wise idea, maybe you should seek advise from the equal opportunities commission?" Mitch added.

Doctor Low nodded his head in agreement.

Annie continued, "You want me to document everything, every horrible thing that I have seen? And has happened to me, on every ward, in that hospital?"

She screwed her face up.

"Yes everything that has happened to you and everything you have witnessed in that hospital, everything!"

"God," Annie sulked, "I will have written a novel by the time I've finished.

"Look what it has done to you Annie. You were always so happy, organised and motivated. In the last three years, I have watched you change, I wasn't sure why, but I did notice a type of personal change in you, your personality going down hill, in front of my eyes, at least I know now, it wasn't all in my imagination. You haven't been your happy self since working in that bloody Lake View Hospital. Now I understand why. Surely there must be better hospitals to work at?"

Mitch pulled his chair closer to Annie's and grabbed her her hand.

"Oh alright," Annie agreed. "Looks like I'll be putting a complaint in then. What about the stuff that happened to me on the other wards?"

"Everything . . . . ," Mitch said, "I want you to document everything, all the things you think are inappropriate, go by your instinct, behaviours that you have experienced by all your boss's, on all the wards you have worked on. I'll be ringing the hospital as soon as we get home and make an appointment for you to see the hospital counsellor."

Doctor Low began properly examining Annie. "You certainly are a strong young lady," he sighed. "A real battler. You have made an exceptional, miraculous recovery."

They left the Docs and on the way home in the car, Mitch lectured Annie about how she shouldn't have let them walk all over her like that. "You are such a nice person Annie, no one needs or wants to be treated that way." He was no sooner in the door and on the phone to the Lake View Hospital.

Annie took a deep breath, a very deep breath of relief but at the same time she was extremely saddened that her other work mates didn't seek moral support in time to survive. But for her and all her spirit ones, it was still a relief that this was now finally to be brought out in the open. She had been sitting on a personal time bomb but one that involved a connection to many other beautiful souls. Although the time bomb had already exploded, it hadn't quite totally disintegrated everything.

Mitch didn't take long to get through to all the appropriate departments. He even rang to make an appointment with a lawyer and the equal opportunities office for legal advice.

For now it was time for Annie to get some well-earned rest. She ran herself a bubble-bath and had a good soak. Then she put pen to paper, she began to write and write and write and write. Annie could not believe how much she remembered, how much was hiding in her subconscious mind, until she brought it back to her current memory and her conscious mind. Even some of the smallest details were imprinted heavily in detail, the smallest detail, position, facial expression, tone of voice and words that were spoken. Along with this, she saw and heard from other nurses who had been bullied. And worst of all the words and actions of the bullies themselves.

She got up early the day she had her appointment with the hospital counsellor. Mitch had brought her one of those small portable hand held recorders, the same they used at his work for the police interviews, he had purchased it from Dick smiths electronic store at West Lakes.

It was a lovely day for a nice stroll along the beach, she took the opportunity to lap up a bit of vitamin D before going to her appointment at the Lake View Hospital to see the hospital counsellor, Donald Tulip.

She had no idea what to expect. As she arrived at the hospital, she felt no where near a confident or relaxed, compared to even the very first day she had her job interview, she felt like a totally different person. As she thought about this, she realised just how much this place had dragged her down. She got to the ground floor office, where the counselling rooms were. She knocked quietly on the staff counsellors door. A very tall man, quite young, with a King George beard answered the door.

"Annie."

"Yes."

"Hello Annie, I'm Donald, come in and take a seat."

As Annie walked in, she felt the presents of other six glowing spirits accompanying her, Lindsy, Andy, Demi, Adam, Cassy and Marie, all entered the room with her. Three sat around the desk, another on a spare chair and two stood behind Donald's high back office chair.

They all looked beautiful, they were glowing so vibrantly now, so radiantly, almost like they were getting the strength of their spirited souls back. Annie could feel their positive energy surrounding her, the same way it did the day she had collapsed, except, this time she wasn't going anywhere.

Annie asked Donald if he wouldn't mind her recording their conversation?

"No not at all, go right ahead."

Annie pushed play and recorded on the little tape recorder.

"Now, I will ask you again, do you mind me taping this meeting?"

"No, he repeated."

"Annie asked him, "Could you state your name, the date and time please?"

He did so without hesitation.

She stated her full name, date and time the meeting commenced.

Donald asked her several questions about her home life, Annie kept telling him that it wasn't her home life that was the problem and we weren't here to talk about that. She stated that she was there to put an internal complaint in about the harassment and bullying of herself and several other junior staff members, by senior staff members. Things that she had witnessed, not only experienced by herself but also witnessed others being harassed. It was a long tedious, drawn out conversation.

She could feel emotions welling up inside, as he kept trying to divert the conversation back to her home life. Away from the real subject of problems. He kept seeking explanation and excuses for these staff members inappropriate behaviours.

"CLICK."

The tape stopped as one side had already been completed, forty five minutes had flown by already.

Annie felt quite uncomfortable, she kept moving around. And Donald noticed quite alertly that the tape had turned off.

"Sorry," he said, "but I can't help you with this."

"Annie," Lindsy whispered from the side lines, "turn the tape over and start recording again, ask him to repeat what he just said."

Annie followed her instructions, as she took the small recorder in hand to take out the tiny tape and flipped it over.

Once again she pushed play and record.

"So, you can't help me? Is that what you just said after the tape turned off, can you please repeat what you just said please. Now that I've poured my heart out to you and given you all the information, which you'll probably use against me, now your telling me when the tape turns off, that you can't help me? Is that right Donald Tulip?"

"No, No, it's not that," he stumbled to find words, stunned at Annie's forthrightness and confidence.

"Well, you just said to me a moment ago when the tape turned off, that you couldn't help me?"

"No, no, I didn't mean I couldn't help you, we just don't get involved with or mixed up in legal matters."

"Will you be taking your complaint further?" He asked.

"I'll have to think very seriously about that, now won't I." Annie answered.

All the white, vibrant, glowing spirits knew there and then that it wasn't anywhere near the end of the matter. Annie knew they would be seeing this man again, even if it was in court.

They all filed out of the room surrounding Annie with uplifting strength she hadn't felt for some time.

She had no idea where all this was heading but she put her trust in God and all his messengers. She knew in her mind, heart, body and soul, that she was at last doing the right thing.

Annie was very breathless by the time she got home from her little so called counselling session, Mitch was waiting for her.

"I'm getting you back to the Docs," he insisted.

He took her there in a great hurry as she had become extremely short of breath. Doctor Low put her straight into the private maternity hospital and called Doctor Larvy her Obstetrician. He worked from the Women Out West Private Maternity Hospital or the WOW as some people called it. This is where Mitch and Annie planned to have baby from the very beginning.

"But I'm not due for another three days," Annie contested, "I want to get my husband out of bed in the middle of the night and cry out, my waters broke, get me to the hospital," she laughed. "You know, just like you see on T.V." She laughed again, still quite puffy with breathlessness.

"Well you are going to need strict bed rest for the next few days. Tomorrow if you haven't started to dilate on your own, I'm going to have to start your induction. So we will give you some prostaglandin gel tonight, to see if we can give you a little encouragement."

Annie made herself comfortable, fluffed up her pillows and surrounded herself with some good reading materials. Lindsy and the gang were also there keeping her company.

They all seemed so at at peace now they knew the matter was finally being dealt with.

Mitch had organised a lawyer to see Annie but he wanted to wait until after the birth of their baby. He also sensed that she knew a lot more than she was letting on. All in good time he knew she'd sort it out.

An exceptional nurse, by the name of Sally, came in to place the baby and mother on a monitor. She was a pretty nurse, a little older than Annie, with glossy blond hair, a pleasant smile and a slender figure. She was very thorough in explaining the whole birthing procedure to Annie and Mitch, in a very professional and thorough manner.

Mitch had to pop home to sort out a few last minute things before the baby was born.

Annie was reassured when she heard the strong and steady sound of her unborn child's strong little heart beat. As soon as Sally was out of the room, they all reappeared. Annie was getting very used to them being around.

"Wow Annie, you must be getting pretty excited right now," Lindsy said. "I'm sorry Lindsy, about what you had to go through, you are welcome to be as much of a part of this as you can, it's what I wanted to share with you anyway. I know it was awful for you."

"I went through it, the same as you Annie, only mine turned out to be fatal." Lindsy said. "We couldn't let the same thing happen to you as well. Don't worry Annie, my little soul still glows safe within me."

Annie spoke genuinely, "I should be thanking you guys, matter of fact, I don't know where I would have ended up, if you hadn't been there to guide me and encourage me to come back."

"It's progress and destiny," Marie added. "There is a reason for everything, for every action, is a positive and equal reaction."

Annie was awake all that evening and all the next day.

When the vaginal gel didn't work in helping her on her way, Doctor Larvy ordered the intravenous cytosine to be administered.

Her contractions came hard and fast in the evening, not to mention painful. Doctor Larvy came in to see how she was going. He decided she wasn't ready but the baby was. Then a moment later he changed his mind.

"Come and look at this dad." Dr Larvy indicated to Mitch to come down to the lower birthing end to have a look.

"You see that?" The doctor pointed to Annie's crutch with a huge grin on his face. "That's your babies head."

Mitch stood watching eagerly with tears welling in his eyes. It was time.

Seven hours and thirty minutes later, a baby boy could be heard, not crying loudly but almost chatting away in Annie's hospital room.

"Oh he's just perfect," Annie cried tears of joy.

"And he's a beautiful boy," Mitch said proudly, with his eyes filled with tears. Together they wept.

Annie only spent three days in hospital. She couldn't wait to get baby Jack home. Although the nurses were very good and could see she was so very thorough, she was really enjoying this new experience of motherhood.

She hoped she could continue breast feeding, as she wanted the absolute very best for her child. She was a little worried though, as she had always been quite athletically chested, as she preferred to put it. From what she could see, she was developing quite a decent sized couple of melons.

It was an exhausting time, as family and friends popped in to admire Jack day and night. Her spirit friends were often around, watching over her safety.

She was so overwhelmed by emotions of motherhood, it seemed like she was on a constant high. Annie's mum insisted she come around and help her with house work for the first few weeks, until they had settled into their new life, with beautiful baby Jack. Mitch was very happy, as he loved his mother in-laws cooking.

Annie came to realise, that she appreciated her parents so much more now that she had a little one of her own. One quiet afternoon, while Jack lay sleeping, Annie decided to get back to another one of her favourite pastime. She wrote a poem about motherhood for her mum.

© *A Mothers Unconditional Love*

Being a mother is something to be proud of,
Having a mother is something to keep hold of.
You realise how precious a mother is,
When you become a mother yourself,
For being a Mother is far more precious,
Than any promotion, or any wealth.

Nothing can compare,
To the birth of your own born child.
All the parties, weddings and holidays,
These sorts of joys are only mild.

Even to consider comparing these joys,
You would not even ever know,
What true love really is,
Until you see your babies grow.

Every time you look at your child's face,
So innocent, Angelic and pure.
You realise for all the petty stresses in life,
That this child is the cure.

There comes this feeling from deep in your soul,
That feels like it may explode.
But that is when your eyes well up with tears,
And your heart overflows.

Nothing has your attention,
Except this darling little soul.'
And you hope and pray,
With all your heart,'
That you may play the perfect
Role
"Mother."

Written upon the Birth of her own son for her mum 1996.

Annie absolutely loved motherhood.

But she knew Mitch couldn't cope with the finances on his own, especially if they wanted to continue their great Australian dream of owning their own home. She decided she would get some part time agency work with the N.R.S, nursing relief service.

Annie did see her Lawyer post all the LVH trauma but tried to put more of her positive energy into baby Jack's younger years.

The LVH and the incompetence of their senior staff were severely and intensely investigated. It took a long two years but seven of the seniors involved, appeared in court and pleaded guilty to gross misconduct of junior staff. All seven seniors were removed from their managerial positions and fined $20,000, each serving an eighteen month, non-parole, jail sentence and stripped of their practising certificates. One senior got an even more severe sentence because she'd threatened a young Portuguese nurse with a Voodoo doll, saying that if she didn't do as she commanded, this is what would happened to her, slamming the Voodoo dolls head in the draw with pins stuck all over it. Then the senior proceeded to say, now you know why Adam has back pain. This nurse was a witness and also lived to tell her tail.

Can you imagine the fear and the terror, some cultures actually do believe in this kind of black magic.

As Annie sat in the court room and listened to this young witness, another bullied victim, tell of her experience in the LVH, Annie could still see the terror in this poor young nurses eyes, a glazed look, a cold look, a look of some sort of purity, innocents and happiness ripped from her soul. A broken bone can be healed but a spirit is scarred forever. Sticks and stones will break my bones and bullying will eventually kill me!

"Over my dead body." Annie thought to herself.

The guilty, spending time in jail would no doubt give these monsters a taste of their own medicine.

After struggling to stay in the job that she loved, Annie finally resigned after the court hearing was finalised, she continues to this day working with the N.R.S. She continues her life's work that she so loves and where she is most needed.

While she gained more definite, positive experience, she also supported other victims of bullying and harassment. Encouraging them to speak out, as she had witnessed it as being the silent killer.

Annie was also awarded a certificate for her ingenuity in preventing infectious diseases. As she had been picked on about washing her hands too regularly and using paper towel to turn taps off after washing her hands to prevent the spread of germs. Senior staff had told her she had a compulsive repetitive disorder. Then once Annie had resigned from The Lake View Hospital, they put signs up above all the taps reading,

"STOP

PLEASE USE PAPER TOWEL

TO TURN TAPS OFF AFTER

DRYING HANDS,

BEFORE DISPOSING IN BIN.

HELP PREVENT THE SPREAD OF INFECTIOUS DISEASES."

Annie found out that even others pinching and stealing your ideas and taking credit for them was in actual fact another form of bullying.

Her life was never the same after the Lake View Hospital, she lost a part of her forever, that she never got back. She never took anything or anyone for granted and lived every day as if it was the last one walking on this place we call earth. She continued trying to enjoy every moment as she had always tried to do. Continuing to be inspired by God's wonderful creation.

The most important lesson Annie learnt from this and she wants you all to hear this,

LOUD AND CLEAR

"It is not your fault if someone else has bad behaviour. Do not blame yourself, as you can not be to blame for someone else behaving badly. It is quite sad in this world, that people have become so shallow and unfeeling, especially in positions that require a person to have great compassion and empathy.

Just remember, you can not control their behaviour but you can control the way you react to their behaviour. It's them, not you that has the problem. Please don't take it personally.

LET YOUR HEALING BEGIN.

GOD AND PEACE BE WITH YOU.

© Healthy Mind, Body And Soul.

My mind is part of my body
And connects me to my soul.
And as we feel the freedom in life
This sets our life time goals.

Let positive thoughts surround you
So much life, experience, beauty and love
Let your souls fly high with your spirit,
And you will connect with the Angels above.

The blood streams around my being,
As my heart rate and pulse increase.
I can feel the oxygen saturating me,
as I breath to it's rhythmical beat.

With every push of the pedals,
I feel my body improve.
My body feels stronger and healthier,
With every single move.

Sometimes I ride my mountain bike,
Along the river track.
My little boy Jack giggles with delight,
As he sit on a seat at the back.

We ride beside the horses,
Who along the rivers run.
We feel the fresh air on our faces,
And tingle in the warmth of the sun.

As we ride as free as those horses,
We sing along as we role.
Al the sensations on this journey,
Would be wonderful for any ones soul, soul, soul.

Published in Poetry Anthology Tied of Hours, copyright All Rights
reserves AESwain ©1999

Would you believe, would you believe, he came to me, in a time of need. No need to grieve, no need to grieve, it was hard to believe, he came to me. Oh this feeling of absolute awe and be-wonderment, I knew that this love, was heaven sent, yes heaven sent.

Lindsy, Demi, Adam, Andy And Cassy, under the guidance of Marie, all stood in Annie's garden, side by side, holding hands. They all prayed together.

"Be my guide Oh Holy Spirit, take my hand, Oh take my heart, through the light and through the darkness, Holy Spirit be my guide. Be my guide Oh Holy Spirit, be my comfort, strength and shield, through the mountains and the valley's, Holy Spirit be my guide. Be my guide Oh Holy Spirit, take my hand, Oh take my heart and when my work on earth has ended, lead me safely home to God, lead me safely home at last. And when my work on earth has ended, lead me safely home at last.

All the nurses who were lost in this life changing experience have had their spirits released from limbo and are now in the safe arms of their maker. They returned to their childlike state, were given there Angels wings to return to our Lord, God in Heaven.

The cruel aggressors still walk this earth in their earthly bodies, in their own living hell, I say this with a heavy heart, a saddened heart.

They are no longer Kings and Queens of their power play domain.

Annie watched each and every one of her Guardian Angels change into their childlike state and get their Angels wings, they then diffused into colours of soft pink, white and blue. As they disappeared into the vast dark blue night sky. She recited their destination.

©He Walks With Me

*I shall now walk beside the sparkling stream, As down on me the
warm sun beams,
And the birds sing merry melody, In the distance I hear the hush of the deep
Blue sea.
Lead me to crystal clear waters, Reunite me with myself and others,
Unlike the mere once mortal.
Lead me to a greener place, Where I no longer hunger nor haste,
Where I can be still and calm for a while, To sit and absorb your
Beautiful smile.
For once a lost child I have been, And now am found and so serene.
Look inside your heart and you will find, You will find your heart
Inside your mind.
For I am unique, no one ever to be the same, And now I've found myself,
I Will go back from once I came.
Not a truer word has been spoken, now my spirit once again awoken,
But you don't really know what you've got until it's gone,
And you hope the ones you leave behind remain strong.
Never will you fear, for where ever you look,
You will find me near.
For I am now the earth, and the seed that grows from within.
I am now the tree that grows, free from any sin.
I am the flowers that blossom and the roses that bloom,
I am in a place now, where sadness never loom.
Look inside your minds eye, I'll watch over you from the vast blue sky.
For I am the birds that fly over head and the animals waiting to be fed.
Always remember, Hope, Faith and Love are forever.
Never the end my dearest best friend, always remember my smile.
'Amen.'*

©2000 The Bully Victim No Longer

You may have heard some stories, do you believe that they are true, but this does not mean that I am not a credit to you. What so ever is in my personal life, is happy, healthy and wholesome, with work and other things to satisfy my soul some.

Should you believe everything you hear, I'll leave it up to you, But a tongue can be a wicked thing, so nasty and untrue. I've always expected a lot from myself, sometimes a little too much. These expectations of myself, have left me with a crutch. That crutch is to be a better person, every single day and if you haven't got anything nice to say, then you just don't say.

Education can be a precious tool, to stimulate the mind, enjoying constructive, not destructive criticism, not being cruel but kind. You can always ask some one nicely, to do what you would like and they would gladly help you if your tongue does not strike. Everyone has made mistakes in their lives as perfect as are you, hypocrisies so common, breads procrastinators too.

Let me walk with my chin up and my head held high, for once in my life I was so low, I thought that I would die. It was a place, a hell on earth, alas years long, I wasn't quite being myself, but wasn't doing anything wrong. The rumours flowed, the nails dug deep, the heels dug right in, but the whole time it was happening, I just kept on lifting my chin.

Why should they get the better of me, a wonderful person like me, for I am a compassionate individual, a human so selfless and free. Free of any hate for anyone you see. Even my aggressors, I did feel sorry for, but this you see my friend did not even up the score. The more I ignored it, the worst it became, the gist I did not get, when it started affecting my personal life, it became a reel big threat.

My God, I'm losing my confidence, my good nature has been marred, my character defamed in full, my heart severely scarred. It took me doing nothing, for this evil to prevail. My heart and soul I had to save, at this I would not fail.

You do not have the right, to touch me any where, my ears, my head, my personal space, especially not my hair. Who do you think you are, abusing what's not yours, please, please leave me alone, let me get on with my work chores.

I'm going about my business, to the best of my ability, if I'm not doing anything wrong, then what's all this hostility? Don't chase me down the hall, or lock me behind closed doors, if you've got something you want to say, then please tell me more. Put it down in writing, say it out aloud. Say it even better, in front of a huge crowd.

Don't you think what you're saying, is inappropriate and there's no need for any of this, on any given date. There are more professional paths to choose, many of them ignored and don't take it out on me because you're frustrated and bored. Leave me out of your politics, your vindictive, bitter ways.

My God, My Heart, My Soul are mine, even after my dying day. 'Amen.'
©25/7/2000Written for all Bullied Victims everywhere. Written By Poet Annette Evalyn Swain.

Never The End

© *"Suicide Angels And The Silent Terrorists" was Completed on Easter Sunday 12th of April 2009 at 0400 Hours.*

Written for all the Angel Spirits, Terrorised and Bullied Victims living beyond the flesh and the loved ones left behind.

Bullying doesn't just happen in cyber space or school yards, "Monkey see monkey do, ADULTS can be bullies too." It also happens in work place, communities and families.

May God give you the peace you are searching for.

Always remember, "Only Kindness Matters."

Quote by Annette Evalyn Swain.

"For I believe we are all of one Soul and what ever we pass on to others will affect us as a whole." AKA Anet The Local Vocal Poet.